Running on Empty

S. Amos

First published in 2011

Onwards and Upwards Publications,
Berkeley House,
11 Nightingale Crescent,
West Horsley,
Surrey,
KT24 6PD

www.onwardsandupwardspublishing.com

ISBN: 978-1-907509-19-3

Bible quotations are from The Jewish Bible, The Contemporary English Version and The New King James Expanded.

Cover design: Leah-Maarit

Printed in the UK

Running on Empty

We set off early in the morning to get to Poole in time for the ferry crossing to Cherbourg. It was the beginning of December and weather conditions were pleasant. Fifty miles into the journey, Ted gasped! Keeping my eyes on the road, I asked what was wrong and he told me that he had left his laptop at home. It was in his car. He then displayed what I thought was a mild fit, moving aggressively from side to side in the car seat. He was agitated. It wasn't convenient for me to pull over off the road and I had to try and placate him as I continued to drive. All his contacts were on his computer. I explained that perhaps he didn't need them and anyway I had my computer. He was distressed for some time so I turned off into a service area where we had coffee and breakfast. I suggested that perhaps Father didn't want him to have it, that he must try to rely on Him, instead of his laptop; after a while, he seemed to pull through.

The ferry crossing was about five hours, during which time Pippa, our Staffordshire Bull Terrier, stayed in the boot of the car, very comfortable on her new Dunelm single duvet complete with red patterned cover. I slept for about fifteen minutes while Ted made several journeys to the shop to buy maps. Maps are one of his obsessions. I didn't realise, at this point, just how annoying this would become.

Once in Cherbourg we were able to find the hotel we had booked, without much effort. We stayed at a Campanile off a trading estate. It was dark and Christmas lights were in evidence everywhere. Trees lit up the street and streams of flashing lights illuminated the hotel. It was raining so we took the minimum amount of luggage up the steep flights of steps to the room before making a reservation to have a meal at their restaurant.

The restaurant was a lean-to at the back of the reception area where small wooden tables were crammed together and only two French men occupied a setting in the middle of the long room. Deep in conversation they simply looked up at us as we were shown to a place near the window. The view was obscured by condensation. We both chose similar meals. Five heavily armed, uniformed policemen entered the room and sat near to us. Glasses of beer were brought to them and lots of French conversation took place.

As we left the restaurant after our meal, and passed the reception area on the way out, I noticed a lounge with comfortable chairs, occupied by three more uniformed police.

I felt Father saying, "They are there for your protection," but it bore no significance at that point.

2 Tim 4:5 *Be watchful in all things!*

I didn't sleep much that night because the flashing lights were a distraction and the small room was hot. I couldn't breathe easily although we left a window open and the shutters slightly apart.

Next morning we began our drive through France. It was still raining as we plotted the route together with the assistance of two satellite navigation systems, two maps and the signposts. This was the beginning of my realisation of the extent of Ted's obsession with maps.

We arrived at our next destination in plenty of time, in daylight, so checked into the shabby chateau – the accommodation was spacious - a self-contained apartment with two bedrooms, balcony and en suite. The whole building was badly in need of repair; the carpets were stained and threadbare in places but there was plenty of garden area for Pippa to run around close to the river.

In the evening, we had a nice meal in a newer part of the building and once again I was reminded of police protection when I recognised two men in the dining room wearing similar dark clothing and matching belts. They were obviously in a uniform but an unobtrusive one.

Ps 37:37 *Consider the blameless, observe the upright; there is a future for the man of peace.*

The journey through Spain was quite monotonous. The road was long and straight and the land appeared barren. It should have been easy to avoid Madrid because our route took us on a ring road, but Ted got confused with his sat navs, maps and sign posts so we ended up going up and down the streets of busy Madrid for about forty-five minutes, trying desperately to get out of the maze of traffic and foreign signs.

Horns were being blown at me and mad Frenchmen tried cutting me up. I became annoyed. This could have been avoided if Ted had navigated properly, but I didn't realise that he was confused.

After travelling over four hundred miles I felt uncomfortable about the car and wanted to check the oil level. We stopped at one of the many rest/fuel areas where Ted left me to go to find a lavatory. Here, I was to learn that he needed to empty his bladder very frequently. There was so much to learn about him that I didn't know.

I didn't want to hang around so raised the bonnet of the car and began to dip for oil while he was away doing his business.

Ted was away for some time and just as he came back to the car, a young man appeared from nowhere and asked if I wanted help. "No thank you," was my reply but he then continued in broken English to say, "Yes. Look. You have..." and pointed to a rear tyre which was flat as a pancake.

Ted and I walked towards the flat tyre and inspected it for nails. I couldn't understand why it had happened. I hadn't felt any pressure in the steering at all. It seemed strange. The fellow pointed us in the direction of a filling station (which we realised afterwards was a ploy to keep us focussed on a distraction.) We emptied the car and took out the small temporary spare wheel. Pippa's bed was strewn over the tarmac and the car jacked up – I thought the moment was perfect for a photograph. I couldn't find my handbag! It had been in the rear of the car, placed on top of the luggage on the opposite side to the flat tyre. I took everything out and searched. I knew that I had not left it anywhere on the journey. Then it dawned on me. The 'helpful' foreigner had slit our tyre with a knife in two places. We had been robbed. I cried!

How could I remember everything I had in my handbag? I stood beside the car weeping. People passed by – hostile. I had noticed that the Spanish preferred not to have eye contact. Ted tried to get the bolts undone on the wheel.

A young tanned, well dressed man came over and asked what had happened. I explained to him. He immediately took out his mobile phone and rang the police. He informed me that you have to do that to get a police report. A man and woman, whom, he said, were his colleagues, quickly joined him. They had been on a business trip and were driving back to Portugal. It was a 6 hours' journey for them to get home and yet they stayed with us for two hours until the heavily armoured police had attended. Nobody speaks English in Spain and they knew this, so stayed to interpret for us.

I racked my brains to remember what had been stolen. My purse which contained about six credit cards, debit cards, two cheque books, euros, sterling, mobile phone with all my contacts, my new small camera, my national health card, driving licence, pictures of my family... I couldn't remember everything.

Before the kindly Portuguese people left, I asked for his name and a contact number. He handed me his business card before digging into his pocket and producing a roll of bank notes, which he offered to us. We refused to accept his offer because Ted had a small amount of cash, sufficient for our needs. Nuno, his name, was an angel in disguise.

Thank you, Father, that you promised to send your angels to keep watch over us.

For He will order His angels to care for you and guard you wherever you go. Ps 91:11

It was then dark. We had a further 40 miles to travel to our destination, The *'Abba'* Hotel in Burgos. I could only drive slowly with the temporary tyre. Lorries were blowing horns at me and flashing lights as I crawled along the two-lane highway. Although I pulled over to the right, they just didn't get it! I learned afterwards that it was illegal to drive on the hard shoulder, although it was so wide; it could have been mistaken for another lane.

I remembered when driving in Doha that if it was foggy, or there was a sand storm, they drove with their hazard lights on. Perhaps that was a procedure here. I put them on and we eventually crawled to the hotel later than planned.

There were now a lot of extra things we had to organise. Although we had spoken to the police on the telephone in the hotel and an officer had made a report, I still had to attend the city police station to sign and collect a copy to retain. We also had to order another tyre from a company, where the staff only spoke Spanish.

Ted had booked another hotel for the following night, further south of Spain in Seville and I had a bad feeling about it. Someone had told us to be careful of Seville because it was full of crime. As it happened, our delay caused us to cancel the booking. That was a chaotic procedure because their company policy was to only cancel with forty-eight hours' prior notice, so we were liable to pay for the accommodation. Ted was unhappy about that, so we had to make several phone calls to the hotel, fax them a copy of the police report and other relevant paperwork, before they would agree to cancel the charge. Again, I wasn't happy about faxing a report which contained my passport number, name, address, date of birth and all my personal information to some unknown at the end of a fax line so I blanked out all the private bits before allowing him to take it to reception to send.

The next day we walked about three miles through the town of Bergos to the police station. Under other circumstances I suppose I would have thought it a nice place. The police station was huge and heaving with people. Nobody spoke English.

A young girl stood in the enormous foyer, holding a folded coat over her arms. She noticed the difficulty I was having in being understood and approached me speaking in broken English. She was a trainee policewoman just about to have her break-time and offered to take me into a side room to translate to another officer, who eventually found my report and printed it off. Six copies were produced, stamped and initialled by her, then passed to me to sign.

I commented on the police station being crowded, but was informed that it was quiet today. Usually people are standing down the steps to report credit card crime. It is uncontrollable. The Chinese, Columbians and some Africans have big gangs organised in Spain where the banks haven't yet introduced 'chip and pin.' The criminals do exactly as they had done to us – distract tourists, and steal their documents. The officer advised me not to use any credit or debit cards in Spain.

Fortunately before leaving home I had written down the number of the credit card hotline so we were able to borrow Nuno's phone to cancel them but it was already too late because within six minutes of the theft, my card had been used.

Getting over that ordeal, we walked back to the hotel to spend the afternoon waiting for the tyre people to contact us. Interpretation had been done through the hotel receptionist who had helped us such a lot. His name, Jesus!

Isa 41:10 (emphasis mine) *So do not fear, for I am with you; do not be dismayed, for I am your G-d. I will strengthen you and help you; I will uphold you with my righteous right hand.*

We had lunch on the balcony in the sunshine and were thankful that *we* hadn't been knifed, as the tyre had been.

In the hotel room was an aerial view of the town of Burgos. I felt Father was showing me a bigger picture from a greater height. He wanted me to see a larger perspective. I remembered that He had previously told me to know the enemy intimately. We had lost our focus.

I smiled to myself when I thought:

1 Tim 2:2 *Give thanks to all men in authority (policemen) that we may lead a quiet and peaceful life.*

The next morning we skipped breakfast and left the hotel at 7am while it was still dark. It doesn't get fully light until about 9am at that time of year. It was to be a long haul; because we had intended to stay in Seville to break the journey, then just do the odd 150 miles to the villa the following day. But, we thought it was right to get out of Spain and travel without breaking.

At times I felt myself getting tired, but didn't want to pull off the road. I was still getting over my experience of being robbed. I wasn't afraid, but didn't want to stop unnecessarily other than to let Pippa out of the car from time to time.

The journey was over 600 miles. We arrived at the villa at about 5.30pm. It was not difficult to find but was not how it had been described on the website.

We thought it was set in its own grounds a good way from neighbours but this wasn't so. The approach was up a dirt track fringed with about 20 little shacks on either side. Each shack had a minimum of two dogs, most of them tied and chained but about five of them loose. They ran up to the car and chased us to the end of the dirt track, to the gate of the villa, which was locked. Ted knew where to get the key. We could only just get the car through the gate with the mirrors folded back and about a quarter of an inch to spare. There was no turning space outside the house so I quickly learned that the best way in was to back the car all down the dirt track and into the driveway.

We heard dogs barking throughout the night. Although the garden area of the villa was fenced off, one small dog got through the gate. We attempted to take Pippa for a walk, but it caused such a furore we resorted to taking her out in the car for a walk!

The first day, we just familiarised ourselves with the villa and the surroundings. It was set (as all the neighbouring shacks were) in a vast orange grove. The garden had 36 orange trees and then a further orchard area beyond a locked gate, all surrounded by pomegranate hedges laden with rotten fruit and black rot on the branches.

Every house had great iron gates and fencing with barbed wire on top – guard dogs chained up. It didn't do my sense of security much good seeing how they are all cruelly restricted.

The first days we were there were very cold. It was apparently very unusual for them to have a north wind. One person even said that he couldn't believe they had frost yesterday and got out of the car to feel the grass to check that it really was frost!

John 4:48 *"Unless you people see miraculous signs and wonders," Jesus told him, "you will never believe."*

There were irrigation pipes everywhere in the gardens and orchards. The water for this is free. It seems a shame, too, that although the trees were loaded with fruit, it was going rotten on them. We were informed that the Portuguese have EU subsidies to grow the fruit, but are not obligated to harvest and sell it. I suppose foreigners coming to England might say the same about our apple trees.

Father had already spoken to me about setting before me an open door which no-one can shut.

Rev 3:8 *Look! I have put in front of you an open door, and no one can shut it.*

Whilst investigating the rooms here, I found a lot of pictures of doors. But all of these doors were closed.

Is 22:22 *He shall shut and no-one will open.*

After putting our belongings in the villa and settling down, we visited our nearest town of Tavira, 4 miles away. It seemed a nice little place, set on the river. If you want to go to the beach you have to get a ferry over. We hadn't done that, because we had too many organisational things to do, for example to contact the insurance company and try to get a phone connection to get my laptop online.

Of course, we also discovered that in Portugal they don't accept English credit or debit cards so Ted had to get cash from a machine before we could do shopping.

We were advised to keep low profile because if we look like tourists we are likely to be targeted in Portugal. I found it difficult because I imagined Ted standing in the centre of the square in Tavira, holding out his street map for all to see! Advertising himself as a tourist – 'Here I am – come and get me!'

We met a school friend of Ted's who ran an estate agency in Tavira. I couldn't believe it when I met him. They were like clones in appearance and in mannerisms. I wonder if that is the result of institutionalised schooling? It was interesting.

Anyhow, we had our first rain over night but the sun began to shine.

"Today is a new day and we are going into Tavira again. We discovered that we can get online free of charge at the library which will give us more time than those dongles."

Ps 118:24 (emphasis mine) *This is the day that the Lord has made; let us rejoice and be glad in it!*

Chapter 1

Diary

Thursday December 17, 2009

We stayed at the villa today. The sun began to rise, its warmth evaporating the heavy dew and it looked as though it would be the best day yet for nice weather. It was so warm that we sat outside for lunch, which Ted barbequed, while Pippa sniffed amongst the orange trees. In the afternoon it was quite hot. I found out how to use the washing machine, did four loads of washing and hung it on the roof to dry.

I discovered a mandarin tree in the garden and collected half a bag of them to eat later. Ted squeezed some of the larger oranges for juice.

The oleanders, and roses were in full bloom. It seems that winter here is the time when the plants grow. Not many leaves have fallen off the trees – it all looks very green. The grass is growing and all is as it might be in the summer at home.

Nearby there are cork trees, pine trees, almond, fig and carobs. We have yet to identify them individually.

Yesterday on our return from a shopping trip in Tavira, we found two vans parked in the driveway. One was the lady gardener and the other was the cleaner. I felt it was an intrusion and didn't care for the cleaner lady who told me that she could see my "aura". I had to spiritually cleanse the house after she had gone. She even left us a flask of broth, which I had to throw away.

1 Cor 10:21 *You can't both drink the cup of the Lord and the cup of demons.*

We found out why dogs get poisoned here – it's because they bark constantly all night long and people get fed up with it so throw them poisoned meat.

We thought it was going to be quiet, but dogs are barking all the time. We were told, "You'll get used to it..."

James 1:9 *But let the brother of low position be glad that he is lifted up*

When we went to the new shopping centre called Continent (the maintenance manager of the villa told us to go 'in continent') when I got to the till, I was surprised to hear the cashier say I should have weighed the lettuce. I couldn't be bothered to go all the way back to find out how to weigh a lettuce so we left it. I have never heard of that before! We are learning...!

The sun rises about 8.30am and is bright by 9am. It goes chilly about 5pm and the sun sets about 5.30pm. I saw a strange rainbow today. It was only a small piece of one, standing upright in the sky and another one very, very close to it, but not a double one. It looked strange.

I don't quite know how to put this into words but I am finding it strange being with Ted 24/7. He doesn't seem to have any bearing on the real world.

We have to do everything together now because I am the car driver and he has to come with me to the supermarket as he is the only one with the money, but he is totally disorientated. I asked him if he had a euro to get a trolley. He looked in his pocket and said, "Yes, we're alright for euros, don't worry." He didn't realise that I wanted him to put a coin in the trolley. He didn't know how to do it so I had to do it in the end.

His is the only card we can use here as mine are in someone else's pocket by now. They don't accept English cards so I don't have financial resources. Many times I have looked to pick up my handbag, and realised I haven't got one! It really hasn't bothered me that much though. I have accepted what has happened, prayed for the robbers, forgiven them and moved on.

Luke 6:28 *Bless them that curse you, and pray for them which despitefully use you.*

I know that Father is in control and that His ways are higher than mine! I must trust His ways knowing that His plans for me are to prosper me and not harm me, giving me hope and a future!

We went to the new Continental shopping market, which we call 'incontinent' as the maintenance man had said one could get *everything* in continent. All the restaurants and burger king outlets are located on the top floor, and in between them are popcorn stalls at the entrance of the new cinema. Ted gasped with disbelief (of course you have to have the arm waving as well because he speaks with his hands and fingers) 'Isn't it wonderful having popcorn and so many restaurants!!'

My eyes have been opened and I now see a child, not the husband I thought I had been given.

Yesterday we ate soup on the top of another shopping centre in a place, which we call Ohio because we can't pronounce it properly. It was so windy that it blew the soup out of my spoon all over my coat! ~ The weather has been so cold ~ Easterly and northerly winds, which are cutting. The under-floor heating doesn't work and we had to buy three expensive propane gas cylinders. Ted has brought a calculator along with him and from time to time checks the heating temperature and tries to calculate how much money we have spent. We bought some logs today for the wood-burner and he has been calculating how much per kilo they work out at. These obsessions are unfolding and beginning to irritate me.

I was very surprised to get an email from the woman looking after our home in Wales, saying that all was okay and that the heater for the car was working. I questioned Ted, but he said he didn't know what she meant. I do! He is mean about us being kept warm here but has a heater on all the time for his bloomin' car!

Same thing with the diesel! We drive about three miles (its all in kilometres here which I don't understand) to a cheaper fuel station where he is saving 0.01p on the fuel, when he doesn't realise that he has used up all that he has saved in travelling further for it!

He has his calculator out in the shops, seeing if it's a good buy or not. I am so embarrassed and it also takes so much longer to do the shopping.

We went to the library the day before yesterday to use the computers there because they are *free*. There was only one available and it kept crashing. It wouldn't work in English and we had to leave it. Instead we paid more on the top-up card for the pay-as-you-go dongle. Once we got it home, he wanted to see how much credit was on it and discovered that we are charged in units of five minutes, so, if I use the computer for two minutes, it charges for five. Consequently, Ted stands over me with a stop-watch while I try to type as fast as I can, making mistakes and conscious that he is watching me.

I feel as though I have been stripped of all identity and am looking after a person who has led such a sheltered life that he doesn't know how to operate in the real world. Father is this your way of humbling me?

I have had to warn Ted about putting his wallet in his back pocket, but he can't readily change his habits.

It's not easy and I can see that he will never be able to take responsibility for anything. He spent three quarters of an hour in a camera shop as I sat outside on a seat and watched him. He then ran towards me, sighing, blaming the cashier for taking such a long time (shifting responsibility). Cameras and looking at photographs are another obsession!

It's difficult to get fresh milk here. The milk tastes like that bottled stuff with tin caps, which they used to have in the war. You know, you have to take the top off with a bottle opener. It's horrible. I brought some special tea bags so don't have to drink it. I did notice that they sell red bush here!

We have seen white storks in amongst the orange trees and noticed more nesting on the top of a bell tower in town on Friday.

We drove up into the hills again today. I don't really like staying in this villa and would rather be out except that it was bitingly cold. I brought a hot water bottle with me and am glad that I did.

On the one day of warm sunshine Ted cleaned the barbeque and used it. I'm glad we had the opportunity to enjoy the garden in the warmth. I am hopeful that we shall get some more warm days. When its cold at home you can turn up the heating, or put on more clothes, but when you are away in a place where you don't know how things work, it's more difficult.

Phil 4:13 *I can do all things through Him who strengthens me.*

Lee has bought my sister and brother-in-law a ticket to come out on January 16th for a week. This is for her 60th birthday. A relative of theirs lives here in Tavira so I expect they will want to see her, but I think they will stay with us.

Ted is cleaning the car now. The temperature outside is freezing, but he needs to have something to do. Mostly he sits down and goes to sleep. Boring.

Everything here is a learning curve.

At the top of the house, are two roof levels. One has a built in barbeque, washing line and small sink and the other higher one is just simply a roof where I suppose people could lie if they wanted to sunbathe.

Another barbeque has been built in the garden, complete with sink and water. This is the one that Ted used today when he cooked lunch.

Roses and oleanders are at their peak as well as the orange trees, some of which are mandarins and quite sweet.

Lots of pictures hang on the wall in the study, all pictures of *doors*. An artist's easel is set up in the corner with a huge photograph of a door! Watercolours are left out for our use if we want.....

Rev 3:8 *I know your deeds. See, I have placed before you an open door that no one can shut...*

Chapter 2

We have been familiarising ourselves with our surroundings during this very unusual cold snap.

The under-floor heating in the villa is very inefficient and hit-and-miss. We used three huge propane gas cylinders this week alone, but the effect is like a candle heating an igloo. We found some old wood, which had been used on the barbeque and lit the open fire in the sitting room. That, too, is strange. It has an electric pump which forces the warm air back into the room, but is so noisy that when you turn it off your ears think your head has been chopped off.

I go to bed with a hot water bottle, dressed in clothes underneath my nightie with dressing gown on top. I'm glad I brought Pippa's duvet because we share that. The room is so cold (marble floors) that it has been too cold to have a shower. The bath is a rectangular piece of concrete, covered with small mosaic tiles. Totally impractical from a comfort point of view, but also five men could fit easily into it. It is huge. Funnily enough there is a notice beside it saying 'please save water'.

We have tried to go out most days but that, in it-self, is an ordeal. The gateposts are so narrow that I have to crawl through them with both mirrors folded back. A dirt track allows me no turning space so I have to either reverse the whole length of the road in - or conversely reverse out. I am not so inclined to go out because of this ordeal.

Yesterday we went to our local town, Tavira, to the 'incontinent' shopping mall once again. Instead of coming back to the villa we drove towards Conceicao, which appears to be an area, rather than a town. I wondered whether we might pass Casa du Hera (interpretation Home of Ivy) – my sister's relative – but we travelled miles into the hills on roads which weren't even marked on the map.

I turned left at one junction and travelled about two miles only to find that it ended up as a dirt track at somebody's home. Naturally, about six loose dogs accosted us!

The dogs here are a bit of a problem. Each time we close a door it sets off a chorus from the dogs down the dirt track. One by one they begin barking until you can hear dogs all around the area. A little cheeky one jumps through the bars in the gate into the garden. It makes me be on guard all the time, that Pippa doesn't eat one of them.

We found a lovely beach yesterday at Fuseta and she was able to run free for a few minutes until we realised that the ex-pat community used the beach for their dog runs too. Most of the beaches are unreachable because of a line of swampland they call a nature reserve. To get to the beaches you have to either get a little train across, or ferry over. We have yet to do that because we are unsure whether dogs are allowed.

We seem to be drawn a lot to a village behind us called Santo Estevao, (St Steven) and have been told that there is a nice restaurant there but, when we walked through the only street the other day, the recommended restaurant looked more like a bar to me. One of the villas Ted had been looking at (before he booked this one) was in that village and we didn't realise it until now.

The hilly terrain was amazing when viewed from the highest point. Lots of hilly lumps, covered the land for miles, (or should I say kilometres) rather like huge molehills. There are lots of golf courses here and even a golf village has been built in one place up the hills – very posh looking villas looked a bit out of place in the wild hilltops.

We continued close to the border of Spain to places not even marked on the map and it is doubtful that we should ever find them again. I stopped the car on the brow of a hill to take a picture of some rather unusual looking goats. They had big curling horns and beautiful brown and white patterned coats. The weather-beaten old man looking after them sat on a stonewall hugging his crook and waved his arm as I peeped the horn in a gesture of friendliness.

It was bitterly cold. The wind has been northerly and Easterly for a few days and as soon as we got back to the villa, manoeuvred the vehicle into the drive, the heavens opened and we have had torrential rain since. It is now afternoon on Monday.

We lost our electricity supply last night but Ted came to the rescue with a spare torch. He had brought one for himself and one for me!!!! He doesn't go anywhere without his friend, the torch.

The other day we travelled to Olhao, which we call Ohio. It is a coastal place but we weren't very impressed with it. It seemed to be very dirty and lots of high-rise unkempt looking flats monopolised the streets. We found a new shopping mall, which had been recommended to Ted if he wanted to replace my stolen camera. Of course, spending time in a camera shop satisfied another obsession so I waited outside.

Today, Monday, 21 December 2009, we spent indoors because it is so wet. I am hoping that the weather will change for our trip tomorrow. We are meeting our guardian angel, the lovely man who helped us in our hour of need when we were robbed. We want to take him out for a meal - so are travelling to Setubal (270 kilometres away) midway up the west coast of Portugal.

Chapter 3

Wednesday December 23, 2009

We had an early start yesterday to drive 200 miles to Setubal, which is about half way up the west coast of Portugal. The drive was easy – long straight roads and very little traffic. The cruise control crashed and I wondered what it was to begin with when the car suddenly slowed down! We are only allowed to do 120 kpm on the roads, so I stay to the limit although it is very tempting to put my foot down and could easily do about 150 mph. I have to remember that I am driving without a licence.

We arrived at Setubal in plenty of time for our meeting with our 'angel'. Ted rang him once we were parked up and within five minutes Nuno and his four years old daughter, Maria, who was strapped in a baby seat in the rear of his new BMW, greeted us.

He insisted that we left our car parked in the town and brought Pippa along so that he could show us around. He drove along the coast, round bendy mountains overlooking the beautiful sea. The sand as white as purity acts as a reflector and so many white skinned people get very burned in the summer when the sun is strong.

The scenery was breathtaking. The sands and aquamarine sea were outstandingly beautiful. The wind was rough on the sea and yet, it commanded a certain stillness because of the sunshine. We are used to rough seas being due to bad weather, but here was a seascape beyond description. The sun turned the colour of the sea into liquid silver.

Deut 33:19 *They will summon peoples to the mountain and there offer sacrifices of righteousness; they will feast on the abundance of the seas, on the treasures hidden in the sand.*

The landscape was so different from the barren, dirty, ram-shackled Algarve. It was clean and pure.

We met Nuno's brother, Geito, who travelled separately in his own vehicle so in convoy we travelled to a restaurant overlooking the sea at Sesimbra. They ordered a typical Portuguese meal for us to sample and the waiter brought a trolley to the table laden with a whole fish, which had been baked in salt.

Lev 2:13 (emphasis mine) *Season all your grain offerings with salt. Do not leave the salt of the covenant of your G-d out of your grain offerings; add salt to all your offerings.*

The salt covering had become hard during the baking process, allowing the fish to be tenderly cooked within the protection of the casing. The waiter took a sharp knife to the coat and hammered it open to reveal what was the most deliciously soft and scrumptious white fish.

We drove elsewhere for our dessert – another local dish of almond and oranges rolled in a swiss-roll type cake and filled with a yummy fig filling. Everywhere they drink Turkish coffee. We tasted the sweetness of the place which was, indeed, very good.

Ps 34:8 *Taste and see that the LORD is good; blessed is the man who takes refuge in him.*

We were then whisked off to the ferry and taken over by car to an island about twenty minutes' ferry ride from the coast. Once on the sandy island, they took us through a maze of roads to an exclusive resort to their large, luxurious holiday home.

As we entered the kitchen I felt a darkness being cast over me. The kitchen was dark in the natural, but as we were shown into the large open plan sitting area, a life-size Buddha sat on a huge low, oriental table. Against the wall was another Buddha similar in size. They monopolised the entire area. Woodcarvings of oriental gods were hung on the walls. I hoped they were not going to offer the place to us as a rental!

As the evening approached and darkness was imminent, we took the ferry back to land and said our goodbyes and thanks, hoping that we should meet again.

It was only when we were driving out of the town that Ted noticed a piece of paper flapping on the windscreen. As we moved off, he reached through the window to grab it before it blew away. Reading through the Portuguese, we realised that we had a parking ticket!

The road back to Tavira was long. We approached the peage booth and passed through without being able to get a ticket. This was to our detriment as, hundreds of miles later when we reached another peage, we didn't have a ticket to produce. The operator charged us 94 euros, which Ted proclaimed as outrageous. Thus followed an exchange of vocabulary. Some Portuguese, some English.

A queue of cars was building up behind us as Ted fought his patch. He stated that nearly a hundred pounds was absolutely disgusting and that we had only been charged twenty-six euros the last time we didn't have a ticket.

Adamant that she was only doing her job, the woman said if we wanted to complain we would have to fill in a form. Yes he did! This entailed her looking around in the booth to find the appropriate paperwork. All of this was causing delays for other motorists.

We *have* to pay the money into a bank within eight days and *then* complain. Well we know what that means. In the meantime, she came out of the booth and took details of the car registration number, took Ted's passport and still the cars were joining the queue.

I knew that when I was able to drive off, annoyed drivers would cut me up in revenge for making them wait. Ted was oblivious to this.

Once the business was finished I put my foot down to accelerate away, but as I had suspected, a couple of cars cut me up later as payment for delaying them.

As Ted is the holder of all the money, since I have been stripped of everything I own, the axe is at the root of his tree. He is finding that he is responsible for having to pay for things, which are hurting his purse.

Gen 37:23 *So, when Joseph came to his brothers, they stripped him of his robe—the richly ornamented robe he was wearing-*

Stripped and vulnerable, I feel now that our details have been marked or sealed in this place. My personal details are now on record at the police station in Bergos, Spain because of the theft and now, the parking ticket and toll fee have caused our details to be logged too. We have been sealed here.......

Today the cleaner and the gardener 'ladies' are due to come. We had torrential rain again in the night and the winds are so forceful that they have blown sunshades and chairs into the pool. We have floods all around the villa. The weather wasn't like this yesterday when we were in Setubal.

We need to go out to do some shopping at some stage today. Its midday and they haven't turned up. Tomorrow is Christmas Eve and the shops will close at 4pm, reopening on what we call Boxing Day. The people here apparently open their presents on Christmas Eve before going to midnight mass. We shall be giving all that a miss!

Our new friends had asked why we were not joining in the festivities for Christmas. I was able to explain that Father's holidays are simple. He has seven Feasts, plus the celebrations of Hanukkah and Purim, and the weekly Shabbat—the day of rest with Him. His days begin in the evening.

Yahshua Messiah (Jesus) would have grown up celebrating Hanukkah and Purim, along with the weekly Shabbat and the seven Festivals of Leviticus. Leviticus 23 gives us a general explanation of what these Festivals, or Feasts are. Hanukkah was also called "the Feast of Dedication."

The first four of the seven Festivals picture His death, burial, resurrection, and the coming of the Ruach ha Kodesh (Holy Spirit), The Ruach calls with the Bride of Messiah for our Messiah-Saviour to come (Revelation 22:17). These first four Festivals are in the springtime. The last three are in the autumn. They picture His second coming, His judgment on the nations and the salvation of all of Israel, and the Kingdom of G-d on earth for 1,000 years, and then for eternity.

Why should we celebrate Hanukkah and Purim?

These two Festivals teach us victory over the enemy. They teach us not to compromise with the enemy in hard times. We celebrate them because they show the victory that Father had over His enemies, using the tenacity and faithfulness of the Levites (priestly tribe) and the Jews (tribe of Judah) of that day. Purim, of course, is the victory of our Father over His enemies and the enemies of His people, through Esther and Mordecai. But, that whole story is clear from the book of Esther. We are wise to keep that holiday also.

Both Hanukkah and Purim are celebrations of victories of the past, but also are very important teachings for us about what is to come upon the earth in our day and time.
Hanukkah is a message of hope for our survival in the days ahead!

Hanukkah is called "The Festival of Lights!"
The miracle was that all 7 lights of the menorah burned for all 8 days.

We also celebrate Purim! It usually occurs in February. While Jewish tradition tragically has gone worldly, making it a Halloween dress up carnival time, you can celebrate the real meaning of Purim—past victory and future promise of victory.
It is OK to have the children dress up to enact the story, and to read the story as a family, booing at Haman and cheering for Esther and Mordicai. Jewish tradition has just lost the true meaning of Purim and depth of its importance through making it a carnival-spirited thing, making the story almost a spoof.

Chapter 4

We drove to Tavira this afternoon after waiting in all morning for the cleaning and gardening personnel, who didn't turn up!

Ted needed to pay the fee for the toll road and also go to the Tourist Information place to translate the paperwork and establish what the parking ticket said.

We parked up, got a ticket, which we displayed in the passenger side of the car and I walked Pippa along the riverfront while Ted went to the bank.

It began to rain so Pip and I got back to the car just in time before the deluge. The heavens opened and it rained like I had never seen it rain before. It was as though we were standing under a waterfall. The fast windscreen wipers would not take the water.

Poor Ted came back to the car absolutely soaked through to the skin. He had learned from the person at the bank that he must pay the fee at the post office and as it was Christmas he needed to do it today. He then made the trek to the post office not knowing that he needed to take a ticket to stand in the queue. He waited for ages watching everyone being served before realising that he needed to take a ticket with a number so that he could take his turn. He gave up and came back to the car leaking like a dripping tap.

We had to pay the fee so he should have paid up at the time.

The advice given at the tourist office was to forget about the parking ticket because there was a lack of detail on the paper. He was relieved about that.

The rain subsided for a short time, but continued for most of the afternoon. The streets and gutters were like rivers. I wondered whether it was better to be in UK or here for the rain is the same except that the climate here is slightly warmer today.

It was an amazing sight when the rain subsided temporarily because the warmth of the air caused a thick fog to appear.

Matt 5:45 *...and sends rain on the righteous and the unrighteous*

We were told that Portugal had experienced an earthquake a few days ago – 6 on the Richter scale. We didn't feel anything, but buildings shook in mid Spain.

When we returned to the villa, it was evident that nobody had been. We took the shopping out of the car and put it away, I then made dinner. We don't have to go out again for a few days if we don't need to (or if we can't!).

We ate lasagne to a display of lightning and a chorus from the crickets. They are extremely loud. Storks were in the garden again and I wonder whether they like the wet weather as much as the crickets. The wind is now howling. The weather here seems to be extreme and we have learned that the rainy season is, yes, you guessed it, December and January!

Poor Ted's anorak was thin and soaked through. He hung it on the line on the rooftop. At about 9.30pm he asked if I had taken his anorak off the line because he hung it to dry out. I didn't know he had done so.

He looked upset. "The wind has blown it off the line," he said shaking his head. "I'll have to go and look for it." He then took his torch out into the black of night, the wind blowing a gale that it was hard for him to stand upright. He searched the front and rear of the house and couldn't find it.

I went up on to the roof and found the only evidence of his coat – a yellow magic marker, which had fallen out of the pocket.

After looking around the roof I found it swept up in the corner lying in a puddle of water. It was wetter than when he put it up there. He's now got the instruction book out and is working out how to spin dry it.

Chapter 5

Thursday December 24, 2009

Torrential rain in the night left us with floods around the villa this morning. The water from the orange grove next door was gushing over the drive like a river. The gardens were like a lake and have remained waterlogged all day despite the sunshine and strong winds. It has been relatively warm and we sat outside for elevenses this morning.

Although we brought Wellington boots with us, we haven't felt that we wanted to wade through the floodwater or drive out anywhere, but we might go out later and take some oranges to the English couple we met on our first visit to the supermarket. They are staying on a camping site (in a caravan) near Cabanas, a couple of miles east of Tavira.

The rain beat in through the windows and ran down the interior walls. It has also come under the doors in places. Ted has been investigating and found that the drainage passages under the doors and windows have been filled with ant powder which has prevented the drainage. He cleaned them all out this afternoon.

The pump house for the pool has flooded and water was almost level with the electric pump. Ted called the maintenance man to warn him, but he was aware of it and simply said that the owners had built the pump house to a silly spec and had already moved the pump to a higher level as the previous one had been ruined. His uncaring attitude concerned Ted who wanted to get stuck in and redirect the floodwater.

The villa roof was covered in almost two inches of water that leaked through my bathroom soaking the corner cupboard and some of my cosmetics.

As the car sat in the river outside the front door, we waited for the deluge to subside.

When there was a break in the clouds Ted picked a bag full of oranges from the trees in the garden which we took to the couple, John and Margaret, who had been helpful in showing us where the Information Office is situated. (A place we would frequent almost on a day-to-day basis!)

Their little caravan and awning looked sorrowful in the rain. A small Christmas decoration was pinned to the awning above the zipped doorway which Ted tripped over when he went in. It was too wet for me to get out of the car so I waved through the window. There was little point in us both getting soaked!

They were delighted to see us and with waves and signs from their plastic window, I realised that they were managing well and were dry.

Ted ran back to the car, stumbling over a tent peg, and we drove on towards the borders of Spain finding a couple of nice places on the sea. Dulled by the rain, we couldn't make a fair judgement of them.

On our return eastwards, Tavira looked pretty with all the dazzling lights displayed over the river. We took some pictures of them and then returned to the villa.

One of the loose dogs was killing a chicken on the verge of the road as we passed what looked to be a farm or smallholding. It made me feel sad.

We didn't need heating on in the house today and didn't have to light the wood burner because the temperature was really pleasant.

Pippa found a ball, which had been blown into the garden and demolished it in two seconds.

Friday December 25, 2009

The pope called midnight mass forward to 10pm so that he would be refreshed for mass this morning!! The Portuguese people open their gifts on Christmas Eve so it all seemed quiet this morning. Even the dogs were fairly quiet!

Although the rain still persists, it is quite cold today and Ted tried to light a fire but couldn't get it to go. Instead, we just got smoke in the house. It reminded me of a time at home when he lit oil lamps for Passover and filled the house with black soot!

The fire-grate hasn't been cleaned and there is a build up of ashes but he is adamant that that doesn't matter and he can get a spark out of dead ash.

A telephone call this morning (which we missed) because the phone was too deep in Ted's pocket, was from my son, Al. I asked if we could call him back because the phone belongs to Ted and he keeps saying how expensive the calls are. Of course, my call with Al opened up the way for him to call his daughters. He hadn't given that a thought until now.

When I spoke with Al his voice was loud and clear and I felt the blow of missing him and my family. Mary was very upbeat and proclaimed that next year we shall all be together at this time of year. I agree. I realise how important my family is – especially as the only 'conversation' I have had for two weeks is with Ted and he likes the sound of silence!

The floods which had subsided this morning, are now well in evidence as we have another day of rain. Various people have said that it is unprecedented weather and they have never known such rain. Usually it is sunny and warm.

Hey ho! We must have brought it with us!

We had pate and bread rolls for lunch with some local Portuguese rose wine. It is very nice (and of course cheap!). Pippa is a little princess and occupies the sofa with me and only climbs down when she thinks she can have a leftover!

Tomorrow is another day...

Chapter 6

Saturday December 26, 2009

After another night of thunder, lightning, flooding and being awakened in the night by rain leaking in through the windows, it was so nice to see the sun shining.

All evidence of rain quickly dried up as the sun got warmer and we decided to go out for a drive.

We headed north towards the mountains again, but there are so many different roads it is doubtful we could ever find them again.

Whilst driving through the rugged terrain, across the top of a mountain, I suddenly felt a darkness come over me. I looked to my right, which overlooked a steep drop and commented to Ted how black everything looked. It was only about a mile later that I realised the countryside had been burned *black* by *fire*. The trees were *charcoal* and new growth was bursting from the trunks of the trees, rather than the branches, because the branches had been killed. For miles the earth was *black* – trees were *black*. I looked for houses and there were a couple of ruins but we weren't sure whether they were already ruined before the fire. Road signs had been licked and blackened by the *fire*. It was an amazing experience. But, new growth was springing forth. *New life* after the purging, but it would take time to restore the land again for such a vast area had been taken.

Heb 12:18 (emphasis mine) *For you have not come to the mountain that may be touched (that you can feel) and that burned with fire and to blackness and darkness and tempest...*

12:22 *But you have come to Mount Zion and to the City of the Living Elohim the heavenly Jerusalem to an innumerable company of angels.*

12:29 (emphasis mine) *Because my Elohim is indeed a destroying (consuming) fire.*

Further along we saw some cork trees on the roadside. The cork is taken off the trunks as far as the branches so consequently the trunks are very dark in colour getting lighter higher up. It almost looks as though the trunks have been stained with dark varnish.

In the midst of the wilds, we found a sign in English for a restaurant. We didn't intend to stop there, but just to get some information, but instead, we ended up having lunch there. www.herdadedacorte.com (Herdade da Corte at Santa Catarina.)

They had been closed over the holiday and were really opening tomorrow,

Sunday, but the Argentinean couple were more than happy to cook for us. We had a lovely meal (our first out in Portugal). We started with goat's cheese covered with a small blob of the local fig paste, topped with local honey. It was delicious. I so want to get some of this fig paste. It is the basis for a lot of the local dessert dishes and is thick and sweet. The succulent, Argentinean beef was cooked on a barbeque. We had to give the black pudding a miss (not to eat blood) and I felt very guilty about giving it to Pippa. At first she turned her nose up at it, but thought better of it. Apparently black pudding (or blood pudding) seems to be a vital part of the diet here. It is included in stews, soups, barbeques and fry-ups!

The owner gave us complimentary pieces of Christmas cake which was very dry and stale, rather like stollen cake, with candied fruit and topped with huge thick pieces of angelica. Along with that came a free drink of red alcohol, which was probably a liqueur. We were made very welcome by the couple and asked to return by the husband whose name was Jorge!

By the time we found our bearings (Ted navigating with the help of two maps and two sat navs) it was almost sundown. The sun sets at about 5.30pm and rises about 8.45am. The moon is quite strange to look at because it appears to be upside down to how we see it in the UK.

So this evening is quiet, apart from the crickets, which are making a dreadful row and occasionally the dog chorus starts up.

We don't want a meal tonight, thankfully, and will have an early night asking for sweet sleep.

Thank you, Father, that when we lie down, our sleep will be sweet! (Prov 3:24)

Sunday December 27, 2009

I was hopeful about the sleep! One dog, in particular, cried and yapped all night through, intermittently setting off the others. In the early hours of the morning Pippa jumped up and began to bark. This is the second time she has done this. She sniffs around the house but doesn't want to go out.

Early this morning the men of the neighbouring households took their guns out into the orchards next door and the resounding of the bullets was heart rending.

It is a dry morning! The sun hasn't been able to cut through the clouds, but it is dry and fairly warm.

Ted busied himself checking the oil in the car, pumping up the tyres (or letting the air out of the rear ones) and vacuuming the car with an ancient vacuum cleaner, which won't pick up a hair! Whilst he was outside I began to prepare a meal. THE MOMENT I came up to write, he came in and followed me up to the little room where there is a desk on which we have placed the laptop. Is there no peace?

Thank you Father, that you have established peace for us! (Is 26:12)

I did some washing this morning and Ted came up to the roof to check that the line wasn't tangled. Water is still on the one side of the roof – hasn't drained away.

We didn't plan to go anywhere and just pottered about. I was in short sleeves and Pippa has been queen of the car, relaxing in her place in the boot, elevated enough to be dominant over the stray dogs which are annoying us through the open fence.

Ted has already chased one who uses the garden as a lavatory. It really is a nuisance!

The evening got cold and Ted couldn't get the *fire* to light. Eventually when it did get going, it didn't give out any heat. Bundled up in a blanket and hot water bottle, I decided to go to bed early.

I dreamed:

The details are hard to recover. It was a large building. I was walking up a wide corridor and witnessed a large door at the end bulging out towards me, being pushed by flames. That part of the house was on *fire* and blazing like an inferno. The name here for oven is 'furno'. I don't remember how it was put out but I saw the remains of the house as *black charcoal.*

> Deut 4:20 *But the Lord has taken me and brought me out of the iron furnace (out of Egypt) to be His people, His inheritance as I am today.*

What a wonderful promise!

The lavatory cleaner is called *ash*!!

Chapter 7

Monday December 28, 2009

It was too cold to get out of bed this morning. I slept in my fleecy dressing gown. Oh if I was ever to meet the person who invented fleeces, I should give him a bear hug!

Wearing black socks, nightie, fleece and shawl, I went downstairs to make coffee. The garden was a lake once again and the driveway was a river. Is there no end this rain?

Several people have told us that this weather is unprecedented!

Matt 5:4 *And He sends rain to the righteous and the unrighteous alike...*

I felt a bit like Eve, in the Garden of Eden. There is one tree (and one tree only) bearing a fruit rather like an apple. Of course, all the fruit here has been left on the trees to rot so there were only a couple of these good fruits left hanging on the branch.

Ted reached up to take the 'apple' and brought it inside to cut open. It felt like a lump of concrete so he took the carving knife to cut into it because it was so hard. We didn't eat of it!!

Inside it had the appearance of an apple with a core and pips, but was solid. After making enquiries, we were told that it's a larger version of a quince (but called something else) and the locals boil them up and make a product called marmalada – not to be confused with marmalade. We bought a tub and it is just like quince jelly except that it is solid like a cheese, but quite nice. We have it on the local bread toasted. The bread doesn't stay fresh for more than a few hours so I have *overcome* that by freezing it immediately we buy it.

Prov 7:2 *Keep my commands and live, And my law as the apple of your eye.*

Tuesday December 29, 2009

There is still no let-up on the rain. The driveway is now flooded but we had to go out to get food shopping.

Is 68:9 *You caused abundant rain to fall and restored your worn-out land.*

We parked the car in the underground car park at 'incontinent' and were surprised to see it flooded when we got back. Officials on their quad bikes were looking at the water in disbelief. All nearby roads were closed and the river is now almost at bursting point.

People here have never seen floods like this! Of course, to us, who are experienced at driving through deeper waters than this, it still isn't nice.

We called to see John and Margaret, the elderly English couple, at their camping site to see if they were ok. They were snug in the awning over the caravan with sandbags set all along the base of it.

They had been drinking soup at their little camping table and I noticed a box of Cherry Brandy liqueur chocolates on the table! My eyes couldn't miss THEM!

We then drove east, again, but further than we did the other day almost reaching the border with Spain.

We found a nice restaurant where a lot of businessmen were having their leisurely three hours' lunches, partaking of the wine and local fish. Lunch times here are long and relaxed for the locals.

We have to remember that most places are closed during this season as there are not many tourists about.

I kept my anorak on during the meal because, not realising that we were going to eat out, I put on a blouse, the sleeves of which I had cut open with scissors because they were too tight. The restaurant was up-market and I was conscious of the looks I might get if my torn sleeves were on show so I sweated it out in my coat. Fortunately Ted didn't want a pudding, nor coffee, so we didn't follow the example of all the others and were in and out in about half an hour!

In the early hours of this morning I dreamed that I was somewhere where there was a big swimming pool. On the one side of it were Ted, Paul Royce (his friend) and another of his friends. They were all happy because Ted had just secured a job in a place the name of which was difficult to pronounce. It was on an island in the North – perhaps near Finland where they spoke a different language. His friends said he would be very good at it but in my heart I knew that he wouldn't be able to do it.

Ted hadn't told me of this job and I only found out because they were rejoicing about it. I was on the opposite side of the pool. I felt alone (them and me).

I don't know the meaning of these dreams but do believe that they are significant in some way. I do, quite often, feel alone in this walk but rejoice in knowing that Father is with me through this. He promised:

> *...be content with such things as you have. For He Himself has said, "I will never leave you nor forsake you."* Heb 13:5 (emphasis mine)

Oranges are now being blown over the garden like footballs. The windows, doors and ceilings are all leaking water. Ted has been taking photographs of all the leaks 'for future reference!'

We have just been online to catch up with emails and he is upset because the owner of the villa told him that we are responsible for all electricity used here including the pumps which are programmed to go on for four hours every day for the pool. We also have to pay the standing charges for water, so he isn't happy about it. He won't say anything though but will just grieve about it. The villa has been booked for two months so we are stuck with it!

I understand that January and February are the months when almond blossom is at its best and the whole area has a beautiful scent. That is something nice and uplifting to look forward to.

When we were passing through Tavira this morning, Ted popped in to see his old school-friend, the estate agent. He wanted to thank him for leaving a bottle of wine for us as a Christmas gift. We were out when he called at the villa.

Ted got back into the car, upbeat about the weather. "James says that its going to brighten up this afternoon!" he said with glee.

I have to tell him to inform his friend he ought to stick to selling houses because his weather forecasting is way off track.

Ted is beginning to set himself various routines. I can see clearer now, where his obsessions lie and one of them is *maps*. During the journey he armed himself with two sat navs and two maps. Now, every time we go to 'incontinent' to do the shopping, he walks into the equivalent of Smiths and looks at the maps. He *always* calls an assistant over to help him. And they *always* tell him that they don't have an O.S. sheet for this area!!!!

Another little routine, which he has set up for himself is to open the front door, look out and then close it. He will then walk over to the window, look out and go back to the door. There is nothing to look at. We don't know anyone here. We are not expecting visitors... He is doing this about twenty times a day and I am beginning to find it irritating.

He is also obsessed with the weather. We have to watch the 'weather' forecast on sky tv. It doesn't give us local weather – just gives us the forecast for the UK.

I must go now and take the plank out of my eye. (Matt 7:5)

Chapter 8

Wednesday December 30, 2009

Today is my younger son, George's 26th birthday. He is brought to mind and I have been led to pray for him.

Job 3:21 (emphasis mine) *He will yet fill your mouth with <u>laughing</u> And your lips with <u>rejoicing</u>...*

Pippa and I had a game on the grass in the garden. It's a new game of ball but oranges substitute the ball. I threw them for her to catch which she did and then lay down to lick them. Part of me felt guilty about being reckless over food, but it's going rotten.

It then began to rain with force and when it eased in the afternoon we drove to the little beach again hoping we could take her walking but there were too many other dogs about and the place was heaving with people. One poor German Shepherd was obviously really ill, squatting and walking 'diarrhoea-ing' as he went along. Dogs are so neglected here and roam wild on the streets and beaches.

We drove on to 'Ohio' and then further west to Faro (the capital city of the Algarve). It was our first visit here. Some of the streets were really narrow and necessitated me having to reverse down one. What is this all about? I have to reverse either in or out of the drive of the villa. Does this mean I am going backwards?

When we found the old town within the castle walls, we were able to walk through the narrow streets with Pippa. It all looked very nice and is certainly worth another visit. The castle walls are beside the railway line and a walk way is between them. Lots of little taverns and bistros are set in the square within the castle grounds – all cobbled stones and dominated, of course, by a church.

Instead of driving back to the villa we carried on into Tavira to walk in the brightly lit streets. They were busy erecting a tent-like building in the square in preparation for the New Year celebrations, as they were doing in Faro.

All the shops seem to come to life in the evening and we found shops we hadn't noticed during our daytime visits. Ted bought a Portuguese cookbook written in English. He had agreed to purchase it and was surprised when the shopkeeper asked him, in broken English, for 59 euros! He looked towards me for help, but I had to turn away. He had made a decision and it was up to him to either say it was too expensive, or buy it as he had agreed.

He also replaced my stolen handbag by buying me another from a small shop in a side street where we had a lesson from the lady shopkeeper on how to say 'thank you' in Portuguese. I feel good now that I have a handbag. Just have to get a purse and some money to put in it!!!

Thursday December 31, 2009

A free magazine called The East Algarve Magazine is a very informative mag. Each month it focuses on one of the villages in the East and has lots of adverts. We tried getting the most up to date edition from a newsagent who didn't speak English.

The moment Ted said "Free magazine," she understood and waved her arms in a cross (bit like X-Factor) and said "No Free here…" She understood that ok!

In his efforts to find the latest copy, Ted rang the editor and was told that we could get issues from a place called Quinta Fonte do Bispo near Sta Catarina (www.qtfontebispo.com)

The owners were very welcoming and showed us round their complex of small suites, banqueting hall, gardens and bistro. We discovered that they were also the publishers/editors of the magazine. They both gave up life in the UK for a better standard of life so, together with their family, looked for a place where they could all live and work together. When they found this place, they didn't need to speak because they all knew this was 'the place!'

As we stood in the small reception area we overheard the owner on the phone receiving two cancellations for a New Year's Dinner they were putting on that evening. Immediately I felt we should take the seats. Ted was uncertain and more uncertain when he had to hand over 80 euros! The table was booked for 7.30pm.

We had been placed on a table of eight with four Yorkshire and Lancashire friends and a Dutch woman accompanied by a white-haired German ex-guitarist fellow who had brought his guitar in the hopes of refreshing his ailing career by doing a turn on the stage.

As soon as seated, the Dutch woman produced a STAR-shaped vase from her handbag, struck a match and lit a tea light, which she then popped inside the vase placing it directly in front of her setting. This immediately alerted me as I have been reading so much about STARS in The Nephilim and the Pyramid of the Apocalypse. She later gave her card to Ted and I was astonished to see that her home is called Casa Capricornus. She had printed a picture of the symbol for Capricornus on the card.

After our introductions and the others were becoming mellowed with alcohol, we had a good time. Being the driver I would not join them despite being encouraged by the fellow sitting beside me who wanted to buy me a drink. He said he could play the spoons, so he did that and I played a tune on the glasses all to the rhythm of the karaoke sung by the owner who fancied himself as Elvis. His son, was an Elvis look-alike and the grandchildren were obviously following the line.

It wasn't long before Ted was playing the glasses!

My observations of him copying me were beginning to distress me.

Thank you Father that they will cry to You in their distress and You will hear and deliver them. 2 Chron 20:9

We danced till 1am. Ted was a great source of entertainment to others by his interpretation of dance. We collected five lamb shank bones for Pip, exchanged names and addresses with our new acquaintances and saw the New Year in with *laughter* and *joy*. OK it wasn't holy righteous laughter and joy, but it was fun all the same.

Ted made a phone call to Al to wish everyone a happy new year, but although I think he got through, he said he couldn't hear anything because the music was too loud!

As we thanked the hosts, they said we must get together and talk about doing a Poetry Page for his magazine! I never cease to be amazed at the opportunities, which drop into one's lap in another country. We got home after 2am and woke up all the dogs in the neighbourhood. We went to bed at about 3am. Today is a new day!

Then the One sitting on the throne said, "Look! I am making everything new!" Rev 21:5

Friday January 1, 2010

Oh it seems strange to write a new date – a new beginning – a new day – a new season – a new year. All things are made new.

The sun shone and despite the cold wind we ate our first breakfast of the year in the garden and planned local journeys we would take in the days to come. We spent the day at the villa, both tired after being up dancing the night away the previous evening. I suppose that has something to do with age!

Chapter 9

Sunday January 3, 2010

Ooooh! I drank too much cheap plonk last night and am feeling like that sickly dog we saw the other day.

It is now becoming boring, but I have to say it's raining again.

There was no gas today; no hot water and no hob but most of all no heating. We have used two 8ft high propane gas cylinders, so Ted went out to change over to the spare. It took ages and lots of to-ing and fro-ing before he got it up and running. We have to order another couple of cylinders tomorrow at our cost.

Some, or rather few, shops are open on Sunday for the mornings only, so we went to Lidl to get some supplies then went on to the 'incontinent' shopping mall. We intended to get fresh milk because that is the only place we can buy it here. All other milk is that awful sour tasting stuff they drank in the wartime, but incontinent was closed by the time we reached it after lunch.

We took the glass lift up to the top of the shopping centre where there are lots of restaurants. Loads of tables and chairs are set out in the middle of the mall and one can walk around from the Portuguese equivalent of burger king, to a sushi bar at the other end of the scale. We decided to have the Chinese buffet style lunch where you can go up and help yourself to an array of dishes all for a set price.

We ate inside the restaurant; were shown to a table and, with sign language, were invited to help ourselves. I took a bowl from the one end of the table and selected from various bowls, a soup which I recognised – you know the kind, watery with a slither of chicken floating on the top. Ted, trying to be different today, rather than copying (I told him last night about mimicking me) selected what looked like tomato soup.

We took the bowls to the table and began to eat or drink the soup from the funny wide metal spoons they provided.

He asked me if my soup was okay and I said it was. He then said he didn't like his very much that it was very strong with soy sauce. We continued eating and I emptied my bowl, but he left some of his shaking his head and saying it was too strong.

When the waiter came to pick up the bowls, he stared at Ted and pointed to the bowl, then screamed "Its sauce... You eat sauce!"

What Ted had done was the equivalent of walking into a café in England, picked up a bowl from the side and filled it with Daddies sauce then took it to the table and started eating it from the bowl with a spoon.

It was sauce! Well, I couldn't contain my laughter. I nearly choked and almost wet myself. It was a picture. Ted laughed too – I didn't laugh AT him, but laughed at the situation. I am now laughing as I recall the scenario.

With the shopping all across the back seat of the car (Lidls don't give you plastic bags) - 'incontinent' are very good and pack it all for you as you go along – we drove north of Tavira trying to find another interesting road back to the villa. The River Gilao was still quite high and we followed a road alongside it until it changed direction then noticed some magnificent villas in the mountains. The drive was enjoyable and it had taken us out of the villa for a while.

There were lots of storks on some marsh ground near the river, their nests built high on the top of telegraph poles. I also noted a cattle egret sitting on the back of a donkey. They usually feed amongst the cattle and perch on their backs to peck off insects and flies. The wildlife here is quite prolific.

We then did a car tour of Tavira as it was still raining. Car drivers just plough through the floods irrespective of whether anyone is walking. One can see folks getting soaked from the floodwater as it splashes over them.

We passed the castle in the old Arab quarter on the top of the hill. From here the four-sided roofs that line the Rua da Liberdade are clearly visible. These pyramid-like roofs allow the sudden torrential rain to run off easily. Pity the architect of the villa didn't bear that in mind. The flat roof, here, leaks water through the light switch in my bathroom!

Chairs had been set out in the tent in The Square and a stage had been erected where the New Year's celebrations had taken place. As we drove alongside it on the cobbled street, we noticed people filling the seats and a few musicians getting ready for a performance. It was too wet to get out of the car, so we gave it a miss.

Within two miles of the villa is a village or hamlet called Synagoga (synagogue in English). We passed through with no evidence of a synagogue, and only a few houses dotted about. We hoped that we would find some interesting historical ruins left from the Jewish occupation, but the area only consisted of the road.

Yapping dogs greeted us once again as we returned to the villa. Ted had to get out to unlock the fort Knox gates and guide me through (wing mirrors tucked in because it's so narrow). He cut the hedge back the other day with some blunt tools he found in a plastic container by the side of the house. The gate now stays open more easily allowing easier passage. It then has to be locked again. I still am unable to turn the car round in the driveway and have to reverse it out.

We are going to see an estate agent tomorrow and also might drop in to see his old school pal who is also an agent. We want to see if we can find another villa for the month of February, as we shall be moving on from here on the 12th February, or before if possible.

So, as we close another day, I can't help thinking how this year is whizzing by! We watched the BBC news and weather forecast this evening just in time before the satellite closed down on us. When it rains heavily we don't get any signals and messages come up on the screen from Germany! It's a small world!

Ted carries a dictionary around with him so we can read out words (not phrases) if necessary. I need to get some ingredients to make something, anything; out of that cookery book he's bought. It was so expensive; I can't just let it sit on the table. I looked around for cinnamon today but its called something else and nearly picked up curry powder by mistake. I don't want to follow Ted's example of eating sauce for soup now do I? !!!!!!!!

Chapter 10

Monday January 4, 2010

I wore my handbag today. I wore it as a garment. It was the first time I have used it since 'the robbery'. I think it was made for a 6ft Portuguese woman because the strap is very long. Even with it crossed across my chest like a satchel it almost reaches my ankles. Inside I had my journal, a set of coloured pens, my new camera, passport, Pippa's passport and some tissues. I really didn't need to have a handbag because I don't have a purse, but I felt I needed to get some practice.

The maintenance man came round this morning to tell us that he had ordered the new propane gas bottles and presented Ted with a large bill. Cash is the order of the day. He was astonished to see how the rain had beaten through the windows and under the doors staining all the tiles and flooding the floors. The garden is still a lake and he seemed surprised that the path to the front door was more like a river.

"In eight years I've never seen anything like this," he said in his south Welsh accent, which was hard to detect at first as we are getting used to the Portuguese lingo.

We drove through Santa Barbara to a small village where the estate agent had an office situated on the corner of the main street. We were early for our 2pm appointment so looked around the mini supermarket opposite for fifteen minutes. I was so happy to find corn flour and Bisto gravy granules, which went into Ted's shopping basket. He is still in charge of all finances. Further investigation made me realise that there must be a big ex-pat community here in this little mountain village because a lot of the stock was British made.

Andrew, the estate agent, was a jolly, young person who boasted about his wife and daughter being in the business with him. He was previously employed in the office furniture business and came out here two and a half years ago with no previous house selling experience. It seems to me that plumbers can be estate agents and electricians can be doctors…. Anything goes so long as you know somebody.

He showed us pictures of lots of villas he had on his books for sale. Many of them are on offer from 'distressed sellers.' This means that they either, have ill health and need to get back to UK, or have hit hard times financially. We weren't looking to buy, but were interested to see what was available. I felt that he would tell us where we could get our next villa rental and looked to him for confirmation of our direction. Sure as ever, just as we were leaving, his parting words to us were:

"I will see if I can find you a villa to rent. I don't deal with rentals, but I know several people who might rent their villa. Ring me."

We returned through floods and storms, to 'our' villa, happy, knowing that Father had all things in His Hands. Things were not so bad until the storm woke me up in the night. I really thought an earthquake had hit the house. It shook the foundations and torrential rain, thunder and lightning continued through the night. We had no power this morning. Everyone says how unusual this weather is, but that they need the water for the boreholes.

When we got back to the villa after our villa viewing, I proudly poured the Bisto gravy over the beef burgers I had prepared earlier. This was the nearest to a Sunday lunch we have had! Then I remembered yesterday, and the sauce, and quietly giggled.

We watched Harry Hill's TV Burp and he had a gesture for sauce. He raised his hands up to his head (rather like making ears on his head) and said, "Sauce, sauce."

Ted and I hooted at that so now we have made it our own gesture and when I raise my hands to my head and make pretend ears, he knows that I am referring to his saucy moment in the Chinese restaurant.

Ted collected another map today from his estate agent friend, James. This one is only on loan and is very old, patched up with faded sellotape. He is carrying it round with him everywhere he goes. When we were in the mini supermarket for an awful moment I thought he was going to buy another map! I caught him opening up a local street map. He wants to go to a particular newsagent in Tavira to buy an up-to-date copy of this ancient keepsake, which his friend lent him. I'm hoping it's out of print!

So I am now ready to retire to bed. Pippa has made her way to bed and is lying huddled on her Dunelm Duvet. I noticed a patch of mould has appeared on the wall under the window of my room. That's because there is humidity here in the evenings, not that you would notice.

Lev 14 :33-43 The LORD said to Moses and Aaron, "When you enter the land of Canaan, which I am giving you as your possession, and I put a spreading mold in a house in that land, the owner of the house must go and tell the priest, 'I have seen something that looks like a defiling mold in my house.' The priest is to order the house to be emptied before he goes in to examine the mold, so that nothing in the house will be pronounced unclean. After this the priest is to go in and inspect the house. He is to examine the mold on the walls, and if it has greenish or reddish depressions that appear to be deeper than the surface of the wall, the priest shall go out the doorway of the house and close it up for seven days. On the seventh day the priest shall return to inspect the house. If the mold has spread on the walls, he is to order that the contaminated stones be torn out and thrown into an unclean place outside the town. He must have all the inside walls of the house scraped and the material that is scraped off dumped into an unclean place outside the town. Then they are to take other stones to replace these and take new clay and plaster the house. If the defiling mold reappears in the house after the stones have been torn out and the house scraped and plastered, the priest is to go and examine it and, if the mold has spread in the house, it is a persistent defiling mold; the house is unclean.

It isn't our house to pull down!

What we do tomorrow will be determined by the weather and that doesn't look good!

Chapter 11

Tuesday January 5, 2010

I didn't sleep well last night and remember putting out the light at 4am so consequently I am quite tired today, BUT today is sunny so everything looks different.

We decided to go into Tavira because all of the times we have been there it has been raining. We took Pippa for a walk with us. She growled ferociously showing her teeth at two stray dogs. This brought delight to some young drivers – obviously bullfighting fans. We explored tiny cobbled streets; the old castle built by the Moors in the 8th century and rebuilt after the Christians reconquered the city in 1242.

While Ted made his daily visit to the Information Office, I took Pippa up the narrow street where ruins have been discovered in an area just below the castle. Archaeologists are working on the project, which has been surrounded with stand-alone fencing – the Health and Safety commissioners would have a wonderful time here!

We walked over one of the four bridges which connect the town divided by the River Gilao, to a narrow street which Ted had been told had a newsagent who sold maps.

I waited outside the tiny doorway with Pippa while he indulged his obsession. He was such a long time that I decided to walk a short way up the river's edge to see a restaurant, Beira Rio, which has had a lot of publicity. (www.beiroriotavira.com)

Set right on the riverside with a large paved area for tables and chairs, the old building looks very grand and colonial. It was bought by two Irish families just over 2 years' ago – two brothers who were in the double-glazing industry in Roscrea, Co. Tipperary. (Everything is possible!) When they heard it was for sale, they bought it between them and moved here with their children. The notice on the door implied that they had gone back to Ireland for a month's holiday so it is closed until February but very successful according to recommendations.

Meanwhile, Ted had come out of the shop and 'lost' me. I caught sight of him waving his arms around (with new map in hand) as he danced across a small square in front of a rather imposing church.

It was really quite warm and was apparent who the English tourists were. The locals were walking about with coats and scarves and we, Brits, were sleeveless and one old couple was wearing sandals and shorts!

We moved the car to a shadier place and left Pippa while we looked for somewhere to have lunch. Lots of people were sitting out on the pavements having coffee or drinking beer. We were accosted twice, by begging Portuguese gypsies with babies on their arms and school-aged children taught in the art. I was quick to render powerless any curses they put on us because of our refusal to give.

Further on we noticed a couple that had placed their coat on the pathway for offerings while they knocked back bottles of locally brewed beer!

We came across a strange sight in front of the main church. A German woman had erected a tent on the cobblestones and all her worldly belongings were strewn across the low branch of a tree. Sheets were laid across the stones to dry and an offering box on the wall had filled with rain and caused the cigarette butts to float. I wondered how the authorities would allow her to just pitch tent there and set up home on the footpath! Strange. We later found out that she was conducting a protest.

As Ted hugged his new map, we decided to go inside a small bistro place as Germans and Dutch occupied all the chairs outside. We were a little disappointed because the food wasn't Portuguese so we ordered Italian lasagne and spaghetti bolognese. Two English couples came to sit beside us and asked if we knew where some famous golfer's new golf club was. We said we didn't play golf but thought we had passed it one of the days on our trek into the mountains. They went on to say that they were fortunate to sell their home at the right time and they now only come to play golf.

In most of the coastal towns there are Municipal Car Parks set aside specifically for motor homes. They are able to park up and sleep in these designated places. Sometimes there can be hundreds of these huge vehicles occupying every space in these vast parks. Parking there is free. We noticed, today, that most of them are German, Dutch and French registered vehicles.

On the return journey we turned off to Barril Beach thinking that we would give Pippa one more walk before going back to the villa but any hopes of that were soon dampened. Motor homes and cars were thronging the roadside and stray dogs running in between the vehicles searching for food scraps. The walk was definitely not on for today.

Instead we brought her back and played 'oranges' on the grass. She loves it. I throw a good orange for her to retrieve. The damaged ones are full of ants. She tears about getting them, sticking her teeth into them and then licking her lips! It's a wonderful way of exercising a dog because I don't have to do anything other than throw.

I was able to dry the towels today and have just put some washing on the line on the roof. It all seems very boring and more like doing the chores at home but it is the first day for a long time that I have been able to dry the washing! Yawn.

The sun sets about 5.30pm so I think we will have some bread and cheese this evening. It's been a lovely day. The sun makes such a difference when it's warm and dry.

Tomorrow evening we are going to a Quiz Night at the place where we had the dinner dance at New Year. That should be fun, *for I know nothing...*

Chapter 12

Wednesday January 6, 2010

Ted has another hobby. I noticed him striding around the periphery of the garden this morning and at first glance thought it was Basil Fawlty doing a Hitler impression. He was 'measuring' the boundaries so that he could calculate whether the architect's drawing (which he found in the study) is accurate! It's given him a mathematical exercise to do.

I, for my part, am turning into Mrs Bouquet and am cleaning before the cleaner arrives (if she does).

We sat outside, again, for cornflakes this morning although the dark clouds soon descended. The weather here can change in the twinkling of the eye!!!! That's something to bear in mind.

As we sat, we heard the train go past. It was the first time we had noticed that and then, heard an aircraft taking off from Faro airport. The wind must have changed direction, so we are hopeful that the weather will become warmer.

The three palm trees in the garden make a tremendous noise when the wind blows.

Ted and I talked over 'breakfast'. I had noticed when I took a blouse out of the wardrobe this morning that it was wetter than when I put it in there. I then discovered mould on the soaking wet wall. I said that it would be a good idea if somebody could invent a condensing de-humidifying system, which would run synonymously with an air-conditioning/heating unit. The water could be collected and run through pipes to a master unit somewhere and could be recycled. The unit could be placed on outer walls to reduce the noise and would probably be more cost effective used by solar power.

We then went on to discuss the advantages of having solar power for water and electricity, also harnessing the wind for power. We talked about the new electric car being launched by Renault. It's really smart looking and attractive and will be on the market soon. Laughingly I said wouldn't it be amazing if they invented an electrically powered aircraft. "They have!" he told me. Apparently the Chinese have launched a light aircraft, battery operated. I wouldn't like to trust the batteries going flat on that! But, he said it was safer than conventional aircraft because there are fewer bits to work.

I said that I could now see the need for community living much clearer. There will be a time when we will not be able to get power and telephones will be completely unavailable. He said that we could get a 'ham' radio system but the recipients of our calls would also have to be on the same network. (Bit like skype, but uncomputerised). To be online we would have to have telephone communications so to be self-sufficient that service would be unavailable to us. That is where the community living comes in. All those we love and want to be with would live together in a community, bringing all our skills into the stew pot, as it were.

> *Those who have ears, let them hear what the Spirit is saying to the Messianic communities. To him winning the victory I will give the right to eat from the Tree of Life which is in G-d's Gan-'Eden.'*

Pippa nuzzled up to my legs. She wanted to play 'oranges' again. Ted dashed in to get his video camera to record the score. I felt a few spots, and ran up to the roof to pull the clothes off the washing line.

11.45am (This sounds like Big Brother calling!). The cleaner has arrived.

1pm – The cleaner is still talking to Ted about how unfair it is that we should be paying for electricity and gas and how unfair this is, and how unfair that is…

I think she is only here for two hours and wonder when she will do any work. Actually, the house is clean so there is very little, if nothing, for her to do!

She said that previous occupants of the villa had complained because they couldn't get their BMW through the gates and had to reverse it and leave it in the track. Seems that others have experienced the difficulties we are having.

She is going to bring some bleach next week to "spray all the mould wot could be dangerous to your 'elf. I know all about 'elf and safety cuz I did it in the factory where I worked…"

1.15pm. She began to clean the huge bath. "Trubble is, I've told 'em that this baf aint the right sort for this country. It traps all the mould, see, you can't live 'ere like you can in the UK. It's a different kinda life. In the winter you has to close the 'ouses down 'n leave a de-'umidier on all the time – yes, 24/7 'n then in February you can open all the winders and let the hair thru."

Do we need to know all this information? Are we likely to be spending another winter here? Surely we are not going to *live* here?

She moved her hand over the outer wall of the landing and felt the soaking plaster.

"See I told 'em that these bricks aint pointed 'n if you don't have proper pointin' evrythin' comes thru. In the summer it's a breedin' ground for all manner a insects – they should a put nets up to the winders. Clients complains about bein' bit. I has to bring 'em bottles a stuff for bites. They never thinks to bring anythin' with 'em well they shouldn't 'ave to should they, it should be "all-in" 'n mosquito nets should be provided, that's what I say…"

Ted went to speak but was interrupted :

"I've just done a surprise visit to my muvver on Berkshire/Wiltshire borders 'n I missed all the bad wevver. I was lucky mind you. But they don't get wevver like we do 'ere. When it rains, it rains boy."

Weather being Ted's other pastime, he was eager to get his shovel full in but was interrupted again.

"I know from experience. All a my properties this year 'ave bin soaked. I've left all the 'eating on to dry 'em out for my clients. I'm goin' to send a nice email to these owners and tell 'em its not fair..."

I then overheard her saying to Ted, "I've just bin upstairs 'n bleached the baf it's the only way to get ridda the mould…."

She had been standing in the huge bath with a mop and bucket, slopping it all out with bleach.

She also advised us that we probably had a bird's nest in the chimney. She had brought her rods with her but hadn't time to clean the chimney herself but would get the maintenance chap to borrow them and do it! Here is a superwoman! I think Ted was impressed by her rods and began to show more interest in her non-stop conversation.

1.45pm. Bang on, she prepared to leave. What a relief! With a flash of her gold tooth, she brought forth a prediction that we were in for dreadful weather this afternoon! I wonder if she is any better a weatherman than Ted's estate agent friend?

Ted had another practice of his Basil Fawlty walk – this time around the pool. I think this is going to be the new pastime. He wanted to 'measure' it to see if it was the same size as described in the advert! He has to put on his Wellingtons to achieve the correct result, whatever that is! I hope he doesn't decide to check whether the mapmaker's measurements are accurate. We could be in for some long walks……

We ventured into the dark, wet night prepared for the unknown. The Quiz Night was being held at the same place we had the dinner dance on New Year's Eve.

Pippa lay in the boot while we felt our way across the stony cobbled path following the line of trees now hardly visible. Solar lights don't seem to give off much light. I'll have to talk about that one when we next discuss solar energy!

The small room was filled with tables and chairs only a couple, perhaps mother and daughter, were occupying one near the fire. The small bar was on the right as we climbed the step. The warmth hit us in the face. We have been so cold in the villa that even sitting in the car brought the blood stream to life.

The barman, a large Yorkshire man, displayed huge black tattoos on each arm. Somehow he knew Ted by name and informed us that the 'special' tonight was Lancashire hotpot. Mmmh, no disputes here... I always thought that Lancashire and Yorkshire were at odds with each other!

We ordered the special and headed towards a table at the far end of the room. We sat side by side so that we could observe the others who were joining the group and perhaps assess what size their brains were.

Gradually the room filled and I had the distinct feeling that I was in the north of England with the broad northern accents crescending to an alto.

A few nods were thrown towards us, but that was all. Everyone knew each other but they didn't know us. They weren't likely to either if they were not going to speak to us.

The Lancashire hotpot was quite acceptable and wasn't fatty as I had expected. After a few mouthfuls my circulatory system kicked in and I began to feel a bit warmer.

The door opened and the couple we met and whose table we shared at New Year, headed towards us. The beer was ordered and Karen took charge of the paper work, as she was experienced in the Quiz format.

I didn't contribute much to the effort, but Ted was hailed hero of the night for saying that the unknown warrior was buried under the Arc de Triomphe. Well, what good is that kind of information going to do for me?

We purchased tickets for the draw, which raises funds for young children in the area, or sometimes they are used for sterilising the stray dogs and cats. The prizes were bottles of wine, but the special prize draw, which rolls over each week if not won, was an opportunity to choose a key out of a bag. If successful in drawing the correct key to open a small cash box, the winner would be the recipient of 90 euros, running at that amount this week.

Guess what! I won the opportunity to take a *key*. The bag of *keys* was given to me. I found that so significant. Regrettably I didn't choose the key which fitted the cash box, but I'm glad really because I don't want to be 'winning' things. I'm glad they weren't car keys – I've heard of that game.

So the 90 euros were rolled over until next week when some extra will be added.

Ted was sitting opposite a Yorkshire man, a hardened drinker who kept getting up to buy more beer, each time offering to buy us drinks. I had to tell Ted to buy a round, as I don't think he realised the form.

The scores were counted and our little group came last. Never mind, it was fun. I think we might go next week but I might hide under the table if we do because Karen and Chris are going back to UK on Saturday!

Chapter 13

Thursday January 7, 2010

A cold, but fine morning! I heard Ted talking to a female and discovered that Cassie, the lesbian gardener had arrived. I wasn't sure what she could do because the land is so waterlogged.

Ted was in his elements because he was able to have a conversation about the weather. She, also, professed to be a weatherman! Everyone here claims to have powers to predict the weather and nobody, so far, has been right.

She said that she would pick up all the fallen oranges (poor Pippa will have to have hand-picked oranges for her games now) and prune the trees in the orchard. I suspect that this is a ploy for I don't see any attention being given to any of the other orchards in the area.

I opened all the windows and doors to allow the cold wind to blow through the house. I thought if I 'aired' the place it might slow down the mould growth. We didn't hear the train, or the planes today so the wind has changed direction and that is why it is colder.

To take full advantage of the sunshine we decided to find a beach where Pippa could have some freedom to run without being on her lead. I drove east, again, towards the Spanish border to a township called Manta Rota. We approached the beach through one of those municipal car/truck parks where the mobile homes gather in clusters. Access to the beach was by a long wooden footbridge, which opened up to a long, wide, pale sandy beach.

Pippa ran and rolled in the sand, then headed straight for the sea. The waves were high and she almost had to swim at one point. We took some pictures of her and she is actually smiling and showing her teeth on one of the images proving how much she enjoyed it all.

When she was tired out we popped her in the boot of the car into her cosy bed and found a little local restaurant to have some lunch.

Typically it was just a long room filled with tables and chairs. There were two large families eating, who all turned their heads to stare at us as we entered.

The waiter didn't speak English, so with sign language and two words we have learned, we were presented with olives, bread and sardine pate as something to go on with while they cooked my striped bream (fresh from the boat) and Ted's sword fish.

The puddings here are absolutely delicious. Mostly made of sweet almond and fig paste. It is sheer sweet heaven! I must see if I can go on a cookery course to learn how to make these wonderful desserts. Of course we tried a couple afterwards and shared them between us so that we could savour the different flavours.

A couple brought their very old mother for lunch and sat at a table close to us. The old lady was so small that she hardly reached up to the table. Her appetite was so bird-like that the daughter asked for another plate on to which she removed most of the mother's meal. Why do the old ladies here insist on dying their hair black? I have not seen one grey-haired woman. And, in the supermarkets, they only sell black hair colour. I shall be returning home looking younger – or older. I think having black hair with sallow skin makes one look old.

We carried on towards the town of Vila Real de Sto. Antonio, which joined to Spain by a new expansion bridge. The beach was wonderful. It was miles long and hardly anyone was there apart from a few fishermen so once again Pippa was given another bout of freedom and more pictures!

VRS Antonio, as they call it, has all its streets arranged on a grid system – as straight as soldiers on parade. It is said that the town was built very quickly (in five months) the contingencies of policy towards Spain and the Marquis of Pombal, Prime Minister of King Jose, meant that it had to be! Sardine and tuna fishing turned the town into a major canning centre and a city of wealth.

Ted was anxious to try another supermarket on the way back because he had heard that he could buy garlic sausages. I happened to see this particular shop on a traffic island so pulled in for him to get them. They also sold fresh milk and *cream*. What a treat! Cream!

When we got back to the villa and made coffee, it tasted so delicious!

Since the Quiz Night Ted has been watching Celebrity Mastermind on the television. I think they must be showing it every night. He now has to try to outdo the contestants by trying to answer all the questions. I am wondering whether that Quiz Night was a good idea after all!

We have booked to have Portuguese lessons. If these people can't speak English then we shall have to learn their language.

Our first session is next Tuesday afternoon.

Chapter 14

Friday January 8, 2010

A beautiful sunny day! We had an early appointment with the Welsh estate agent, Andrew, who is a Ricky Gervais look-alike. I had to remind myself that he wasn't a comedian despite his continuous smile and Gervaisian mannerisms, and that we needed to be serious! We had agreed to meet him in The Square at Estoi, a small village in the hills north of the coast.

He was drinking coffee outside a small café with his wife, Lana, so we joined them before setting off to look at various properties he had to offer.

The first was a villa in an agricultural zone in Santa Barbara de Nexe, which was nicely fenced off, but, oh! *so* English. The lawn was manicured and I could have mistaken it for somewhere in the Midlands. The vendors were moving back to the UK to be near their grandchildren but were keeping an apartment here to come back to regularly.

A lot of middle-aged/elderly do this apparently, as in Portugal there is no inheritance tax to pay if you are resident in the country for 183 days a year!

The second place we saw was a holiday villa, owned by a Scottish family, built to a very high spec and quite palatial. We learned that properties here are normally built for occupation only in the summer. They are not properly insulated and therefore suffer damp and rain penetration. This villa had been built to a higher spec suitable for all year occupation. It wasn't 'distressed' as such, but the owners wanted to sell quickly because they needed to secure another property, so it was likely they would rent it for a month.

The third property was set on a hillside so steep that I wondered whether the brakes on the car would hold. I asked Pippa to keep still while we took a quick look round. Owned by an Asian woman, I didn't get a good feel about it. The person who had unlocked it for us was also Asian so there might be a little community there. We wrote that off as a possibility due to the precarious position of the villa propped on the edge of what looked like a cliff!

The fourth and last property we viewed was high on a hilltop. A single storey building (which looked as though it could be two properties joined by glass on both sides.) Within the glass bit was a beautiful large room furnished with a long table at the rear and sun-loungers at the front – both sides enjoying wonderful views. The rear glass doors opened to a courtyard where the barbeque was built into rock. A stone table and benches were set in the paving slabs. The view from the glass windows at the front was spectacular. An infinity pool at the front allowed one to just see the pool water and then the <u>Atlantic Ocean</u> beyond. Paths criss-crossed the land below with ancestral windmills as points of reference along the ancient rural byways.

Infinity pools are built in such a way that there is no side to them – the water cascades down into a channel and is pumped back into the pool, so it just appears that there is only water going on to infinity.

An excerpt from the local magazine:

Right in the HEART of the Eastern Algarve, the municipality of Sao Bras de Alportel is an OPEN DOOR to the mountains and A WINDOW OVERLOOKING THE OCEAN, curiously peeking in between hills – a cheerful land, waiting or us with a smile!"

The owner of the property, a Dutch man whose marriage has broken is now desperate to sell but would consider a short term let in the meantime. Perhaps this is our next stop?

Pippa had lots of investigating to do where the zones were dog-free so we were happy to leave her in the car while we all had lunch in a tiny restaurant in the small, peaceful village of Estoi. It is a traditional Algarvian village with an astonishing architecture and cultural heritage.

When we first arrived there we drove around the one-way system but didn't find a parking place in The Square and ended up driving about a mile around a long wall, which we later discovered was the palace wall. It has now been converted to a pousada. It's a huge building, the exterior is partially covered with tiles bearing floral decoration and depicting a variety of scenes. This is quite common with a lot of properties and at first I thought the tiles were the type we would put on the floor at home. The outside of the houses look quite ghastly tiled with patterned tiles.

The restaurant had simply a door on to the road, but inside it opened up into a long room, which could seat up to 100 covers. The Portuguese owner spoke no English, but Andrew (who has lived here for over 2 years) was able to order fish, again, in the native tongue. I wondered whether we would be as adept after our Portuguese lessons!

We learned that this couple were Believers and he said he was 'hooked' after doing an Alpha Course. I then knew where they were!

We said our goodbyes and continued our adventure towards Faro airport and beyond to a beach recommended by Lana. It wasn't as nice as the others we have seen and a quick walk across the dark uninviting sand was enough for us all. The wind was bitingly cold, blowing through my very bones. I couldn't wait to get the car seat warm!

When we got back to the villa, I realised that I had left my trousers on the washing line all day. I climbed up to the roof only to find that they had been pooed on by a gecko. I remember, now, why I don't like hanging washing on a line. They have to be washed again and hopefully we shall have a day without rain so that I can dry them.

Saturday January 9, 2010

Armed with seven maps (yes, I counted them!) and a dictionary, Ted prepared to go on a journey west. I really wanted to stay at the villa to read, but as I am the driver, decided to go on his leading!

We drove along the only motorway, which cuts through villages and farmsteads. I haven't seen many sheep here and was surprised to see a good flock on some scrubland, but with a shepherd. Another time I had seen sheep and goats together in an enclosure with their shepherd who was armed with a gun. It appears that the sheep are never left without a shepherd. Isn't that wonderful to know. As we, too, are never left without our Shepherd.

I will raise up One Shepherd to be in charge of them... He will pasture them and be their Shepherd... Ezek 35:23

We did a small diversion to look at the town of Silves. Although its commanding position made it an ideal fortified settlement, we were quite disappointed that it didn't have much to offer other than the red sandstone walled castle standing out against the skyline, and a canal. The Portuguese are very fond of their castles and have many of them. We drove through the only street and then continued our journey west.

The soil here is rich with copper and looks bright red. On the hillsides the farmers have adapted the Chinese method of farming by digging terraces deep into the hills.

We stopped at a roadside restaurant for lunch. It was a typical Portuguese local with an awning sprawled across trees, housing tables and chairs. Inside the restaurant, tables were covered with paper cloths and, judging by the amount of people crammed in, we thought it must be very popular. It seems that we are the source of great amazement when we enter these little restaurants because, invariably, the locals drop their forks and turn their heads to stare at us. A silence sweeps the place momentarily while they size us up. It is quite off-putting.

We chose to sit outside; much to the dismay of the waitress who, in sign language, placed her arms across her chest and muttered, "cold!"

The sun was warm on my back as we sat under a tree. It wasn't until we were eating our soup that I noticed we were sitting under a huge lemon tree heavily laden with fruit. It reminded me of Lawrence Durrell's book, "Bitter Lemons" goodness knows why! Perhaps I need to read it again.

We had been heading towards the village of Monchique – a small market town nestling high in the mountains, famous for its altitude (1,500 ft) and wooden handicrafts particularly folding chairs which are believed to date back to Roman times. A painter and decorator who, acting as an estate agent, was offering a rental property and had contacted Ted, so we were curious to see what the area was like.

Ted noticed the name of the agency over a shop window and introduced himself to a scruffy young man inside the shop, who apologised for his dress.

"Sorry for my look but I didn't change. I wear only this and sorry for that….."

While Ted talked with him, I took Pippa across the road to wait. Two stray dogs approached her whereupon she immediately turned into a little lion. Her teeth set and her roar was awesome. Within *seconds* a crowd of six or seven men had gathered to watch with glee. I'm sure they were expecting a dog fight and probably had already taken bets. Even a couple of young lads slowed down their car to get a good view of the proceedings.

We put her back into the car and went into the only little coffee shop to taste the local cakes. It was packed out with people, mostly elderly. We guessed that this must be the pastime for Saturday afternoons. One old man sat in the corner with his bowler hat tilted on his weather-beaten face as he pulled an almond tart to pieces with his fingers. An old lady got up from a table beside me to go to the counter and I noticed she was wearing Nora Batty tights. They were certainly the vogue in this area as most of the ladies were wearing them too!

We felt that we were a bit at the 'back of beyond' and found a scenic route quite by accident. The road began as a fork in the main road but soon deteriorated into a stone track. We had travelled for quite a long time and wondered whether we should continue or turn back. The road ran steep down the mountainside amongst the forest and then we climbed up another ridge.

After a mile or two, the desolation was concerning me. Was there an end to this track or would we have to go all the way back? There were no houses anywhere and at the bottom of the mountains in the valley was a river. We then noticed the occasional shack built on the riverbanks and of course the dogs. It's hard to imagine that people actually live in these sheds.

Then the road seemed to break up and a landslide had caused a blockage. I contemplated, and then decided that the car was capable of driving over rocks and rubble. It was unnerving but I was relieved to get over to the hardcore on the other side, which represented a road.

God is our refuge and strength, an ever-present help in trouble. Therefore we will not fear, though the earth give way and the mountains fall into the heart of the sea, though its waters roar and foam and the mountains quake with their surging. "Selah" Psalm 46:1-3

Those who have criticised the 4x4 are the ones who have been grateful for their services during the snow in England. Perhaps they might take a different view of their versatility in future!

In the course of time we did reach an absolutely fabulous bit of new tarmac, which led us on to the main route once again. As we headed for Portimao, the countryside seemed to be a bit more civilised.

Portimao, one of the largest towns in the Algarve, is a coastal tourist town consisting mostly of high-rise apartments and large sea front hotels. Rebuilt after the earthquake in 1755, mostly on a cliff edge, access to the beach is down hundreds of very steep steps. The waterfront and marina, further along the coast, is at sea level and lined with restaurants serving sardines and sea bass fresh from the boats.

We took Pippa along the headland where lots of little restaurants were preparing for the next season by decorating the frontages in readiness for the business they hoped to generate. We imagine that it would get very busy indeed judging by the amount of accommodation we saw.

Time was passing and it was almost dark so we began our return journey. As we approached Loule, I turned off the motorway to just drive through the town to see what it was like. We were taken by surprise! It's an attractive market town and thriving craft centre. Each street was decorated with the most beautiful themed lighting. In one street the palm trees had their trunks lit up – in another street large green iron leaves had been erected in the trees and were lit with green bulbs. Ted tried to take a picture of them but it was difficult to capture the sheer beauty. We were told that on Saturdays the area is particularly lively when gypsies run a simultaneous outdoor market. I'm so glad we did that detour.

We joined the motorway again and headed towards Tavira.

"*Right!*" said Ted, so I turned the wheel furiously to take a right turning, which I had almost over run at 80kpm.

"Straight on! Straight on!" he shouted correcting me. "*Right*, I've now sussed out where we are!"

I was glad to get back to the villa after 200 miles of driving I was tired!

Sunday January 10, 2010

I came downstairs to see Ted stooped over the kitchen floor shining a torch on the tiles.

"Ants!" he exclaimed.

"We've got ants…"

A trail of tiny, weenie, little black ants that looked like poppy seeds had made a line from the architrave on the door to Pippa's food dish.

Prov 6:6 *Lazy people should learn a lesson from the way the ants live. They have no leader, chief or ruler but they store up their food during the summer getting ready for winter.*

It amazes me that they are able to detect food from such a distance. They have obviously been awakened from their sleep to take advantage of an opportunity. I must stay awake.

"Where's the ant powder?" he asked.

I didn't know where they kept the ant powder, but had a much better idea and boiled the kettle to pour over them, then mopped it all up. I think we have resolved that matter now.

The heavens opened this afternoon and heavy rain caused a much bigger flood than we have had to date. Ted got the video camera and went paddling outside to film the current gushing past the front door.

We watched 'The Boy in Striped Pyjamas' this evening when Ted had discovered how to get the DVD player working. Let's hope it doesn't rain tomorrow.

Chapter 15

Monday January 11, 2010

The moisturising cream and a few cosmetics I had brought and placed in a cupboard in the bathroom were standing in a pool of water this morning. Rain has leaked through the light switch in the ceiling and poured down saturating the cupboard and soaking the floor. The roof above is flat and flooded so the water is finding a way through.

There are mirrors everywhere. I haven't had mirrors on the wall for years and prefer not to look at my image. Vanity profanes!

Catching a glimpse of myself in an opposite mirror, I saw the scars on my back.

"Mmmh. So that's my scar. I have never seen it before. Two parallel lines running up my spine look like a highway. A highway of scars. That sums my life up, I suppose."

But I am thankful that I am in the process of being healed from all that stuff. It's an ongoing work, but I know I shall be perfect one day!

I press on toward the goal to win the prize for which God has called me heavenward in Christ Jesus. Phil 3:14

An army of ten thousand ants was marching across the black granite worktops in the kitchen this morning. Who thought of having black worktops? I can't SEE them clearly. Have they been there all the time and I just haven't noticed them? Have we been *eating* them?

I now want to alienate myself from the kitchen and don't want to eat here any longer. It all feels unclean.

Several boiled kettles later and frantic mopping seemed to do the trick. Out came my spray of Limpa Vidros, I assumed it was the equivalent of Dettol antiseptic spray. Closer inspection revealed a tiny window on the label and I realised that I had been cleaning the surfaces down with window cleaner. We need to understand this language - it's a barrier. We need to break down these barriers! So, having been sprayed with window cleaner and boiled, we thought we had won the battle.

Ted wanted to see Loule again in the daylight. It was so 'enchanting' when we drove through the other evening so we set out on our journey of discovery.

We noticed a sign for "Garden Centre" and thought we would go and say 'hello' to the English couple who had opened it about eighteen months' ago. It seems to me that this part of the world has only created a lively ex-pat community in the last two or three years.

The couple had, in their past lives, lived in the west of Scotland and then the north of England. His career was working for a Pound shop. We think he was a delivery driver who knew where to go to get supplies. The couple decided to purchase a large villa with plenty of land here and started up a garden centre. It was a bit stock-light and the shelves only displayed English food – all the items that one wouldn't find in a local supermarket. The rear of the premises was set out 'Pound shop style' with cheap lines of almost everything you could think of.

The entrepreneur told us that his father is building a villa on another parcel of land near to their home. Here is another example of someone changing career and seeking 'prosperity' in another land.

On entering the town via the new bye-pass (lots of new roads and bridges have been built with EU funding) and passing the big supermarkets of Modelo and Lidl, we came into the heart of Loule. It seemed larger and dustier – drabber than we had expected and was overrun with cars. We were disappointed. It was very difficult to find anywhere to park as the streets were lined with cars, some double-parked. After circling around for a couple of times, we decided to go to Modelo, the large French supermarket with an underground car park. We needed some supplies so it was convenient to go there and also see what they had to offer.

Inside the complex and alongside Modelo, were smaller shops. It wasn't quite a shopping mall, but a photographer, farmacia (pharmacy) and vodafone had set up outlets. I had been told that prescription drugs are available here over the counter so I asked about my cholesterol reducing tablets. The woman in the pharmacy didn't understand me so I didn't pursue. I shall need some more and only have another month's supply. Perhaps I can ask Ricky Gervais where I can get them. He said his brother in UK was a pharmacist and sent him stuff out.

> Jesus turned and saw her. "Take heart, daughter," he said, "your _faith_ has _healed_ you." And the woman was _healed_ at that moment. Matt 9:22 (emphasis mine)

I wanted to buy ground almonds and have not been able to find them anywhere. It then dawned on me that the women collect the almonds and then grate them, as we do nutmegs. That's why I haven't been able to buy them in that form.

I kept losing Ted as he felt the need to explore the aisles ahead of me. He was in hot pursuit of glue. It needed to be water resistant. He caught up with me waving a package with such delight; you'd think he had won the lottery.

His card was rejected at the checkout so he had to pay cash. He had forgotten that our cards are not accepted here. I haven't handled a coin so would be hard-pressed to understand the currency.

We did another circuit of the town and found a shady parking space up a narrow cobbled street just at the end of a line of cars with enough space for us to squeeze in. Having thought about it, I felt we should take Pippa with us so that we did.

A few chairs and tables were set on the corner of a crossroads at the edge of the town so Ted went inside the establishment to see if we could have something to eat. The Portuguese owner spoke with broken English telling us he had very nice chicken so we took him at his word.

When the very nice chicken arrived, it was simply chopped pieces on the bone covered with an orange oily sauce, fringed by fried potato. It was so oily that I'm glad Pippa was at my feet so that I could drop my portion down to her as well as dripping most of the oil down my sweater. I was annoyed really because I had washed it and it took about 3 days to dry and wasn't completely dry when I put it on because all the clothes in the wardrobe are damp. I hoped I would find some way of getting the oil stain out – perhaps I could use that all-purpose window cleaner?

The nearby businesses were closing for the three hours' lunch and a lot of people walked inside the restaurant, some not bothering to extinguish their fags! The smoking ban is non-existent here, although they are very much in favour of the subsidies they get! They appear to pick-and-choose the rules they want to abide by!

Conscious of the fact that the shopping had been left on the back seat of the car and that the sunshine, although not directly on the car, was quite warm, I wanted to return so began to walk Pippa while Ted paid for the lunch.

She caused much amusement to teenagers who were sitting outside a pizza café eating their lunch. I suppose they hadn't seen a dog of her breed and all stood up to take a good view of her. Pippa, however, was undeterred by the commotion and continued sniffing the footpath where I've no doubt that many strays had left their mark.

We passed an old lady shepherd with her goatherd. The shepherds usually sleep with their herds, often in shacks.

When we returned to the villa and began to unload the car, we were greeted by a secondary army of ants. Our battle procedure recommenced and when we thought we had conquered, Ted fished around in the polythene bags to get his glue.

"What are you going to do with that?" I asked.

"I'm going to glue up the hole where the ants are coming from."

"*Glue??*"

"Yes, glue!"

I left him to it. Armed with his torch he set about gluing the hole up. We still have ants!

Tuesday January 12, 2010

I am finding it much easier to write 2010. I quite like it and favour it over 2009. Perhaps there is significance there?

A ferocious wind is tearing across the land today bending trees almost double. Fruit has been blown off the trees and the garden looks like a ballpark with oranges everywhere. When it all subsides Pippa will have a wonderful time sniffing out the ones she likes. She doesn't eat them, but likes to lick the skins especially if they have been split. She then spends a lot of time licking her face and rolling her tongue round her cheeks.

Our first Portuguese lesson was at 3pm in Sao Bras. Ted had taken directions from Lydia, the teacher, so we set out in the rain and wind in plenty of time.

We turned right, as directed, at the Fiat dealership in the town. One would have expected a large glass building with cars displayed on a forecourt but this was merely a small shop front with the Fiat logo above the window.

We didn't know which of the apartments she lived in and so didn't know which button to press on the intercom. After looking through the letterboxes at the side of the large security door, we deduced which apartment was hers by guessing what mail she might receive.

Lydia was a slightly built woman probably in her fifties. She had dark red dyed hair and eyebrows pencilled in black semi-circles high over her eyes, Edith Piaf style. She invited us through the dark hallway of the apartment into a small, dark sitting room filled with large paintings and pictures on the walls. The shutters were closed at the long window and a huge chandelier gave a dull light.

She beckoned towards a small round table tucked away in the corner of the room, gesturing for us to be seated. The table was dominated by a large vase of dead flowers, which she had to move in order to see me.

The lesson began by Lydia explaining it was necessary to learn which words were masculine and feminine. She produced a sheet of paper containing verbs for us to learn. It all seemed like very hard work to me and I am wondering whether I shall be able to persevere.

We said we would see her again at the same time next week, but in the meantime Ted made contact with another Portuguese lady who teaches the language and lives closer to where we are staying. She may have a different teaching technique and after all, we only want to be able to have a conversation. We don't want to write a dossier. An appointment for a two hours session with the new teacher was made for Thursday week. Ted cancelled our lesson with Lydia.

This evening we began our homework. Lydia had suggested that we watch a 'Soap' on Portuguese TV as an excellent way of learning everyday language. It's a pity that we only have Sky TV and can only get BBC. Another method of learning to speak the lingo is to buy a local newspaper. It's all so challenging and time consuming for somebody my age!

Chapter 16

Wednesday January 13, 2010

Goodness! I am morphing into an alien! Or, have I digested the contents of the book I have been reading, The Ahriman Gate? My big toe nail is disintegrating and changing into pure calcium. It looks like talcum powder. This calls for deep cream treatment. Is nothing sacred?

If only I could spend more time online, perhaps I could investigate the cause of this but, as it is, Ted's antennae bring him to the laptop each time I open the lid. The dongle we have to enable us to get online is rather like a pay-as-you-go phone. It eats up the credit and as a consequence, he has decided to use the stopwatch part of his wristwatch to calculate up to the nearest five minutes of usage. We are charged in units of five minutes so his mathematical brain kicks in to continually inform me of how long I have left!

It is most irritating trying to dance my fingers over the keyboard and more often than not I can't risk using the shift key for capital letters in case I lose everything. It's a rush against time. That, also, is significant for isn't life a rush against time? Time is short. We are in the days of Noah when all the earth was corrupt. The circle of life on earth is turning and going back again in time towards the Garden of Eden.

There is a disturbance in the track at the front of the house. Five men of differing ages are arguing with our direct neighbour, an old, Portuguese lady who wears black. This indicates that she is a widow. Complete with black hat she is waving her arms about while they stand in awe of her. I wondered whether two of the men were strangers (opportunists maybe) and then the older, local men joined them.

I'm out of hearing range, but wouldn't understand what they were saying anyway. Our language lesson has only given us verbs and adjectives to learn, oh, of course and the alfabeto. I might buy a child's reading book – a story I know and can relate to – to see if that helps!

It's Wednesday again and the weeks are flying past. Rene should come today. I haven't done any preparation as I did last week. The kitchen hasn't been used because of the ant invasion so everything is clean so Mrs Bouquet is on holiday!

Ted is out again checking the oil on the car. You would think it was an old 'knacker' the way he keeps dipping. I suppose we are knocking up a fair mileage as we drive about 100 miles every day. We filled up again with diesel yesterday and he remarked how the price had risen since last week. I wish there were a way that I could make the car run on fresh air! We then revert to our conversations about self-sufficiency!

Rene arrived at 12.30pm with her bucket filled with bottles and sprays. Immediately she walked into the room she began to talk and so talked and talked and talked.

An hour later she took the bleach (which she had promised last week) up to the bathroom and I heard her scrubbing the bath. She also scrubbed the wall beneath the window where the rain leaks and has made the most astonishing pattern of black mould.

She was soon back to begin talking again. I asked her how old she is and she told me forty-one. She seems to know a great deal about every subject under the sun.

Putting on the hat of weatherman (again) she informed us that we shouldn't expect a change in the rainy weather until after at least two days because there is a full moon and the tides don't change until after that! When asked how she knew that, and who taught her this method of predicting, she said her grandfather followed the moon and stars. I believe she is from gypsy stock, right down to her gold tooth!

She began to lecture us on how we should be self-sufficient as she is. She makes all her own medicines (medicine man?) out of herbs and plants and when the "crunch" comes and we can't use money, people will come to her to barter for medicines.

Her partner has built a cistern for storing water and she is not going to have a chip embedded in her forehead nor hand, "No bl***** way, man! They aint getting' me on that! I knows all about it man. They'm watchin' you now through the telly it's all connected by them sat-lites. I turns my cellphone off at night, man. I aint 'aving nun a that stuff comin' intu my 'ead! I leaves it in the car."

She told us that she can "go in and see" (whatever that means.) She has 'seen' a lion and a lamb and the lion's head manifest into *Jesus Christ* and a rat came out of the lamb's mouth.

"Folks don't know about rats. The Iranians am goin' to send rats and it only takes three drops and all our water'll be contam-nated. There's no hope. Shwwwh!" and she sliced the air with her hand indicating that we shall all be cut off!

"But I shell be alright Jack. I'm goin' to be one a the 144,000."

What a lot of bunkum. I became exhausted. I felt sad that she was being deceived. I have to confess that I don't feel comfortable with her. Her demeanour isn't good; she twitches and sways as she stands. Her big eyes flash about as she stares wickedly.

She overstayed her time here by an hour. For three hours she only washed the bath, the rest of the time she commanded our attention.

It was almost as though she sucked the very breath out of me. I felt like a rag doll after she had left but despite how I felt, I immediately cleaned the threshold of the house leaving no trails of whatever she had delivered here.

We have both decided that we need to leave this house. Ted had paid upfront for the rental until February 12th but we both agree that we need to move on. The house is damp and terribly expensive to keep warm.

Rene said that she had told the owners that we were going to get pneumonia, which I dismissed immediately. She is not going to put stuff on us by words of her mouth.

Who has helped you utter these words? And whose spirit spoke from your mouth? Job 26:4 (emphasis mine)

I have been coughing and Ted has begun to do the same. I am concerned because I cannot discern whether he is copying me, or seriously has developed a cough. So, our next move is in the hands of Andrew aka Ricky Gervais. I have left it that we are guided by what he says. He phoned Ted last night to say that both houses we liked are available for a month. Ted is undecided and 'logically' wants to take the Scottish couple's house, which is solidly built and probably warmer. I don't know which we have to take. I believe the agent will give us the answer in the next couple of days.

...but those that wait upon the LORD, they shall inherit the earth" Psalm 37:9

Diane and Clive are coming on Saturday so we shall certainly be staying here for them and I believe we are to move out at the end of the month.

It was Quiz Night at Quinta but I didn't have the energy to go out in the lashing wind and rain. Instead we sat and talked as Pippa lay on her rug on the small sofa, which is only big enough for her and me. It was good.

Massaged cream into feet and went to bed!

Chapter 17

Thursday January 14, 2010

I am so proud of Pippa! She went out into the garden to do her business this morning and was confronted by the little grey dog from next door, cocking his leg up an orange tree. He had gained entry into the garden from under the fence and was standing crying. Pippa stood tall, a ripple went down her back and her hairs stood up, but she just turned her head and walked inside.

I learned yesterday from Rene the reason why heads turn when the locals see Pippa and how bets are definitely exchanged in the streets at a second's notice when they see her growling and ready to fight.

Pit bulls, Staffies and bulldogs are banned from Portugal. They are only allowed here if, as visitors, they are brought for a temporary stay. And, if in the streets, they should be muzzled. It all clicks into place now. Here is little Pip, prancing around the streets in her diamante collar, unmuzzled, showing her teeth and roaring like a lion, it gets the blood pressure rising in the local men who have an in-built fighting instinct living next door to bull-fighting country.

We heard a chorus of about five dogs all crying this morning. It was such a weird sound. They sounded like a barbershop choir.

Although the fierce wind is still with us, its much warmer today and the sun is shining. I don't know how long it will last because it can change instantly without warning. (In the twinkling of an eye! – again!)

I have done a load of washing and put it on the line on the roof hoping that I have anchored it down well and that it doesn't blow away, hoping also that it will dry. We have opened all the windows and doors to allow the wind to blow through the house and have been informed that it takes about 4 months to dry out a house after the winter!

The propane gas ran out last night so Ted had to step out into the rain, wind and darkness with his torch to switch over to a spare bottle. The bottles are located at the end of the drive, some distance away from the house and seem to last only five or six days. He has spent most of the morning making out a spreadsheet to calculate how much gas we use a day and how much it costs! So successful was the spreadsheet, that he has now made out a similar one to assess and monitor the costs of the electricity.

I had no idea that he was logging the dates and times we have been putting on the heating and the time that it has been turned off. He knows exactly how many hours the heating has been on. So, on all the occasions I have seen him screwing up his face and staring into the thermostat with his torch, he has been monitoring the temperature and keeping notes.

We decided, this morning, that no English language will be spoken in the house from now on. This is going to be difficult because we don't know any Portuguese words!

Ted is walking around with a dictionary in his hand and all I can say is "Sim!" which means 'yes'. Well, I suppose that's a positive word.

Pippa responds to her name being called with a Portuguese accent. When I shouted, "Pee-pa" she seemed to understand.

This new method of communication has brought shrieks of laughter between us and on one occasion when Ted was trying to explain why he had put a piece of writing paper in the bin, I simply had to rush for the loo. It was all too much for my bladder.

"Nao compreendo!" is my favourite phrase. It then excuses me while I flick through my exercise book for more enlightenment.

We have laughed so much. This little exercise is hilarious because neither of us knows what we are saying.

Occasionally, well, frequently, Ted says something to me in English and I quickly respond with,

"Desculpe. Nao compreendo Ingles!" (Sorry, I don't understand English) which makes us fall about.

I'm sure the little old lady next door must be amused listening to highly accented versions of Portuguese trailing over the fence telling Pee-pa that she is a 'Bom Cao!!" (good girl)

It was pleasantly sunny this afternoon. Not warm enough to be out without long sleeves, but lovely nevertheless. Ted busied himself by oiling the lock on the gate, which leads to the orchard, in between shining the torch on the temperature thermostat of the heating system. He also collected a few broken branches from the orange trees to fill in the gaps in the fencing where the loose dogs are getting in, watched carefully by 'Pee-pa'.

We are beginning to sing our conversations now. Our monotones become baritones as we have adopted a foreign accent. Ted is slipping back to Ingles and I am constantly telling him I don't understand English! It's all so funny.

The bookshelves here, in the villa, are well stocked with books ranging from a complete set of John Grisham, to books on People Watching and Mind Reading. Whilst scanning through them this morning I felt drawn towards a book called 'Driving over Lemons' written by Chris Stewart, the ex-drummer of

Genesis. I have only just begun to read it but it appears to be an account of his life in a remote part of Spain where they moved to live and survive on a farm. Perhaps this is a substitute for 'Bitter Lemons?'

So, as the sun goes down, Ted is sitting in a deckchair by the side of the house reading a book with a Pina Colada at his elbow. I don't really think he is enjoying it (the drink, nor the book!) but he likes to sit in the sun whenever it comes out. After an exhausting day of to-ing and fro-ing from the temperature gauge and computer I suppose he is entitled to relax!

I, for my part, have to go and find something to cook. Last night's attempts were disastrous. Apart from the gas fading on me, the salted codfish I cooked according to the recipe in the new, expensive, cookbook nearly made me sick. The method quite clearly stated to wash the fish and not soak it. After all the preparation of cooking onions, tomatoes and rice, the fish spoiled it all. It was like eating Saxa Salt out of a tablespoon. I threw it over the wall into the orchard next door and even the stray dogs haven't touched it.

I dearly want to go on a cookery course to learn how to cook the wonderful almond, orange and hazelnut cakes. The recipe book says to use 20 egg yolks then use the skin of the eggs .... it's all too complicated. Eggs, here are very cheap to buy and that's perhaps why they use so many in their desserts. But, they are delicious!

Massaged foot. Big improvement in condition of toenail!

Chapter 18

Friday January 15, 2010

Another day and NO RAIN! How wonderful!

I made coffee for us, which I normally do, while we sit and get ourselves together and decide what we are being led to do for the day.

Having had the windows and doors wide open yesterday to air the house and treat the mould, we now have flies.

Ted walked into the sitting room and remembered that we are now Portuguese.

"Bom dai!"

"Bom dai!"

I pointed to the flies and in sign language showed my disapproval.

He found the fly swatter and began slicing the air saying,

"Oui destructionadoo….."

Well I nearly burst with laughter. We are making our own language, filling in with made-up words heavily accented. We both collapsed with mirth at our efforts.

So far (with dictionary in hand) we have managed not to speak English. I am beginning to understand what he means when he says the odd Portuguese word packaged with a bit of French and Teddyism.

We are off to Estoi, the place where we met the estate agent, because we have been told that there is second-hand shop there where we might pick up a CD to help us with our pronunciation! We are taking this very seriously indeed.

We parked the car in a narrow street quite close to the church and walked Pee-pa up towards the small restaurant where we had coffee with the agent the other day. Directions given to us by the Portuguese language teacher, Lydia, meant that we were to walk alongside this little restaurant and the second-hand shop would clearly be seen on the left.

We walked up the street and down another street but couldn't see the shop we wanted. Estoi is a drowsy little town with only a couple of shops, mostly closed. Ted noticed the post office. He now recognises the Portuguese word for Post Office because he has been into them so many times. As one of his favourite places he felt sure that he would be given concise directions from one of the clerks in there.

I waited outside with Pee-pa holding her tight on the lead. Two unruly loose dogs approached her and we had the now familiar growl. A fellow turned his head and looked very interested. One of the strays pooed in front of us and then moved on.

Pee-pa was biting at the lead a bit, but soon calmed down. She is getting used to my new accent.

Ted came out of the Post Office humming and aaahing.

"Ohhh. They don't know. They don't understand English!" he was exasperated.

"Nao compreendo Inglese!" I replied. He laughed.

We gave it one more try and retraced our steps towards the church and then walked beside the pousada. There, on the left, was the small shop with a notice on the wall saying it was closed until February 2nd.

We then decided to travel on to Loule where we know they have large supermarkets. I wanted to buy a babies' reading book, but Ted kept putting it back on the shelf.

When we went shopping the very first time, here, in Tavira, I wanted to buy hair conditioner. I picked up the bottle and he was very quick to point out that it was over five euros. I put it back on the shelf.

Today, he bought a co-axial wire to put in the back of *their* television to experiment with the channels and see if we can get a local one, which speaks our new language. It was over twelve euros, but that's okay!!! We won't be leaving *that* behind.

After shopping we took a wrong turning somewhere and although Ted was navigating with the aid of his seven maps, two sat navs and a partridge in a pear tree, we had great difficulty getting out of the mountains again. As a result of this mis-hap, we ended up doing 92 miles before getting the shopping back to the villa. I'm glad that I didn't buy milk today.

Pee-pa had been in the car for over four hours, and I was tired. We binned our plans for going to the Quinta for their steak night and will do that next week.

Instead, we spent the evening trying to read Portuguese newspapers whilst listening to Portuguese television. It really is so funny. We don't understand a word, but the adverts are English dubbed Portuguese!

Ted now has his dictionary stuck to his thumb. I bought a dictionary for myself today. It had a label on the front for Name: School: and Age: I managed to slip into the shopping a child's cardboard book about Bobo the Cao. (Boo boo, the dog).

Anyone looking through the window this evening would have roared to see me reading this little six-paged book and Ted with his nose in the foreign newspaper only popping it down occasionally to go and look at the thermostat to register the temperature!

I spoke to Diane today on the phone. I wished her happy sixtieth birthday. She's looking forward to coming out tomorrow. I'm moving out of my room for them to have it, so hope they don't find it too cold.

There is great improvement with the nail. It might be good enough to paint soon!

Chapter 19

Came down to see Ted standing in the sitting room looking lost.

"What's the matter?" I asked.

"I've forgotten some of my numbers!!" he said quietly as though his whole world had caved in. For several days he has been practising his Portuguese numbers, um, dois, tres, quarto, cinco, seis, sete, oito, nove, dez …… and, this morning, he had forgotten them!

The battery had also gone on his torch so he was having a bit of a struggle! I did catch him in the corner of my eye as he was stooping over the heating thermostat. Obviously finding it hard to see properly without his torch.

I practised my new language on an old man who lives at the end of the track.

"Bom dai, Senhor!" to which he answered with a great barrage of words, not one of which I could recognise. Realising I was out of my depths, I was partly relieved to notice his eyes drawn to an envelope in the front of the car. It was to be mailed to the UK.

Without hesitation he flagged down an oncoming car driven at snail's pace by an old local. Stopping in the middle of the road a conversation took place between them. The car stayed in the road and the first man returned to knock up a couple of younger men who spoke Pidgin English. After several minutes I was told, "Blue." The only word that they could communicate was 'blue' so we assumed that we should post it in a blue mailbox and not a red one!

Ted seems anxious to go out. I have to strip and make the bed for our guests and move all my worldly belongings to the room downstairs. He turned the heating off in that room so I have had to put a hot water bottle in the bed to air the damp bedclothes.

He began to put on his waterproof so I took that as a sign that he was ready to go out. After a short conversation we decided that we should go into our nearest town and seek out the second-hand bookshop. We thought we might be able to add to our increasing library of Portuguese language books.

We just caught the second-hand bookshop in Tavira before it closed. It is located in a corner of a room used as a church for a Christian fellowship. There were banners on the walls, of crucifixes and dead men hanging from them, in front of which were rows of clothes and a few books. Some were still in cardboard boxes so we looked through in search of our pot of gold.

I asked one of the volunteers if they had any Portuguese language books but she didn't think they had. Another volunteer began to talk to us saying that she had been living out here for several years but still hadn't made up her mind whether they want to stay here or go back home!

On recommendation from the first lady, who couldn't find anything for us, we tore up the road to catch another bookshop before it closed for the three hours' lunch break. Run and owned by an American lady, we were allowed to mooch about. She was very helpful and showed us various books, which were relevant, but not appropriate. I turned around to see Ted unfolding a huge map!

"Oh no! Of all the things to find, not another map!"

"Well this one's got much more on it than the others. See, look at this little road which isn't even marked on the other maps…."

"It is a very good map," encouraged the American. I was outflanked. He bought it to add to his collection. We shall soon be able to open a map shop.

Whilst we were in Tavira, we thought we would try the Four Aqua's restaurant. An eating place which sits on the four rivers. We tried out our Portuguese language there, much to the amusement of the waiters who kept correcting us. We don't understand each other and neither does anyone else!

I thought I was ordering strips of chicken, but when the dish arrived, it was chicken livers! Our meals out seem to arrive as surprises because they are never what we think we have ordered!

We were invited to go up and choose a pudding. The Fig Surprise looked good and tasted good too. Ted chose jelly and blancmange. He didn't know that he was going to get that. I suppose it reminded him of schooldays because he didn't seem to like it much.

Pee-pa isn't very well today. She is quiet and her tummy is upset. She's had diarrhoea and I'm wondering whether I am spoiling her by giving her bits of cake as treats.

Our journey to the airport was uneventful. We had only travelled five miles up the road and Ted decided it would be nice to 'suss out' a beach, which we haven't been able to find yet. It was dark and I was anxious to be at the airport on time to meet Diane and Clive. Their flight was ten minutes early. It was lovely to see them walking through Arrivals.

We all had a drink and ate cake in the airport before our trip 'home'. Whilst we were in Faro we gave them the tourist version of a sightseeing tour of the old part of the town and walked around the floodlit castle, sauntering gently down the jetty to see the moored boats.

We then took the coastal road towards Tavira, which is more interesting than the motorway. Diane and Clive were hungry so we stopped off at a restaurant we hadn't been to before. JJ's is right on the roadside quite near to the villa.

As we pulled off the road, the headlamps picked up three men hovering over the back of a pickup truck with guns slung over their shoulders. They later walked through the restaurant into the kitchens and I wondered what would be on the menu tomorrow after the big shoot.

We ate well anyway and then had a flying visit to Tavira to give them an idea of how big it is. We toured the main streets and pointed out various landmarks and then took them back to the villa.

The dogs gave them a musical welcome as we drove up the track towards the gates of the Casa, which will be their home for the next week.

Diane cut her birthday cake, which I had been able to buy from the supermarket yesterday. She loves the yummy cakes here as much as I do. I think we are going to have a good week!

Sunday January 17, 2010

The kitchen floor was flooded this morning. Neither of the men could find out where the water was coming from. Ted wanted to get down on his knees and investigate, but we exercised wisdom and persuaded him to leave it alone and get the manager to deal with it.

We had made plans to have a 'Sunday lunch' at Quinta but had to abandon those when the manager-cum-plumber said he would be with us in an hour. That, of course, could mean any time and, then, we didn't know how long it would take for him to rectify the problem.

We all had coffee and yoghurt while we listened to Diane singing the praises of having a good night's sleep. They didn't hear the dogs. They didn't hear a sound!

I was so pleased that they had been able to have complete rest. I didn't tell them that I couldn't sleep in the damp, hard, single bed but had crept out and slept on the sofa instead.

The maintenance man arrived almost on cue and began to dismantle the kick-boards in the kitchen. With instructions to flush both lavatories, he discovered that the drains had been blocked by twigs and bits of greenery swept into them by the floods we have had. An hour later he bade us goodbye promising to come tomorrow at 4pm to change the faulty lock on the front door.

It was lunchtime so we went to the American Restaurant at the bottom of The Square, near the riverside. It wasn't at all American and we were able, once again, to practise our Portuguese much to the amusement of the proprietor. We ordered our meals and my steak arrived on a hot stone complete with plastic bib for me to wear whilst cooking it at the table! They joked to the waiter about giving me a job and we enjoyed good company and food. Ted remembered the poo-bag used to take Pippa some titbits for being a good girl, or bom cao!

The weather was the best we have had in all the time we have been here so after lunch we walked leisurely over the old bridge and into the other part of town. The sun was warm and Pippa was in good spirits, particularly when meeting another dog at the end of the bridge. Heads turned! She then began barking furiously at a litterbin. It's funny how she barks at strange things.

We then decided to travel to Faro de Luz where Clive's relative lives. Ted had the map sprawled out across his legs and was trying to find the location when Diane said she had seen a signpost. I turned the car round and drove back to take the turning which course of action threw Ted completely. He had a different route planned and was then completely confused.

I pulled in front of a pickup driven by a small, old Portuguese man and asked him in the best way I knew if he knew of Casa Hero. He didn't but asked me to follow him to the café where he thought someone could help. I really don't know how I understood him.

He stopped in the road outside the 'men only' café – some were inside but most sitting outside in the sunshine with their beers and port chasers.

Not one word of English was uttered. A lady from behind the bar came out and took me to the hoard of post boxes erected on the bend opposite the café and asked me to find the relative's name but it wasn't there. The weather had baked most of the names off the boxes.

Ted then had the brainwave of asking her if she spoke French and she did! She hopped in the car and directed us to a small roadside property she thought was the home we were looking for. I followed her around the back, fighting off a small dog, as an old lady appeared in the doorway pulling up her pants.

An exchange of dialogue went on between them then the bar lady threw her arms in the air and began to walk back to the car. It was the wrong house.

After all that, we couldn't find Casa Hero but it didn't deter us from having a nice afternoon driving up the mountains and looking at the spectacular scenery in the sunshine rather than rain.

When we came back, we tucked into the birthday cake and had a peaceful evening talking about properties and how they are constructed. We are looking forward to moving on to our next property now. We shall contact the agent tomorrow about signing the paperwork.

Chapter 20

Monday January 18, 2010

We had breakfast together and discussed our plans for the day. The weather was dull and overcast – most likely we would have rain. What a letdown after yesterday's glorious warm sunshine. Even the almond blossom is beginning to flower after those few hours of sunlight.

As Ted pawed over his maps we finally decided to take Diane and Clive to the English Garden Centre, which is on the way to the estate agent's office. We could then pop in and make an appointment with him to sign the necessary paperwork for the rental, and ask if we could take our guests to view.

When we arrived at the garden centre, a few people were milling around but there was nobody available at the till. It all appeared to be a bit unprofessional. I looked through the array of miscellaneous products on offer and saw a set of huge keys. They are rusty ornamental keys, but looked so interesting. As I picked them up to look at them more closely, a Dutch woman beside me told me that I was picking up *the Keys of the Kingdom*. I had to have those! Ted didn't really want to pay for them, but I insisted on having them. We were eventually offered coffee for free. Whilst the girl was making it, people were waiting to pay for goods.

As I sat watching the scenario, I thought of how I would manage it so differently. I would change the stock to open it up for larger catchments. The business part of my brain began to function and I concluded that if he continued to run it as it is set up, he may not be able to make it profitable.

I left the others sitting under the awning and went to find the lavatory. There was no flushing system in operation and rust had discoloured the filthy pan. However, when one is desperate, one uses whatever facilities are available.

I washed my hands with soap provided and dried them on paper towels. That was a plus – give me towels any day rather than wind machines.

Having finished my toilet, I attempted to open the door and found that it was jammed. I could not move it one bit. I pulled and pushed, twisted the knob, rattled the door and shouted for help but nobody heard me. I was resigned to staying there. I opened the window, which was secured by iron bars, and called for Ted but there was still no reply to my calls.

I thought I would have to wait for a customer to arrive, or leave, to alert their attention as the window faced on to the car park.

As I screamed through the open window, the dog began to bark and came to the window. It stood making a row as it looked up at me and brought the shop assistant to my aid.

"I heard the dog barking," she smiled "and wondered what the noise was!"

She rattled the door, turned the knob and pushed the door towards me and it opened with a start. Another relief!

When I returned to the table, nobody had heard my cries and just thought that I had wandered off to talk to somebody.

We were able to see Andrew, the agent, and his wife in their offices. It didn't appear that they had much to do and agreed to meet us all at the usual coffee place in Estoi tomorrow morning at 9.30am. I wonder if this is where most of his work is conducted sitting out in the street sipping coffee. As it was lunchtime when we left his offices, we drove into the countryside to the hotel that the Argentinean couple runs. They made us so welcome the first time we met them that we thought Diane and Clive would enjoy the wonderful views seen from their building.

When we approached, it was evident that they were very quiet. There were no cars anywhere to be seen and the place looked closed.

Jorge, the proprietor (and also the chef) waved at us; and soon his wife, Adrienna, was kissing us and inviting us in.

"Of course we can make you somesing," she smiled, her long dark hair falling about her shoulders.

"Come in. Sit where you like. I will make a table by the fire, or you can sit in the window. What you like!"

She brought us fresh bread, pate, cheese and salami as a taster while we waited for the Argentinean beef to be barbequed. The meal was delicious. They treated us so well.

There was ample for Pippa too. We saved some meat, in our black poo-bag, which she soon demolished.

Our appointment with the manager-cum-plumber was at 4pm at the villa. He was to change hats and become a locksmith. As soon as we got into the drive, he appeared. The lock couldn't be replaced today as his friend in the village didn't have another, so he said he would be back on Thursday. The lock is faulty and Ted almost locked himself out of the house. Another case of being locked out (or the door closing shut)!

I will place the key of David's house on his shoulder; no one will shut what He opens; no one will open what He shuts... Is 22:22

We had a cup of coffee, then, went back to Tavira to do some shopping. We hadn't been to Pingo supermarket before so Diane and Clive were able to experience a first, as we did. By the time we returned to the car it was raining.

Our plans for having a drink on a pavement café were scuppered and we returned to watch Ted's homemade videos (mostly of our grand-daughter and the floods).

We all retired for an early night knowing that we need to be ready for our appointment with Ricky Gervais tomorrow morning.

Chapter 21

Tuesday Janeiro 19, 2010

We had an early start to the day as arrangements had been made to meet the estate agent and his wife in Estoi at the restaurant near the pousada. We arrived before them but the coffee place was closed. A bag of bread was hung from the door handle waiting for someone to open up.

When Andrew aka Ricky Gervais walked across the square, a quick decision was made to view the properties straight away. In convoy we followed them for several miles up a mountain to where the Scottish couple's house was. Parking on the roadside was difficult for two cars and poor Clive had to crawl up the wall to get clear of the car.

We noticed two wet towels on the balustrade. The usual format of viewing took place. We were kept outside with Andrew showing us the outside, whilst Lana went indoors to put on the heating, lights and open blinds. Today it was evident that she had also mopped up a leak. Perhaps that's why there were two wet towels hanging to dry.

Diane and I observed sweet smelling freshener as we descended into the basement room, described as a suitable annexe. Lana had sprinted around spraying the room hoping to disguise the fusty smell of damp but we were like a couple of detectives on a case! There was no fooling us! These are well-known tricks of sales negotiators.

Ted, equipped with camera around his neck, strolled around like Lord Snowdon taking pictures of cracks and leaks while Clive did a mental structural survey. Our eyes met once and he shook his head with disapproval at the house. I walked away hoping that he wasn't going to say anything within earshot of the agent, or his wife!

Mission accomplished, we continued to the other villa with the spectacular views and the infinity pool (and room for a pony!)

It was very quickly condemned by Clive, which I knew would be the case, as it needs a lot of costly repair work. After inspection we all drove off through the electronic gates and back to Estoi to have the coffee we hadn't had before.

At the table in the little café, Andrew's attitude towards the letting agreement changed. He intimated that the owners didn't normally rent out the property and would only consider a rental if we were interested in buying. This was not what he had said previously and we were taken aback at this and decided against any further negotiations. We were more disappointed because we had trusted him as a believer to be honest with us.

We parted amicably and drove through Olhao where Diane noticed a MacDonalds! It was such an occasion not to be missed so we drove through and tried to order in Portuguese. It wasn't successful. Our efforts and Ted's sign language got us nowhere and we were waved to drive on to another window because of the build-up of traffic behind us.

The choice of menu was quite stark compared with what is on offer in UK so with assistance from Ted's dictionary, we all opted for cheeseburgers and fries. We hadn't expected them to be baby cheeseburgers! They were so small that we demolished them in one bite.

Ted, who sat constantly with the map open on his lap, wanted to take us to the Natural Park of Ria Formosa – a nature trail with stopping points to observe the birds. In our endeavours to find the place his navigational skills were put to the test and he, sadly, failed by taking us up a long sand track, deep with potholes, which opened up onto a beach.

We turned round in the sand and drove back taking another route peppered with so many craters that the car was moving up and down like a tug on rough seas. We were ready to throw in the towel when he said we should give it another go. Eventually we found the place and took Pippa out of the car, not knowing for certain whether she was allowed to join us or not.

We began the trail; both men kitted with binoculars and cameras, walking along the boardwalk to the dunes and salt marsh towards an old tidal mill. Pippa in her excitement ran ahead and bounded up the steps alongside the building up to the roof where she joined Clive who was bird watching.

There were several stopping points for bird watching, one was near the ruins of old Roman salting tanks which we passed on our return route. We also walked beside the Bird Hospital, a low building where they nurse poorly birds back to life. Unfortunately access to the Portuguese Water Dogs was not available to the public until further notice. We weren't given the reasons. Water Dogs have webbed feet and were once used by fishermen for fetching in the fish.

We were quite tired after our walk, so were glad to get back to the car. Pippa had been drinking stagnant water and wouldn't drink fresh water so we popped her into her Dunelm bed and headed for the villa.

Ted suggested we did a detour and so drove through St Lucia and stopped at a roadside café for ice creams. The weather wasn't cold for us, but was overcast so we gained a few looks from the locals as we sat outside licking ices in what they consider mid-winter! Mad Englishmen but not out in the midday sun today!

I cooked the evening meal and we all just chilled out. Diane was peeved about her hairdresser winning 1.5m on the lottery. She thinks she's now lost her and will have to find another!

The dogs were still barking past midnight. In desperation I opened the door and screamed into the night with little effect on the dogs. Perhaps they don't understand Inglese? But it brought Ted running into the sitting room (where I was sleeping) in his pyjamas, thinking I was crying for help. How sweet!

Wednesday Janeiro 20, 2010

Almond blossom has suddenly appeared almost overnight sending forth its heady fragrance filling the air.

We had an early appointment to view a villa owned by a friend of Ted's estate agent school friend. It was located only about a mile away from where we were staying but could have been difficult to find despite having written directions. Often places are tucked away miles down tracks which look like mud paths. This one, however, was a little more straightforward and, being shown the way by the owner, a small ginger haired lady, standing at the top of the hill waving furiously, it wasn't hard to see.

She soon introduced herself and began to show us around the house she had available for rental. A detached property, standing in a large garden area, it was square and quite ordinary – could easily have been mistaken for a house on a housing estate in UK. There was absolutely nothing spectacular or characterful about it, but it is a functional, warm house.

Diane and Clive wandered around taking it all in. Olivia, the strange little lady, invited Diane and me down the footpath to her home, which also stands in the grounds. She told us that she had identical houses built for letting, one of which she has sold. Her much larger villa, (a separate entity), sits comfortably in the hillside overlooking Tavira and district.

She is seventy and has a new 'partner'. I asked her how she had met him as they had only been together for three years. She explained that she had picked him up at a café in Tavira. He had just lost his wife and she was lonely (looking for an odd job man more likely) and within a few days he moved in with her.

We decided to take the villa for a month. The deal was a laid-back affair and she said we could move in today if we wanted to! We needed to go back to the present villa and as the men talked, so Olivia's 'partner' shared with me how he has managed to get Olivia to go to church. He spoke about his faith and how they go to church regularly every Sunday now. Hmmn. I heard her swearing and taking the name of Yeshua in vain! Also living in sin? Why are we here?

For in the same way you judge others, you will be judged, and with the measure you use, it will be measured to you. Matt 7:2

Seconds after our return to the villa where we are all staying, Rene, the cleaner arrived with her bucket of soaps and substances. She passed no comment about our visitors and promptly went upstairs. Was she actually going to do some work today?

As soon as Cassie, the gardener, turned up Rene finished work and went outside to chat with her and to light up a fag. They chatted for about half an hour and then she continued her chitchat when she came into the sitting room.

"'Ers luvly," making reference to the lesbian gardener.

I heard the same rubbish this week about my having a yellow aura around me and that I was an angel. That my husband doesn't have that nice aura, but his is dark, purplish.

"You knows a lot more'n you makes out," she wagged her finger at me grinning and flashing her gold tooth.

"You aint nobody's fool me daaaarlin'"

She was getting very familiar. Afterall, she was referred to in the website advert as a maid.

I thought she was packing up to leave when she walked behind me and I became aware that she had her hands cupped around my head – not touching me, but performing some new age practice on me. I moved away.

"Haaahha," she screeched. "You'm frightened. I know you can't take it. You'm frightened."

In a huff, she collected her bucket and waved goodbye assuring me of her presence again next week. I knew better.

I felt unclean. I needed to be cleansed. I needed to get lunch too, but it was far more important for me to be released from whatever she was putting on me.

I showered. Washed my hair to my toes. Cleansed, I returned to make lunch, which we were able to eat outside in the sunshine. Clive contemplated buying plots of land and ruins while my thoughts were of my other son, Al, and Mary, his wife. Diane was already saying that Lee would love to live in Portugal but she didn't think Zena would!

It was Quiz Night at the Quinta. We arrived at 7.30pm and ordered a meal before the quiz. The wide screen television over the log fire was behind Clive, so I changed my seating arrangement in order that he could see Match of the Day. He is football crazy and it happened to be his favourite team playing. Most of the people at the Quinta are from the North of England and also support

Bolton so Clive's attention was divided throughout the evening between the questions and the goals.

Ted took charge of the paperwork as the room began to fill up for the quiz. They take it so seriously and friends come in to join tables and make up teams.

We were given pieces of paper to write down our answers to submit to the person elected to complete the questionnaire. As Ted had, without consultation, assumed this office, we were surprised when he forgot to keep silent and began to shout his answer across the table to Di. Normally his voice is so quiet that it's hard to hear him!

Without realising, I had morphasised into one of the crowd also and was taking the silly game too seriously. Once again we came last but were given a bottle of wine for participating! On leaving, Clive was presented with a bottle too for being the best loser! We mustn't take that seriously either!

We were all tired so said our goodnights and Diane and Clive went to bed. It was then that I saw a new trail of ants. Out came the kettle of boiling water but it wasn't for the hot water bottle this time!

Thursday Janeiro 21, 2010

Another army of ants was making a trail this morning marching behind the sink to a dish of potato chips left on the side overnight.

Ted appeared shining his torch (with new battery) up the wall and on the floor checking their progress before shining it on the heating thermostat to take his daily reading to record.

Our second Portuguese lesson was at 10am at the Quinta so we left at 9.30am to be on time. The weather was dry and fine but very ominous looking clouds covered the mountains.

Maria was a very jolly young lady who had a completely different attitude to teaching than Lydia. We sat under the veranda in the shade and drank coffee while Diane and Clive amused themselves in the gardens looking at the exotic birds.

Our lesson was great fun. She even asked us if we wanted to learn swear words so that is how relaxed she was. We obviously declined that offer. Instead, she wrote out a recipe for sweet cakes. I don't think I shall be baking in that kitchen though. She also had a recipe for getting rid of ants. Cucumber. She instructed me to slice the cucumber and leave it around the kitchen because they don't like it and soon leave.

The two hours went past very quickly and we drove back towards the villa and called in at O Forno for lunch. O Forno (The Furnace) simply has a door off the main road opening up into a large busy restaurant. It was very nice and not at all what we had expected from just seeing a doorway off the street.

The plumber turned maintenance manager arrived to fit a new lock on the front door but after manoeuvring and jostling, it just wouldn't fit. He couldn't understand why it wasn't the right size; after all, he had drawn around the original lock and faxed the drawing to the makers!

In the evening we walked around Tavira starting by climbing the steps near the Information Office which Ted now can walk to in his sleep, up the cobbled street to the Roman ruins and around by the floodlit church.

Our journey brought us back to The Square where little cafes have their chairs set on the path, different styles and colours delineating their individual patches. We chose to sit and eat ice cream whilst watching the few people passing by. Pippa sat quietly at my feet believing that she would get the end of my cornet.

Ted and Clive then began what was to become a pastime of looking in estate agents' windows for plots of land. Never being able to remember all the fine details, but adept at finding a way to do just that, Ted took photos of the particulars in the shop windows. I don't know what people thought about him bending with the lens of his camera resting on the shop front.

The cucumber didn't work.

Friday Janeiro 22, 2010

Ted squeezed freshly picked oranges from the tree for breakfast. He stood at the table outside as the sun's rays crept slowly towards him. What a beautiful day!

Our plans were (as of last evening, but subject to change at any moment) to head east to the Spanish border to Villa Real de Santo Antonio.

Ted wanted to go over the suspension bridge into Spain because somebody told him that the diesel is cheaper. Let's hope we have enough fuel in the tank to get us there!

When we arrived at VRS Antonio we drove up the causeway and on to the beach where we witnessed about a dozen men in the sea, clad in diving gear and operating machines sifting mussels. I let Pippa off the lead after ensuring that there were no other dogs about and she delighted herself by rolling into the sand and scratching her back on the grains before running into the ocean.

I made a big mistake by throwing a seashell to her. There were no stones on the beach – only millions of shells. She ate it and got the taste so then ate one after another.

After her little game, and when Clive had taken in their methods of fishing, we drove into the town. We were a bit disappointed with the shops, but were impressed with the large square and had sandwiches at one of the snack bars set on the periphery.

When we returned to the car we were confronted with the result of eating seashells. Pippa had been sick in the back of the car. At the roadside I pulled out her bedding and did my best to clear up the mess. The smell of regurgitated fish shells stayed with us for ages.

Our trip northwards took us through several little hamlets or areas of very small population. One such place was, according to Ted's map, supposed to take us to the riverside. A small road-works sign was placed at the side of the sand road. Little did we realise how much a small sign can mean! As I drove on, the road got narrower until I could almost hardly get the car between the houses on either side. Retracting the mirrors was not a complete solution for the road just disintegrated. I simply could not turn round and would not have been able to back out.

A small red tape had been tied to a stick secured at the side of the road in concrete and attached to a hook on the other side of the road. In sign language this indicated that the road was blocked.

It was now evident that workmen were laying a new road. The usual tarmac machinery would not have been able to get through to resurface the road in the normal manner, so the answer obviously was to send in workmen to pave the road manually.

Exasperated and hot, I asked Ted to get out and pull out the stick so that I could drive forward. He did so and I was able to get the car on to a wider bit of road but was hailed by alarmed workmen waving for me to go back. How could I go back? I couldn't even turn!

Sitting behind me I heard Clive remark that he would have been mad if I had driven over tiles he had laid because their system was such that any movement on them would mean they would have to be ripped up and the work started again. I still don't quite know how I managed to get out of there, but with waves from old ladies in black and mouthfuls from very old men, we exited with a vow not to enter any other 'interesting' villages.

Relieved to be on a better road, we continued up the mountains to Alcoutim, a town recommended on the tourist map. They described it as a town but it was really only a road but Ted spotted a Tourist Information Office so we couldn't pass without him visiting. I parked and waited at the roadside for him to bring back a leaflet about the place and, yes, another map!

Our sightseeing tour brought us back towards Tavira just as the sun was setting.

We made our last evening with Diane and Clive a momentous occasion by celebrating at The Piano Bar, an upmarket restaurant situated in the shadow of the main church high above Tavira.

The waiter was meticulously aiming for perfection as he kept coming back to the table to set the drinking glasses in line. It took him several seconds to handle the cutlery and position it. All he needed was Ted's tape measure to make the job perfectly accurate.

The experience was certainly one to remember when Diane and Clive's tomato soup arrived in a teapot and was poured slowly into their bowls by another waiter.

During our main course, a small dark, curly haired man in his fifties, entered the room and sat at the piano. He placed his coca-cola on the top and adjusted his clothing in preparation for his concert. As he played the piano, Diane and I both said we had been thinking of Al. There were no tit-bits for Pippa that evening!

Sabado Janeiro 23, 2010

It's interesting to note that the Portuguese word for Saturday is Sabado and Monday is Segunda (second) indicating that the first day of their week is Sunday therefore the Sabbath is Saturday.

The heavens opened before 6am and once again the driveway was flooded very quickly. It was a pity because on their last day, Diane wanted to go shopping. We thought if we went to 'incontinent' it would be under cover and she would in all probability get everything she wanted from there.

After waiting to see if the rain would subside it was obvious that if we needed to go shopping we would have to go without any further delay. I left Pippa in the back of the car in her nest, noted where the car was parked and we all set off in the lift to the shopping centre.

As it was lunchtime we thought we would go to the Steak House within the complex but were told that they only had one steak! They didn't understand us although we are now quite proficient at Portuguese. It was another of those occasions where we thought we had ordered chicken and along came egg! It must be Ted's accent!

Diane and I left the men to look in an electrical shop so that we could buy some of the delicious Portuguese sweets for her to take back. We thought we would take the treats to the car so that we would be free to walk about without baggage.

When we met up with the men we decided to go back to the villa to collect their suitcases before the airport trip but we couldn't find the car! Diane and I had been down to the car park once and the car was there, but now it had disappeared. Thoughts of how we had been robbed on our journey came rushing through my head. Pippa! Pippa was in the back of the car! We paced up and down, returned to the shopping centre and tried another lift, but the car was not to be found.

I was certain that it had been stolen and couldn't understand it because I had prayed for protection before I left Pippa.

What seemed hours later, I had the thought that there was another car park across the road. What if we ran across the bridging road and tried that one? Success! But we had left Diane and Clive somewhere stranded. Mobile phones are wonderful inventions. We asked them to stand out on the road where I could see them. Sure enough they were huddled together in the rain, waiting for me. I felt dreadful. What a way to end their holiday.

Taking them to the airport was a time for reflection for me. I was silent for most of the journey. Sad that they were leaving for in a strange way I had felt they were a connection to Al, Mary and the children. We said our goodbyes and watched them go through to the departures, Clive holding out his arms like the Angel of the North but still setting off the alarm bells. The journey home was quiet.

Chapter 22

Domingo Janeiro 24, 2010

Ants invaded us again! This, our last day at the Casar, the house in the orange trees, and we were being driven out of the kitchen by these little perishers.

I had to take all the food out of the cupboard and throw most of it away. The slices of cucumber, placed as a deterrent, were blackened by the little creatures eating away as though it were some gourmet dish served up by Marco Pierre White.

I needed to wash the covers and dry them before relinquishing the keys. Today was to be very busy for me but as the clemency of the weather was favourable, we went to the Quinta to their car boot sale.

A stone's throw from our 'home,' we witnessed a party of about seven men cutting open two pigs in the field beside a shack. The pigs were laid on their backs on wooden trestles as an old man cut open the stomachs from the neck downwards with a dirty Stanley knife. Another old guy stood at the feet of the animal with a plastic bucket and scooped out the blood, which was then transferred into a plastic bowl. The bucket was then used to gather up the internal organs. All transactions were operated in the open under a lemon tree. We took some pictures of this bizarre scenario.

Only half a dozen cars were participating in this well advertised function called 'Car Boot Sale.' A range of articles were being displayed, some on tables, others strewn over the ground.

I caught sight of a small boy who had lots of his toys placed on a tablecloth near the entrance. His younger brother was jumping around in the back of an old Range Rover fully equipped with tow-bar and horsebox, which the family had travelled in when they came from UK and most likely brought their entire car boot junk with them.

Jack was eight years of age and had moved to Algarve with his family five years ago. Fluent in the Portuguese language, he was keen to negotiate a deal for some of his old reading books. At 50 cents each I felt it was a bargain to buy Portuguese versions of Sleeping Beauty and Snow White and the Seven Dwarfs. Good bedtime reading for me!

When we drove on to Santa Catarina to basically turn to go back in the direction of the villa, we were astonished to discover a 'Fayre' being held in a field. The roadside was swarming with parked cars and people walking in the middle of the road unaware of vehicles. Like an enormous car boot sale, these fayres are held regularly and anything under the sun can be purchased from the local vendors.

We thought it was a shame that it coincided with the little car boot sale at the Quinta, but that is life apparently!

I managed to get another load of washing done before sundown. We packed up our suitcases in readiness for our move tomorrow. Pippa suspected something was in the air as she slowly mounted the stairs for bed, looking behind her to see if I was still here.

Monday (Segunda) Janeiro 25, 2010

We were up early. I took the last load of bedclothes from the washing machine and pegged them on the line on the roof to dry whilst we packed up the car. I'm sure we now have more than we brought with us!

Whilst I was cramming suitcases, Wellingtons, sunhats and books into the rear of the car, Pippa sat on her throne in the boot scrutinising every move, wondering what was happening. The neighbouring dogs made one last attempt to get at us as we drove away to the next chapter of our adventure.

We arrived at our next Casa at 9.15am. I thought it was too early, but Ted didn't feel the same way. He walked down to Olivia's home to tell them that we had arrived. Very soon afterwards they all traipsed up to the house jingling the keys. These were new keys. The lock at the other place needed to be renewed and would have new keys. Are these the keys to that door which is being opened to us?

The house was warm. The shutters were opened and sun flooded through the windows exposing the shiny red tiles and reflecting patterns on the crisp white walls. There wasn't a trace of mould in this house.

I left Ted and Pippa to familiarise themselves in their new surroundings whilst I returned to clean out the other villa and ensure that the place was just as it was when we took possession. It was a wonderful feeling to drive just that one-mile down the road on my own – without Pippa – without a passenger! I felt freedom lifting me high into the clouds. I ejected the sat nav CD from the player in the car and played one of my own praise CD's - turned up the music loud and wound down the windows so that the breeze could take my hair with it.

I took the opportunity to prolong the experience by driving further for about ten minutes before tracing my steps back to the new villa.

Pizza was on the menu for our first meal on the patio in front of the swimming pool in blinding sunshine and, later, as the sun went down, Ted cooked supper of chicken and burgers on the barbeque. When he brought the offering to the table, there were four tiny black pieces of chicken breast and two biscuit sized black burgers. He had left them for too long and it was like trying to eat rock. Pity he hadn't taken his stopwatch outside!

Tuesday (Terca) Janeiro 26, 2010

I spent most of the early hours of the morning wondering whether it was time to get up. The shutters at the doors of the bedroom were keeping out any light and I am used to seeing the morning sunlight. The room was dark and I was surprised to see that it was 8.30am.

Ted was coughing badly and was very chesty but insisted on keeping our appointment with Maria at the Quinta for our second Portuguese lesson.

She took one look at him and said in her forthright way:

"You don't look good today. You looks like you have something with your face!"

Denying that he was under the weather, she was insistent and ordered herb tea and honey for him to drink. She warned him about getting pneumonia. Rene had already warned about that. Maria told him to go to the hospital where he might have to wait 2/3 hours but he needed to get anti-biotics. He is getting worried now.

I have not been able to give the language learning much attention this week so my performance was not very good. Maria brought one of her small son's reading books for us to borrow. We read some words and sentences from it. She laughed.

"You sound like Portuguese gypsies because the way you speak is emotional!" she laughed. Still laughing she said that Ted sounded Spanish.

We took a final visit to the old villa to leave the keys in the secret place. Ted found it difficult to let go and wanted to know whether we should keep them "just in case." In case of what? We wanted shot of it. Just entering the place felt cold and damp – eerie. A single caterpillar was rolled up on the kitchen floor beside a piece of cucumber, which had been dragged from behind the cupboard. Goodness knows what other wildlife had occupied the place since we left yesterday.

That afternoon the weather changed and turned to rain. It was cold. Ted lit the log burner in the new house but didn't see it out. He went to bed at 8.30pm. He really must have been under the weather.

Wednesday (Quarta) Janeiro 27, 2010

Ted only had cold water this morning so his shower was very refreshing. He phoned Olivia to tell her and she arranged for her Portuguese plumber to give the boiler some attention at 10am.

I knew that she would be coming with him and knew that she would be looking to see how we were looking after her property so began to clean the kitchen floor. Ted disagreed with me and said it would be okay and that she wouldn't come. Wrong! She escorted the plumber into the kitchen and opened the cupboard door for him. Showing off her language skills she gabbled away to him in Portuguese then stood back for him to look at the boiler.

Exactly as I had envisaged, she stooped down to pick up a tiny piece of something off the floor, magnified by the sunlight, and promptly put it in the bin, a procedure she repeated. She then puffed up a cushion on one of the chairs. This isn't going to be any holiday for me. I can see that I am going to be brushing up on housekeeping skills, not language ones!

After the plumber had replaced the nozzles on a couple of taps, they set off for the other rental villa next door to check that place out too. Arriving unannounced, I wonder what the residents thought.

It was important to get to that Farmacio to get some anti-biotics for Ted so we went into Tavira taking a superb parking place right outside the shop. We waited in a line to be served and a young girl pawned us off with some 'expectorant' that she said was what he needed. Not wanting to argue, he kindly accepted the local version of cough stuff he already has, with the comment, "I'm much better ......" cough, splutter, loss of voice.

I had the desire to look around a small Mercado (market) where I had often seen an old lady standing on the steps outside waiting for business. As I wanted a lemon squeezer, I thought this might be just the place to find one.

The shop was just as I had imagined - crammed with stock. The shelving was so close that the 'aisles' if you could call them that, were really narrow and I needed to walk sideways to get around. The items were too close to my eyes that I couldn't focus clearly on what was on offer.

I suddenly felt extremely claustrophobic and needed to get out. As I walked towards the door, I saw a cardboard box rammed with plastic lemon squeezers. They came without a dish so I grabbed one and passed it to Ted, as he is the money-holder. Better to have half a squeezer than none at all!

Our shopping expedition to Pingo Doce, the cheap supermarket over the bridge, was a disappointment too. The only good thing I was able to get was a fresh chicken for £2. It was simply delicious and meaty, just like chickens used to be in the olden days! Pippa enjoyed it too. Ted coughed his way to bed. Why is he so stubborn?

Thursday (Quinta) Janeiro, 28, 2010

Maria, our Portuguese teacher, was due to take our lesson this morning at 10am but arranged to come to the house this time. The last lesson at The Quinta was held in the bar and several people were making such a noise, that we found it hard to hear what she was saying. Besides, where we live now is closer to Tavira so it meant that she wouldn't have to travel so far.

The arrangement was that Ted would walk down the narrow lane, which is better described as a concrete track, to the main road (which is only marginally better) and wait for her at 9.50am. Considering that the Portuguese people are very laid back over timekeeping, she is very good at turning up on time.

Still coughing, he left the house to meet her and she was prompt.

As we sat at the table in the sitting room, I began to feel that the lesson was long and I was losing interest towards the end. I had not been able to give enough time to the project and more important things had to be done this week. I had to get my priorities right and learning a new language wasn't on the top of the list.

She picked up on this and suggested that, perhaps next week, I have an hour alone with her and then Ted has the other hour with her. He didn't seem to like that idea. I suggested that we go to her apartment for the next lesson. I'm not quite sure why I made that suggestion, but it might open up something interesting.

Once again she commented about his health and said that he needed to get better attention and possible treatment rather than swigging cough mixture. He insisted that he was better as he reached for his handkerchief. I wish he would use tissues.

After a simple lunch of bread and cheese eaten outside in the warm sunshine, I felt weak; rather like a football being deflated slowly. Although the sun was warm, it was cold. That sounds a real contradiction, but can you imagine the situation? Warm sunshine and yet my body was cold, particularly my back. I needed to get that fleece. I am still contemplating about who invented it. It must have been a woman!

I wonder if Ted has forgotten my name. He has been calling me 'darling' for a couple of days. I suppose it covers a multitude doesn't it? I heard him calling Pippa 'darling' today.

I thought I would try another attempt at making rice again after the disastrous mess I made the other day. I found a large frying pan in the cupboard and eventually got the old gas ring to light with the aid of a 'spent' igniter. I began to fry the onions in oil and the aim was to slightly burn them to give that lovely flavour to the rice.

I was unaware of the smoke but it set the sophisticated fire alarm system off. The bell was ringing and echoing down the valley. I couldn't turn it off and tried opening and closing the front door to fan the smoke out but that didn't work.

It really needed to be reset. It wasn't just an ordinary smoke alarm, but a complete fire alarm panel. The noise resounded for about ten minutes so I tried to ignore it. Ted sat outside near the pool, fast asleep with a book falling off his knee unaware of a thing.

I returned to the panel and tried pressing buttons but nothing happened. I had a quick look outside to see that nobody was running up the road thinking there was a fire. Satisfied that no one was being affected by the ear-splitting sound, I went inside the house. I then had a brainwave. There was a note stuck on the panel which read:

In the event of a false alarm press Button 1 once, Button 2 twice and Button 4 once. To reset the alarm press Button 2 twice.

Why hadn't I seen that before? Resolved! I pressed the buttons accordingly and silence fell. My ears felt strange and then I heard banging on the door. As I opened it I saw Olivia and her 'partner' looking anxiously in and asking if everything was ok. The person occupying the neighbouring house had been concerned about the fire alarm going on for so long and had gone down to them asking if they should investigate. I explained about my culinary skills being able to set off the system and they laughed. Ted slept through it all totally oblivious to all the activity raised by my onions!

I don't think I want to cook anything else. We shall have to get to like the local cheeses. The tomatoes are delicious and the lettuces have to be weighed. I read somewhere that raw vegetables are good for you too!

Chapter 23

Friday Janeiro 29, 2010

Rather an uneventful day – warm in the sunshine but a cold wind cut across the top of the hill where the house is located. I made a couple of attempts at sitting out, but had to go indoors because I was so cold. Ted spent most of the day dozing out on the patio wrapped in a woolly pullover. I must get to grips with his method of reading with his eyes closed.

The wind blew his straw hat into the pool, which he had to fish out with the fish net. He tried pegging it to dry on to the rotary washing line but because the rim of the hat was stiff and circular, he had great difficulty in attaching it to the plastic rope.

Pippa was sick on her rug again which I had to wash in the bath. Yes, we have two baths here but because of the altitude of the building, and something to do with the tank, the water doesn't get hot in the upstairs bathroom.

I managed to haul the heavy padded dog rug out through the house leaving a river of water behind me. Heaving it over the fence was quite a task. I must be losing my strength. I can't understand that, as I haven't had my hair cut!

The house needs a revamp. It was fitted out 15-20 years ago and is dated, showing signs of rental unlove. The gas hob doesn't ignite automatically taking ages to light. When it does, it bursts and bangs like a small explosion and I have to draw back from the flames to avoid getting singed. The elements in the electric oven only function on the right side. I discovered that when the pizza came out scorched on the one half and raw on the other.

The old dishwasher door is so heavy that it falls to the ground if I don't hold it. I am wary of it after it nearly took off my kneecaps. But, most things are functional and as we don't know how long we are staying here, I can tolerate it.

After raising the fire alarm, I am doubtful about cooking in general. There is a machine, which looks as though it's an old microwave, but as its buttons are marked in Portuguese, and none of them seem to operate, I can't use it.

The Quinta was holding a Jazz night advertised as 'Chips, Salsa and Jazz.' I suggested that we should go, as I needed to have a change of scenery and company.

The room was set up with large tables in the same format as at the New Year's dinner. I like to sit somewhere and then see who comes to the table, but

Ted chose to take a table near the lavatories where we were joined by a couple originally from Cornwall. I recognised the accent immediately.

The woman of the partnership had short canary yellow hair and didn't stop talking throughout the night. Her husband sat silent while she gave us a potted history of how she had lived alone for *twelve* years and then met 'Don.' They had been together for *twelve* years. They built their house here *twelve* years' ago. She knew everything there was to know about the family who owned the Quinta. I had to let Ted get on with it as he was sitting beside her. The remaining four places on the table stayed vacant until later on in the evening when the three jazz players came to eat at their break-time.

It wasn't jazz as I know it. Three old men performed in the corner of the room – one played the keyboard, another played a set of drums and the third played a flute!

I caught sight of a Paul O'Grady look-alike and wasn't sure if he was the real thing.

Isn't it strange that some people look amazingly similar to others? I know whose image I want to replicate!

For G-d made human beings in His Own Image... Gen 9:6

At the end of the evening the yellow-haired lady, called Jane from Moncarapacho, claimed Ted as a friend and insisted on exchanging phone numbers and addresses. Why do people do that? I must have at least five contacts imposed upon me in this way, some, whom I shall never see again. Little did I know at this point, that she would become a close friend?

Saturday Janeiro 30, 2010

A cold, chill-out day spent mostly hugging my hot water bottle whilst curled up with my books. I am so thankful that I brought this item. I wonder if the same person who invented the fleece, invented the hot water bottle? I love her (or him).

Sunday Janeiro 31, 2010

Ted's birthday! I felt bad because I haven't been able to buy him a gift. He is with me all the time so, apart from also not having any financial resources, it has been difficult to find time alone to look for anything.

I slipped a card with Portuguese greetings into an envelope and left it by the door for him to pick up when he came downstairs. Pippa and I had written it together but I had no idea of the meaning until we looked it up and translated it meant Congratulations!

He had an envelope from Angela, his daughter, which had been sent to the other villa ten days earlier, but that was all. I wanted to try to make the day special for him but was limited in what I could do.

He wanted to drive to a vantage point somewhere close by so we set off to do that. Once again it entailed turning round and retracing our steps several times, advancing up sand tracks and past illegally parked motor homes. When we eventually found the place, others had a similar idea and were walking their dogs up the stony path towards the summit. We had to abandon that idea. Sunday is a family day here and one should expect lots of Portuguese to be out and about amongst the tourists so finding a suitable dog-walking place is hard work. I do wish that Pippa were more sociable with other dogs.

We stopped for birthday cake and coffee at a small roadside snack place about a mile away from where we are staying. It was an extremely local place and the small dark skinned (and dyed dark haired) old lady behind the counter only spoke Portuguese. The food counter was one of those thrown out of shops in the UK about twenty years ago, propped up by a sixties type Formica bar which she used as a tray. The cake was delicious. Happy Birthday Ted!

We did a detour on the return journey for Ted to open the mailbox at the old villa. He had failed to relinquish the key for that. I suspect he was hoping to get some birthday mail. A wet card was retrieved sent from his brother and a slip of paper from which we guessed the writing meant he needed to collect a 'voluminous' letter from the post office.

I put the cards up on the mantelpiece when we got back. Angela had sent a letter with hers, which he read and put away.

We were so cold. I filled up my hot water bottle and put on my anorak, then lay on the sofa snuggled up to Pippa. Ted stretched himself on the other sofa and had his first official 'old age person's afternoon sleep.' We all slept for about a couple of hours and darkness fell whilst we were in dreamland.

Ted had phoned the piano restaurant we went to with Diane and Clive on their last night. It wasn't necessary to make a booking. We understood why when we arrived there for his birthday meal. The place was empty and we were given first choice of where we wanted to sit. We sat where we overlooked the town, watching the lights glimmering over the water in the shadows of the church.

We chose tomato soup because we wanted a re-run of the teapot presentation. It wasn't quite the same as the experience we had before. Ted's choice was the lamb stuffed with soft cheese on a bed of spinach. My decision to have deer was a good one. Succulent and lean, the meat was sliced on a bed of potato with blackberry sauce! Yummy!

...Both the ceremonially unclean and the clean may eat it, as if it were gazelle or <u>deer</u>.
Deut 15:22 (emphasis mine)

The big disappointment came when the raspberries in my dessert had been hidden under a biscuit and were mouldy. Because of the soft lighting it wasn't easy to detect by looking, but the bitter taste alerted me to scrutinise each one. When I told the waiter he simply said he was sorry and took the plate away. That was disappointing. I don't think we shall go there again.

We have seen so much rotten fruit here and to be presented with it was displeasing to me. There were no tit-bits for Pippa. She had waited patiently in the car for us and was expectant, but there are times when we all get disappointments.

Monday Fevereiro 1, 2010

FEBRUARY already! We are almost halfway though our adventure. I feel that I am at a bus-stop waiting. But waiting for what? Adventures bring excitement but I don't always feel excited about this 'adventure.'

I brush my hair and put a clip in it to hold it back. I am reminded of my grand-daughter and how she has her hair clipped away from her pretty little face. I open the shutters and the sun begins to stream into the bedroom. It's warm and inviting but outside there is a cold wind. There seem to be such extremities here.

I brush the dog hairs off the duvet cover. I am spoiling Pippa since Charlie's demise. Charlie was my first Staffordshire bull terrier who passed away last year. Her own Dunelm duvet is now placed on top of my duvet serving two purposes. One that Pippa sleeps on her bedding and, another that her extra bedding keeps me warm.

We had a visit from the owner of the house just wanting to know if everything was all right and asking how long we intended to stay. We said that we would stay for a month and so far as I knew that position remained unchanged. She wanted to know if I had changed the bed linen. I feel her eager eye is overseeing me!

Ted told her again that the water wasn't getting hot in the upstairs bathroom. She then went on to repeat what she had said earlier that this is how it is in these houses built at an altitude. He then asked what the big switch was for on the bedroom wall. At that she headed towards my bedroom to see what he meant. My bedroom was a tip. I had books and papers everywhere – my suitcase was open on the floor; Pippa's bedding was on top of the bed, the cushions from one of the sun-loungers was substituting as a rug for Pip to sit on. How could he do this to me?

I don't know now what I said to bring the enquiry to a halt. I distracted her as she approached the door. I am finding her "helpfulness" a bit overawing.

As she left, she said we must go out for supper one evening. They go out for all their meals. She doesn't cook. They go to 'O Forno' and I suppose have a regular table there. Hey ho!

Ted wanted to find the post office in Luz de Tavira, the village next to our old villa. He wanted to surrender the note, left in the mailbox, for his 'voluminous' letter.

Not knowing where it was, he asked the way of a woman who was sitting in a car with the window open. She looked very shocked and then began to talk twenty to the dozen and I was proud of myself for being able to pick up enough words that the teacher had taught us this week, recognising them as 'on the right' and 'continue to the centre.'

The post office was exactly where she had said, set back from the busy main N125 road that runs through the village. With a small paved garden to the front, the post office was just a tiny room. A customer was seated in front of a table and the postmistress stood behind the table opposite him. She talked non-stop for about four minutes, totally disregarding our presence. I took the paper from Ted and put it in front of her face. Still speaking she took it and walked to the back of the room where she grabbed a parcel from the shelf. Bringing it back to the table she muttered,

"pass poor!"

Ted looked nonplussed. It occurred to me that she was asking for his passport. Looking bewildered he felt down his right leg and then the left, trying to locate his passport from his filing cabinet trouser legs. In exchange for the passport he was given a parcel sent from his daughter.

Pippa had been left in the car. There wasn't a cloud in the sky and it was warm in the sunshine. I had to go back to take her out of her nest before she cooked. My intention was to take her back to the post office with me but I turned round and Ted was there, behind me. Pippa, by then, was geared up for an adventure so I took her across the road and sat in the shade while Ted ordered coffee for us from an 'outlet.' A couple of men tried asking me if she was a pit bull. 'Pit bull' was the only word I understood. Shaking my head and telling them 'nao,' their interest dissolved pretty quickly.

A shaven headed man parked his old car beside us and took a seat at the neighbouring table. He ordered Turkish coffee, which he drank intermittently while drawing on a cigarette. Dressed in black from tip to toe his black sunglasses seemed to mould around his face, I felt something different about his presence. His black suede shoes were clean and showed no signs of dust. He was a policeman! It was his break-time. After a mandatory phone call he lit up another cigarette and puffed smoke towards me looking shiftily at Pippa. I was, at that point, unaware of her illegitimacy in this country!

We stayed in the villa this evening. The television reception was dreadful and so we were unable to see the news. This bothered Ted more than me. I don't particularly want to know the English news.

I cooked soup and, as my computer was set on the only table, thought we could have it on our laps. That didn't exactly work out as planned as I did a Julie Walters take of delivering the soup all over the floor. It spilled down my fleece and trousers, but was quickly licked off the floor by Pippa.

I didn't particularly want to do washing in the evening and had to hang my precious fleece on a coat hanger in the bathroom hoping that I wouldn't need it tomorrow.

I noticed that Ted's right thumbnail is black today. I asked him what happened and he said that the lavatory seat had fallen on it.

Terca, Fevereiro 2, 2010
Tuesday February 2, 2010

The sunshine must be having some effect on my clothing because nearly everything I wear seems to have shrunk!! I'm quite sure that it has nothing to do with the almond tarts I have been testing.

We spent the day at the villa, me, doing washing and Ted sleep-reading on the patio. It was a swift, chilly breeze so the washing dried, thankfully. I think I am more domesticated here than ever I was at home.

I draw the line at some wifely practices I have witnessed here, for example, stewing fresh rabbit. When we came back to the house a couple of days ago, we saw the old man and woman from one of the small shack/cottages in the lane, pulling something which was hanging from a branch in a tree. Closer examination revealed that he was skinning a rabbit while the wife waited to pot it.

A lot of animal slaughter takes place in the back yards of the little shacks – no EU Ruling adhered to here! It makes me realise just how over-the-top we take things in the UK oblivious to the flouting going on elsewhere in Europe. I can understand why people want to get out of the UK now fast becoming a 'police state.'

The pace, here, is peaceful and I am, indeed, soaked in that peace but whilst I play the waiting game becoming unpurposeful – without purpose.

You will keep him in perfect peace, whose mind is stayed on You, because he trusts in You. Is 26:3

Pippa lies on the stone patio watching an ant crossing towards the pool. I hope we aren't due for an invasion. I won't miss these if they come indoors – he is huge!

I am reading, 'The Olive Farm' by Carol Drinkwater, an actress who played in "All Creatures Great and Small." I am paralleling my life at the present time with hers when she moved to the south of France to a small, neglected cottage with land. She bought the place jointly with her lover and describes breakfast times spent out in the open, suppers cooked on an open fire in the waning French sun. There is an emptiness in my life as I reflect her days knowing that she has found love with someone she is able to share everything. Sadness rises from my heart, manifesting in a few salty tears, which are quickly wiped away and caught in His Bottle.

You have recorded my troubles. You have kept a list of my tears. Aren't they in your records. Ps 56:8

Reflecting on my own day, it has been strange. I have spent the day indoors reading and Ted stayed on the patio. No exchange of words has taken place today – perhaps tomorrow will be another day!

Chapter 24

Wednesday February 3, 2010
Quarta Fevereiro 3, 2010

It's raining! Thought I would make some fine coffee this morning as a treat from the Nescafe equivalent, GranArom, Highland GOLD a wonderful copy of the real thing without the taste! We keep the jar of coffee in the fridge. That's where we found it so there must be a good reason for it.

Were my eyes deceiving me? Did I see little specs of white in the coffee grains? Surely not! I know that little teeny mites accommodate themselves in flour, but coffee? What can they do to me? I prayed over it and then poured boiling water over them. Who could survive that type of treatment – the ants certainly didn't. And, anyhow, I can tread on scorpions and they won't harm me!

I poured out the liquid into two cups. Delicious!

As the weather was wet, we decided to go on a trip because sometimes, although there is a chilly wind, the sunshine hits the car and makes it too hot for Pippa. There are times when she can't come with us, for example, some snack bars will allow us to keep her tethered by our feet if we drink out of doors, but generally 'no dogs' signs are stuck on the windows of eating places. Pity they don't adhere to the notices for 'no smoking.'

We set off along the motorway, heading west then north to Sao Bartolomeu de Messines. This is a strange busy, but run-down little place. We walked through the main street and found a coffee shop displaying delicious cakes in the window so took our coffee with a gooey accompaniment! I did wonder whether that had anything to do with my shrinking clothes. The cake I chose consisted of beaten egg whites, which appeared raw to me, wrapped in a swiss-roll fashion with a coating of crushed almonds and hazelnuts. Mmmhmmmn!

As I looked around the small café I noticed a very old couple sitting nearby with whom, I assumed, was their daughter. They were definitely English. They had the look. I then heard one of them say, "Yes, it's very good indeed!" Why do the English stick out like sore thumbs? Is it because they often wear shorts and tee shirts when everyone else is wrapped up with scarves and overcoats?

Moving on, we drove up mountains covering a route we had previously taken to Monchique. I hadn't liked this place when we visited before and as we were driving through, I had an attack. I couldn't breathe. I pulled into the side of the road and undid my underwear releasing any of that tight shrunken clothing and sat slumped at the wheel of the car. Gasping for breath I thought I was having a heart attack. After a few minutes of slow breathing, I was able to take off again and get out of that place. I understand that new-agers regard it as a place of healing!!

The heaviness lifted once the landscape opened up and we were out of that area of mountains and thick forest. We meandered downhill to Marmelete, which was quite an insignificant little place, then on towards the west coast to Aljezur, another small town located in the next region of Alentego. So, out of the Algarve, we saw a different open land, flat and fertile with green fields and remote farms. It was almost like driving through France.

Aljezur consisted of a church with a small paved square in front of it, with a few water features fringed by two rustic restaurants with tables and chairs set outside the frontages. We walked down a narrow residential street – all the terrace type cottages leaning against each other in a row each painted in a pale shade distinguishing the boundaries by colour.

We were hungry, again, well it was almost 2pm and lunchtime here is any time from midday until 3pm. We opted for the more Portuguese, rustic type place where the workmen had come in to watch football on the huge television slung at ceiling level. They leaned across the small tables, dipping their bread in the olive oil and spitting out olive stones as they washed it all down with vinho tinto (red wine). I smiled as I thought of council workers back home, stopping for three hours and lighting up a primus stove on the side of the road to cook fish then knock it back with a carafe of red!

We ordered chicken and chips Portuguese style. Batata fritas (chips) come with most things and are mostly very thin. The chicken was simply pieces of neck cut into two inch pieces. Looking for the meat was like panning for gold. Occasionally, amongst the orange oily 'juice' I found a piece of breast no bigger than Ted's black thumbnail. It was disappointing, but, then, we couldn't expect gourmet dishes in a transport café!

After lunch we headed to the coast and discovered some breathtaking beaches taken over by surfers. A couple of camper vans had found their way down the cliffs and parked on the sand. Camper vans do appear to be a nuisance in the Algarve and locals complain about them parking illegally and taking the water. Water has to be paid for by meter so the residents despise the campers, mostly northern European and English, for taking free water.

Both agreeing that the scenery was beautiful and we liked the area although it was quite unpopulated, rustic and remote, we began our trip back to the Algarve, as it was now dark.

Rain began to lash and it was difficult to distinguish the road. There were no cat's eyes, no white lines, the road was black and it wasn't a dual carriageway. Headlamps were blaring into my eyes and the roads were full of potholes. The last thing I wanted to do was hit one of these with speed and end up having to get another tyre, or, at worst, damaging the wheel.

Ted, still navigating, resisted directing me on to the motorway despite my sighs and despair. He had remembered having to pay 94 euros for not getting a ticket on the pay road and was steering clear at all costs.

"Keep straight," he directed as we approached the sign for the motorway.

"It's right, isn't it?" I say, still keeping my foot steady while I negotiate the rough road.

"NO. Straight. Straight!" he yelled.

I wasn't going to overturn the car or get involved in a brawl at this time of night. I was tired. I would have driven over 300 miles if we ever got back to the villa.

And so I continued on this strange road, straining to see through the blackness. When we stopped the car outside the villa, I wondered how I had managed it.

....in all your ways submit to him, and he will make your paths straight Prov 3:6

Quinta Fevereiro 4, 2010
Thursday February 4, 2010

As we were leaving the villa this morning for our Portuguese lesson at 10am, the owner, sheltering under an umbrella, approached us in the drive. She informed us that someone would be coming to clean the pool tomorrow morning and to be careful because he brings his dog. Also, that her agent would be showing someone around the property in the afternoon.

"Is it for sale?" I asked.

"Yes," she replied brushing raindrops off her shoulder, "I'm selling both of them."

She invited us to join her and 'the partner' for supper tomorrow evening.

We waited for over half an hour at the appointed destination, the public swimming pool in Tavira, but the teacher didn't appear. Ted tried to find her telephone number in the contact list on his mobile phone, but couldn't. I suggested he looked through his texts and he then found it. When he called her (it's his phone – mine was stolen) she said we had the time wrong. It was to be 11am and not 10am. However, she agreed to bring it forward and turned up in her little car to meet us and show us the way to her apartment.

It was high on the third floor of the block, which had no lift. We all traipsed up the steps, she, being heavily pregnant, was obviously used to it. I breathed quietly so that nobody could hear that I was panting like a dog. Pippa, who trotted up with us didn't even pant.

Pippa was led to the balcony where she sat and waited for two hours whilst we had our lessons at Maria's kitchen table. The small kitchen had a sea view between the roofs of lots of other buildings, all erected after she had paid for her sea view.

We proudly told Maria, the teacher, of the instance where we had to ask the Portuguese lady where the post office was. Ted related what he had said and she raised both hands to her face in horror.

"What did you say to her?" she asked.

"Ond carrier?" he replied.

"O I don't know. I don't know that you said that to her! Oh my goodness, do you know what you said?"

"I asked where is the post office?" said Ted innocently.

"NO. You didn't!" she exclaimed, "What did the woman say to you?"

"She looked puzzled and shook her head," he answered.

"I don't be surprised. You know what you said?"

"No?"

"You ask her, 'where do you want it?' 'where do you like it?'

I don't think he even understood the meaning of what he had said! He looked puzzled.

After the lesson we were hungry (always hungry) and headed towards St Lucia where the road runs alongside the beach and lots of tiny fish restaurants lie on the side of the road. Selecting one was easy because we chose a parking space in the shade and walked opposite to a speciality fish diner. A couple of disabled people were sitting in wheelchairs made by Sunrise Medical. That brought a glint to Ted's eye as we used to make parts for their scooters when we worked before retirement. I could see him drifting into euphoria so reminded him to look at the menu. We seem to be eating a lot of fish here because it is so fresh, brought in by the fishermen in all these little coastal towns. Dish of the Day was written in Portuguese on the menu, and Ted was all for ordering it until the waiter translated it as octopus.

We had our pudding at the ice-cream parlour a little way up the road from the restaurant and sat outside just as we had done with Diane and Clive a week or so ago. As the cream dripped down the sides of my cornet, the clouds cleared and the sun came out.

I needed to go back into Tavira to get worm tablets from the vet. Maria had described where the vet's surgery was so we had to pass the cake shop she had described as being the best place in Tavira to buy cake. I wanted to get a letter weighed to send to Turkey so parked opposite a post office close to her beloved shop. I was annoyed that Ted had to accompany me to the post office. It seems like I can't even post a letter without him.

Having handed over the envelope to the woman behind the box-like counter, we made our way down the steep hill, over the bridge and to the surgery. Ted, again, got out of the car to accompany me and I almost screamed. I had money that Diane had left me and wanted to have an opportunity to buy something for myself, even if it was a couple of worming tablets. For all the time we have been here I haven't handled cash. I told him that I wanted to go in by myself, which resulted in him sulking. I had to make a stand for myself.

Once inside the vets I asked, in Portuguese, for the pills and the woman smiled and told me, "Just one minute – you want worming tablets, I will get. How heavy is your dog?"

I didn't know. I described Pippa as being small but heavy and was able to bring her in to be weighed but my offer was refused.

"It's okay. Just guess. 20 kilos, 15 kilos? Just guess."

I don't even know what a kilo is. Oh to bring back currency that I understand. Guessing I said she was about 40 kilos. In return she produced two tablets, which she tucked in an envelope with a picture of a cat on it. She then brushed the packet with the back of her hand, saying, "Don't worry, it's not a cat!"

She asked me for 6 euros. I fumbled in the glasses case which was makeshift for a purse (my purse had been stolen, remember) where my little stash of euros were and brought out cents and notes. It was so apparent that I didn't understand the value of the coins that she assisted me by taking a ten-euro note and giving me some change. I had no idea if she had taken the correct amount, or not.

Feeling good that I had achieved my first purchase since the beginning of December last year, I popped the pills into my new handbag and walked out to the car. Ted was pacing up and down. I am not going to bite.

Father, grant me the serenity to accept the things I cannot change, Courage to change the things I can, And wisdom to know the difference. (Reinhold Niebuhr.)

Chapter 25

Sexta Fevereiro 5, 2010
Friday February 5, 2010

I was awakened by strange noises only to find that the 'pool man' was busy cleaning out the pool. His large golden Labrador pressed its nose to the glass kitchen door to say hello, tail wagging, but was confronted by Pippa on the inside of the door going into lion mode.

She went berserk! Well, after all, this dog *was* on her territory and I felt that the guy might have taken this into consideration. However, he did come to the door and shout, "Shall I put him out?" meaning should he close the gate and leave the dog to wander freely around the rest of the garden.

I had a running commentary from Ted on how the guy was progressing.

"He's using the vacuum now!"

"He's putting a solid thing, rather like a tablet, into the holes in the side of the pool!"

"He's now got the net and is sweeping it across the top of the pool!"

"The dog's walking beside the fence........ I think he's going next door! How long do you think it will take him to do three pools?"

There he goes, calculating again!

I had to clean the house and wash the floors in readiness for the agent's viewing this afternoon. The warm, hazy sun dried up the wet puddles left by the 'pool man' so I was pleased that Pip wouldn't walk wet paws all over the floor.

The beautiful almond blossom began to fall like snow, resting on the newly cleansed pool making confetti patterns on the azure blue water. The almond trees are particularly attractive because they have no leaves, the branches loaded with delicate pink flowers.

Once the house was cleaned, we went out for the day to avoid being obstacles in the way of a prospective house sale.

Our route wasn't planned but we headed towards Loule, the place, which we have now learned, is ripe with crime. We by-passed the town and headed towards Almancil, just south of Loule. Not too impressed with that, we had been informed that Vilamoura was the rich boys' playground and it's nice to just sit and have a coffee in the marina watching the wealthy on their yachts.

We approached the marina side of the town through golf greens and large apartment blocks. Huge magnificent hotels dominated the area with pillars and domes not unlike hotels I have seen in Dubai. It was all very opulent, but very nice. I suppose we had arrived when it was fairly quiet, but one could imagine it heaving with sun worshippers in the summer.

We walked Pippa along the water front peering down at some of the boats. We didn't see many people about despite the weather being sunny and warm.

As we were leaving the area and driving along a tree-lined fast road, we saw a roadside fish restaurant with a large car park and shady trees where we could leave Pippa. Inside was very clean and, again, occupied by a mixture of road workmen and business people.

Ted ordered fish of the day and was surprised to get a platter of five fishes! I think he struggled with the bones, but persevered only to be presented with another platter with two large pieces of salmon. It was a case of eyes being bigger than belly!

It might appear that we have all our meals out, but we don't. It's only since we have been in the second villa without a working microwave and an oven which only half works, that cooked meals have been difficult. There is a barbeque, but the weather hasn't been good enough to get that started and the meals here are very cheap.

We timed our return to the villa to give the prospective purchasers time to leave so it was approaching 5pm and was soon dark afterwards.

Ted got out the maps and retraced our journey calculating (from the map) how many miles we had travelled. I believe he is now working out how many miles to the litre of diesel the car uses!

Sabado Fevereiro 6, 2010
Saturday February 6, 2010

A quiet day spent reading and resting. Ted sat outside all day sleeping and dropping his books. His glasses fell off his face whilst he was in dreamland waking him up with a start, looking around to see if I had noticed!

In the evening we prepared to go to The Quinta to their Quinta's Got Talent night!

And I won! Actually it was quite sad because apart from another couple, we were the only ones there!!! Not only were we elected as judges, but also I was the only person to present something different to the show.

The owners' family and grandchildren were there and the form of the evening took shape over singing into the karaoke microphones, so my effort was the only unsung piece! Although, they did drag me over to do a duet with the owner and I sang the female part of 'Those boots were made for walkin' . Ted sang a Frank Sinatra number but I couldn't hear his voice because he held the microphone somewhere down by his waist.

The editor of the Eastern Algarve magazine, a nice glossy publication, afterwards had a long talk with me about publishing and asked if I would help them out, also asking if they could publish my poem. I was delighted.

We watched the children performing until almost 11.30pm - way past our bedtime, but some of the kids were beginning to wane by that time. We are back there again tomorrow for lunch with the yellow haired lady who struck up a friendship with Ted!

Domingo Fevereiro 7, 2010
Sunday February 7, 2010

Sunday lunch today at the Quinta! We kept our appointment with Jane and her husband Don. We arrived before them and I wondered whether we were there under false pretences.

The dining room was very quiet indeed and only four couples were occupying the large room. Business was indeed very slow.

When she walked in, Jane's bright yellow hair had mellowed and it was a softer paler shade – much more befitting. Her Cornish voice was raised above the gentle whispers of the other diners as she swigged down her glass of white wine.

When she left the table for a cigarette break, I followed her. We sat on the bench outside and she opened up to me about her sad life. Her son is a drug addict. She has bailed him out so many times and it began to affect her health that is why they came to live here. I just felt that I was there to listen at that moment.

She went on to say how they had gone back to Cornwall at Christmas time and had their meal at the Old Oak, which I have been to. It seems such a small world sometimes.

Our coffee was getting cold so we went back to the table where we had left Ted and Don. I realised that this was the first time I had been able to conduct a conversation with anyone without Ted being present. She had suggested that we meet up for coffee one day, which would be nice, but I wonder how I could work it.

After our meal, and after she had finished the bottle of wine, they invited us back to their villa. We followed them for several miles on the main road and then further down a track. Their home is absolutely delightful and in a wonderful position. She explained that they would never be able to afford a place such as this if they were still in the UK. They had it built to their own specifications so it wasn't damp like the other places we had seen.

Set on the hillside it had three storeys and, of course, the obligatory pool. Completely double-glazed with special doors having no exterior handles (for security) and five sets of patio doors at that, she invited us to sit on the terrace and asked what we would like to drink. Coffee was fine for me and of course Ted would have the same. She poured herself another glass of white wine from the chilled bottle, which had already been opened and was waiting for her in the fridge.

We took our drinks out on to the balcony overlooking the rolling hills and almond orchards. The sun shone warmly and it was all very pleasant.

She disclosed to me that she was taking valium because of the traumas she had been through with her son. Umm. Valium and wine don't mix, do they?

She had explained to me that they keep the heating on inside, as most people here do, just as a deterrent against dampness. She had closed the kitchen door to keep in the warmth and as we sat together I noticed that the door behind us was open. Only meaning to be helpful, I got up and closed it. It clicked. She screamed.

"We haven't got a key to get in! You've locked us out!"

I had locked the door. I had *closed the door*. There was no way in. Normally Don would leave his keys in the car, but today he had left them in the kitchen so the only spare key was sitting on his key ring in the house!

We looked around the house and found that a small window in the cloakroom was open but it was far too small for anyone to climb through. Apart from that it was double-glazed and had a plastic frame. A lot of contemplation took place between Ted and Don while I apologised to Jane, not knowing what to do.

The men produced a ladder and began to unscrew the window frame. Ted brought the window frame round to where we were sitting and placed it against the wall. Now, the house had a small hole instead of a window. There the struggle began. Ted elected to try to get through. First he tried getting his legs through, but that didn't work and he almost split himself in half. He then tried heaving his shoulders through and got stuck.

Jane began to laugh. I suspect that it was the alcohol, which played a part in that. I didn't know what to do. I felt so sorry. I was only trying to be helpful.

"We've been meaning to hide a spare key for ages," laughed Jane.

After almost half an hour we were startled to see Ted standing behind us. He had managed to get through the small hole and opened the kitchen door. What a fright! The men then had the job of putting the window frame back into its cavity. That took even longer than it did to dissemble it.

Once inside the house again, Jane claimed that she needed a brandy after that! Did I want one? No thank you! The fact that I am a driver lets me off quite well.

She said she had enjoyed our company so much and wanted to meet up with me on our own. I hope I shall be able to do that. Who knows what door was closed today!

Chapter 26

Monday February 8, 2010

We got up really early to take Pippa for a long awaited walk. Usually the beaches are taken over by the motor home crowd and their dogs.

We were able to give her a good run on Fuseta beach at 7.30am before the Germans brought their dogs out. She ran up and down the beach, testing the ocean and rolling over and over delighted that she could at last be free. I think I can witness to her feelings! I can't, however, see myself rolling over in the sand with my belly in the air!

We were really surprised to see how dirty the place had become since we came during our first days here. Camper vans were now sprawled over the car parks taking up to four places each. Litter was everywhere and, despite professing to lead Europe with fine rules and regulations, they don't pick up their dog mess.

After the beach walk we drove to Olhao (since having Portuguese lessons, we now know how to pronounce it as formerly we called it Ohio, it is Olly-how) to buy food shopping but found that the shopping complex doesn't come to life until 9am.

We ended up at 'incontinent' in Tavira, after all. It was the first time we had been back after 'losing' the car in the car park so made a careful note of where we had parked it this time.

We had a coffee in the quiet shopping mall whilst the shops opened up. I needed to fill up with diesel but felt bad about asking. Why do I feel this way? I am, after all, a taxi driver.

My hair is a mess and I would love to buy some hair straighteners but feel like a child having to ask permission, risking the outcome of being questioned about how necessary is it. In goes the hairpin again and I screw the long fringe out of my eyes thinking of my baby grand-daughter. Ted's hair is growing long. Perhaps we can pin his or, even better, give him a ponytail to go back with!

We unloaded the car. I pegged out the towels I had washed and hoped they would dry. Boring. The weather is now much warmer and the nights are not so cold.

Ted spent the afternoon carrying branches back to the villa to saw up as firewood. As the days have been mild, I don't envisage having another fire! He found a saw somewhere and took to hacking up small branches. He could have made better matches. I hoped the owner didn't see him collecting her wood.

The rest of the day was quite uneventful. I sat on the sofa looking out of the glass door at the pool and the trees beyond. It is so beautiful, but the picture doesn't change. It would be nice to see a bit of activity. I suppose the grass has grown since yesterday!

In the evening, we watched a television programme about the radicalisation of young muslims in Bradford. The satellite dish must be faulty because after a while the picture froze and we lost sound as well.

Ted pretended not to be asleep throughout the bits we were able to watch and ended up knocking his glasses off his face again. Time for bed!

Chapter 27

Tuesday February 9, 2010

I was expecting Olivia, the owner of the house we are renting, to call to 'just see that everything was alright' and also to collect the bed linen for laundry.

We had breakfasted outside in the sunshine. Leaves appeared on the almond trees over night and grass has grown on the stony soil giving us a lawn of sorts. A thing I particularly like about being here is, that the only trees which lose their leaves in the winter, are the almond and fig, so the countryside is very green in winter.

It was almost 10am when I went for my shower. Having a shower entails sitting in the bath (we do have a proper sized bath this time) and holding the nozzle where the water is fairly controlled. Without warning it runs boiling hot, or then changes to cold. I thought that being able to have a bath would be a delight, but the way they install the baths here, is to set them in concrete. This means that all the heat out of the water is lost immediately as the actual bath cannot retain it.

Sure enough, as I was getting dressed Olivia appeared.

"Is everything alright?" So predictable!

I passed the laundry bag to her before she could ask for it, trying to hold Pippa back with my foot in the door.

"The people next door have gone out to play golf if you want to look over the house," she offered.

I wasn't sure what to say. It seemed an intrusion to look over a house, which is being occupied but, then, she had allowed the agent to show unknowns over the place where we are renting.

I wasn't sure what her motives were. Did she think we were in the market to buy her property(ies) from her? Ted was already changing his shoes to go with her.

We walked across the pebbled pathway to the house next door. She produced a master key from her pocket and entered the property beckoning us to follow. The house had been built to the same specification as the one we are staying in but was a mirror image. Ted gasped at the sea view from the flat roof. Built at an angle from ours it had the advantage of seeing the setting sun and an altogether more expansive view of the ocean.

She told us that her agent had both properties for sale at 380,000 euros each but she would 'do a deal' because the estate agents' fees here are 6% plus vat at 21%. She then offered information about the electricity for each property being 120 euros a month, water 20 euros a month and their equivalent to council tax is 500 euros a year. Why was she telling us all this?

I made it clear that we were not thinking of buying property in Portugal but she seemed undeterred. Perhaps she wanted to show us her material wealth? I believe her new 'lover' has something to do with her decision to sell. It all seemed strange.

We returned to 'our' villa and I prepared a simple lunch of cheese and wine from a box of wine Ted wanted to buy from the Mercado (supermarket). I am sure that fine wine isn't stored in a cardboard box, but it wasn't fine wine so it didn't really matter.

Since we had been shown the boundaries of each property, I took Pippa for an extended walk of the grounds. The garden is big and laid out in a maze of footpaths leading nowhere. Some are laid with tiny shells, some small pebbles and others with golden shale-type gravel. We have two huge carob trees and an enormous fig tree after which the house was named. The fig tree looks dead but I am assured that it will flower and fruit will be picked from it in September. Shame we won't be here!

Wednesday February 10, 2010

It's raining!

We spent the whole day just sitting watching the rain beating on the windowpanes. Even Pip didn't want to go out in it.

Ted wore his 'Jim Fish' hat and speculated that it was clearing up over there as he paced from one window to another – but it didn't and continued all day.

We had asked Olivia and partner, Martin, if they would like to come with us to the Quiz Night. They seemed keen so we drove down to meet them at Olivia's villa that is located at the end of the drive overlooking the valley.

I drove us all to the Quinta. We arrived at 7.30pm and the quiz was to begin at 8.30pm. We were surprised to see that the room was quite full already and were able to take the only available table. The meal was ordered and took almost an hour to be served by which time the quiz had begun.

One bottle of red wine had already been consumed by then so Ted ordered another, which he shared with Martin. It was amusing watching them getting drunk, slurring their words and getting sillier and sillier.

Martin fell asleep at the table leaving us to answer most of the questions.

When the results were announced, we were surprised to learn that we hadn't come last this week but were joint 4th with a score of 46/50. We are getting better!

Thursday February 11, 2010

We had a fairly relaxed morning. Our Portuguese teacher, Maria, was coming to the house this week and the appointment was made for 2.30pm. She arrived at 2pm. I was so tired and didn't really feel one hundred per cent. I didn't feel like spending two hours at the table but thankfully the time sped past and I perked up during the pronunciation bit.

I have difficulty knowing when to accentuate parts of the words and Maria has already laughingly joked that I sound like a Portuguese gypsy because I apparently 'sing' the words.

A French waiter asked me whether I liked music because my pronunciation of the little Portuguese I know sounded like music!

Oh that my words should be a pleasant song unto your ears!

Ps 40:3 *He has put a new song in my mouth.*

As she left, Maria predicted four days of wet weather. Tavira is holding a carnival for three days beginning on Sunday.

Friday February 12, 2010

Maria, in her capacity of weather forecaster, was right. Today is raining again and it is set for the day.

Ted lit a fire with the wood he had collected. Did I say I thought we wouldn't need another fire?

We drew the sofa closer to the wood-burner, which doesn't throw out heat very well due to the design. The stove is raised above the ground and, like the bath, set in concrete forming a chimney. All the heat from the back and sides of the stove radiates into the cement walls and the only heat escaping to the room is through the glass door.

We sat like statues watching the flames lick the sticks. Every now and then Ted got up to stir the embers with the poker. There are people who continually poke a fire and some who leave it to burn its own course. He is a poker. He's also a biter and not a sucker of boiled sweets. I am neither a poker nor a biter. Is that significant?

He unintentionally put out the fire by placing quarter of a sodden tree trunk on the top of red-hot embers. Instantly they lost their colour and the wet log blanketed the heat. And so the rain continued. I was glad that we were not still in the first villa. For sure that would have flooded. Being high on the top of a hill here, we do get the full blast of the winds, but don't get floods.

I was freezing cold all day. Wrapped up in two fleeces (I love the inventor), I had a splitting headache, toothache, face-ache, cheek-ache...

116

We ran out of milk. I made coffee with natal – a type of cream. Cream as we know it cannot be purchased in quantities as it is at home. The most that we can buy is a small cardboard carton similar in size to those small orange drinks back home which have in-built straws attached to the packets.

Ted got out the camera again to take a picture of something on the computer. Is there no end to his artistic talents? I'll make sure he leaves the camera downstairs tonight when he goes to bed!

Two huge black Alsatians crossed with bears came into the garden sniffing the railings around the rear of the house and pool. The boundaries of the garden are unfenced so Pippa cannot be let out without supervision. These monsters looked like nephilim.

I nurture my aching face and pull the big collar of the fleece over my cheeks. Poor me.

A thump startled me. A log, which Ted had put on the fire, fell through the open door of the stove and on to the floor. He stood looking in amazement!

"Get it up quickly! We don't want it to mark the floor!" I screamed.

We made a phone call to Al and Mary. When I heard my grand-daughter's voice it caused my heart to flutter. She won't know me when I return.

Took two painkillers. That is an indication of how bad I felt because I don't normally take them.

Bill Clinton has been admitted to hospital with suspected heart problems. I feel poorly too!

Saturday February 13, 2010

A pack of hounds barking outside the house at 4.30am woke me up. Pippa didn't seem to react. They continued yapping for almost an hour. In desperation I opened the door of the bedroom, unlocked the shutters and felt my way out towards the rails avoiding the pool. The dogs, all stood by the rails facing the house confronted me. I wondered whether they were trying to have a conversation with Pippa?

She wasn't interested and I managed to shoo them away so that I could return to bed for a few hours.

Maria was wrong! There were no signs of rain today! The sun rose and played hide and seek with the clouds, but there was no rain.

I thought we would have another quiet day, but Ted suggested going out to see if we could find the village where there may be another villa for us to move to next month. I don't know the name of the village but our trip was rather like the one we had when we tried to find Clive's relative's house.

We drove, or rather; I drove up mountains and down narrow lanes not really knowing where we were going. With a couple of maps strewn over his lap, a portable sat nav in his hands and the sat nav blurting out from the inside of the car engine, Ted was not able to direct me in any particular direction. It has occurred to me that we almost always have to turn round and retrace our steps when we go on an expedition navigated by him.

We approached a level crossing down a very narrow lane. The barriers were down and red lights were flashing. We joined the queue and were surprised to see a tractor coming across the railway lines from the opposite direction. Then, the white van in front of us moved forward. The driver hopped out of the vehicle, lifted up the barrier and drove over.

A Belgian couple crossed in a similar fashion and spoke to Ted through the window saying it was taking too long and we would probably be waiting for two or three hours. With that information, Ted jumped out and lifted the barrier for me to cross. He is becoming a regular law-breaker, breaking into people's properties by getting through windows and causing me to aid and abet him by flouting railway signals! What next!

This time we actually drove in a circle and ended up back at Manta Rota where we began. Pippa hasn't had a decent walk for days so we took a chance of being able to walk her on the beach.

The car park was crammed with camper vans mostly from Denmark and Germany. Although the sun was shining, it was a cold wind, which didn't deter the campers from sitting in their deck chairs alongside their huge vehicles sporting hardly any clothes in an endeavour to keep their skins tanned.

We passed a couple of walkers who looked Danish in appearance with blonde hair. The woman's face looked like the soles of a "Hotter" – deep with lines from too much sun.

There were lots of men fishing on the beach – presumably campers. I could see only one dog so was able to let Pippa have a run, roll and dip in the ocean. She loved it.

Happy, we took her back to the car before the dark clouds approached. It was so nice to see the sun shining today after the day of rain yesterday.

We stopped at a small Portuguese eating-place and had a snack whilst families were enjoying slap up meals. Their eating habits leave me cold. It seems to be a normal thing to swill food around in their mouths while they talk. Closing mouths when eating just doesn't apply here. Knives and forks alike are both tools for transporting food into the mouth. Knives are licked and food is spat out on to the plate.

I didn't really want to do shopping today but we were out of milk and other necessities so visited 'incontinent' on the way back. Ted seems to have taken a liking to the local beer and picked up a cardboard carton of ten bottles. He thought there were ten in the package. There should have been ten in the package. Actually there were only nine, which made the carton imbalanced.

He lifted it up to put it on the carousel at the checkout and the odd bottle fell and smashed. He stood numbed with shock. I have noticed when something unexpected happens, he paralyses.

The checkout assistant told him to go and get another package. The mess was left on the floor. We were told to just walk around it. He scooted off to get a replacement and I waited for him to come back to pay. He slipped on the wet beer – I caught the new package. We should enrol for the juggling act in the carnival Tavira was preparing for. Fairground rides were being erected and loud music was being played in the streets. Maria told us that the school children participate by wearing fancy dress and some of them play instruments. Quite what it is in aid of I am not sure.

Large trees have obscured the satellite-dish so the television reception is intermittent. We couldn't get any sense out of it this evening so our early nights are getting earlier. I shall soon be going to bed when it's time to get up!

Chapter 28

Sunday February 14, 2010

I didn't sleep for one minute last night. I had those dreadful pains in my stomach, which recur from time to time. I paced up and down the bedroom, stood, lay, knelt but couldn't find a position to ease the pain.

At some time between 8.30 and 8.45am after putting Pippa out, I fell asleep and didn't wake up until 10.30am.

Still in my dressing gown, I had yoghurt for breakfast hoping it would caress my tummy. We had agreed to go to the Quinta again for Sunday lunch as we qualify for the greatly reduced Old Age Pensioners' Special! As mid-day approached I began to feel better so we stayed with our plans.

The fields are almost effervescent green carpeted with green/gold Belgian Buttercups. Everything is alive and growing at such speed.

On the way to the Quinta we noticed the Guarda at every road junction. I wondered what might be happening. Then, without warning, a convoy of Guarda (police) motorcycles appeared gesticulating to me to get off the road. I pulled into a driveway and waited. Another Guarda car approached and beckoned for me to come forward and drive into a lane off the road completely.

Was this an extra wide load coming along? We didn't see many lorries or trucks on these roads so the chances of that were remote.

We waited and waited. Guarda patrol cars, motorcycles and marked cars passed us, all with flashing lights and, then, we saw a mass of cyclists appear like a swarm of flies. Hundreds of them took up the whole width of the road. They were followed by a convoy of thirty cars, vans, some television camera crews, other media and support vehicles, including an ambulance. This must have been a race!

Eventually a stray Guarda motorcyclist gave us the signal to move on and as we did so, we passed groups of people in their doorways that had come out to witness such an event.

We were surprised to find the tables were splattered with fake rose petals – a remnant from the St Valentine's Ball that had taken place at the Quinta the previous night. We were informed that lunch was also a special event to mark the occasion.

It amazes me how this tradition is upheld worldwide!

As we were waiting for our puddings Ted told me through clenched lips that Olivia and Martin had arrived. She headed towards us and greeted us. This was a signal for the old guy acting as headwaiter to bring another table alongside ours so that we could be all together. My heart sank. They had been to 'church' and were eager to share with us that the minister had been explaining the origins of St Valentine. He was really a good man, apparently! So good that he made it into the church records fit enough for a sermon.

We made a quick getaway and, rather than go back to the villa, went for a drive into the countryside where we could take Pippa for a walk after her lunch of tit-bits, served to her in her nest in the boot of the car.

Ted tried to get the television to function by going out on to the roof to fiddle with the satellite dish. When he came down he had white paint all over the sleeve of his anorak and the television wouldn't work at all!

Monday February 15, 2010

A terrific rainstorm during the night had left the garden soggy despite having a lot of gravel everywhere. Large pools of water formed ponds around the front of the house and Pip didn't want to go out until it began to dry up.

We thought we should visit Sao Catarina and Sao Barbara today. We didn't quite know why because neither of these little places appears to have much to offer. Both places are quite near so we set off for Sao Catarina first. It is a very run down place with a few narrow cobbled roads off the main narrow street. We walked up one of the cobbled roads, wide enough only for a horse and trap to pass, and saw the post office tucked away behind the main square. Every village and hamlet has a 'square' where local functions are held.

Moving on, we stopped at the English Garden Centre, run by the ex-Pound Shop employee and made a dash to get inside out of the heavy rain. We wanted some sticky labels or 'post-it notes' and the back of his shop seemed a good place to begin hunting. I think his stock is well past the sell-by date, but as most of it is junk the greatly reduced prices were attractive to Ted. He dusted a pack of four very pale coloured pads, pale through fading, and took them to a large Scottish woman who was 'filling-in' as she put it, for the owner. Delighted with his single purchase, and a reduction in price too, Ted sprinted to the car to open the door in true gentlemanly fashion, forgetting that I had the key!

Before we arrived at Sao Barbara, we stopped off in Estoi, the famous place where we met the estate agent who looked like Ricky Gervais. Whilst we were out and about it began to rain again and the heavens opened up. I ran to get the car and picked Ted up from a sheltered spot because he hadn't got a coat. Despite the rain, we were all set to go on to Sao Barbara when Ted had a phone call from Olivia. Her estate agent was on his way to our villa, bringing some people to look over the house. Would it be okay? Well, what can you say?

I had left the laptop on the table with papers and various things all over the table. One of the covers for the sun beds was placed beside the bed with a bath mat over it for Pippa's convenience. I couldn't remember whether I had made the bed or not...

With so many robberies, I didn't like the idea of strangers looking over the place unannounced and was beginning to feel that all this was an intrusion. After all we were paying for the use of the house and she hadn't told us that it was on the market when she showed us over.

We began to drive back to the villa. The fast windscreen wipers couldn't cope with the amount of rain. Roads were flooded bringing the dark red soil down from the hills on to the road. The roads were like rivers of blood.

God showed them all kinds of wonderful miracles near Zoan in Egypt. He turned the rivers of Egypt into blood, and no one could drink from the streams. Ps 78:43,44

I hoped that we wouldn't get hundreds of frogs sent upon us, as we had the ants!

When we got back to the villa, Olivia was waiting in the house and had re-arranged the furniture, put all the lights on, opened all the doors and some of the shutters. The agent had not arrived.

She opened the door and greeted us, inviting us into our own place! Well, ours while we pay the rental! Her red hair had been "set" in true sixties style with rollers and the white roots re-coloured in readiness for her trip to the UK tomorrow. I noticed she had a black eye and immediately asked how she got it. I knew by the way she replied that she was lying. Her complete eye and eye-lid was black. She said she had fallen out of bed and, then, she told Ted that she had walked into the wardrobe. I am concerned about this relationship she is having with the 70+ years old lover. I recognise that type of bruising.

We spent the evening sticking post-it notes everywhere; windows, curtains, chairs, saucepans as *aide-memoire* with Portuguese names for each item so that we will learn them.

Tuesday February 16, 2010

Post-it notes fell off the washing machine and sofa so Ted got out his sellotape as reinforcement. We now have the Portuguese word for 'tap' stuck over the tap as well as the appropriate words for light switch, doors, knives, forks and kettle all sellotaped over them so that we don't forget what they are called.

It's Bank Holiday today so the shops are closed for the carnival. The rain continued and had filled the level of the pool to the brim. The strong wind made currents almost blowing the water out and on to the patio.

Olivia and partner Martin have gone to the UK so there is a certain feeling of freedom for the next three days.

I persuaded Ted to take off his 'filing cabinet trousers' so that I could wash them. He wears them every day because he keeps all his worldly belongings in the legs. Ask for a nail file – out comes his red Swiss Army knife which converts into a bottle opener, tin opener, toothpick, scissors, hair dryer ….. anything you like! This is filed in the bottom pocket of his right leg. Sellotape, notebook, paperclips and a pencil are kept in the pocket above. Chequebook and wallet are kept in the back pockets on either side of his bum. So infrequently are they used that they have made an imprint on the backside of his trousers. A handkerchief is usually wrobbled up in the front pocket making a large bulge and whatever else is tucked away is only for me to imagine. So, I was successful in getting him to empty the contents and change into a more respectable pair whilst I washed them. And it began to rain!

There is no dryer here and although the wind is keen, I am doubtful that they will be dry enough for him to wear. The last time I washed them, he put them back on wet – so eager is he to replace his security blanket…

We heard a terrible banging noise in the kitchen only to find the washing machine jumping towards us. It wasn't that the load was imbalanced, so we had to turn it off before the cycle had finished. Soaking, I carried the dripping load out to the washing line hoping that the rain would eventually give over.

I gave Pippa her flea and tick treatment today. She is amazing! I carefully opened the sachet and left it on the mantelpiece ready to use it at the right moment but she watched me and then kept one eye on the mantelpiece. She just sensed that I was going to do something to her. She is so clever!

The electric kettle, or a chaleira, as it is now called, is situated under a wall cupboard, now known as a comada. The steam had loosened the insulation tape holding the wiring to some small strip lights under the comada. I found wires and insulation tape hanging over the chaleira so, again, Ted's sellotape came in useful to do another botch job.

We decided not to go to the carnival. We had already seen a bunch of about a thousand balloons walking over the bridge by means of a pair of feet. The Portuguese gypsies come out in force when there is an opportunity to do a bit of trading. They also send their well-trained children out to pickpocket. We don't want to re-live that experience and, anyway, don't want to see people parading about in fancy dress. I can liken it to driving through the mountains. When you have seen it once, you don't want to see it again!

Another day with no signal on the satellite dish so the television didn't operate on all channels. We spent some of the evening watching local children's programmes in Portuguese trying to pick up a few words. It must have been a funny scenario – two elderly folks watching kids' programmes! If we get desperate we shall have to go to a bar and watch wide-screen television football.

We practised and practised and I had an opportunity to test out my prowess when I had occasion to reply to an email from one of the Portuguese men who helped us when we were robbed. It was nice of him to ask how we are getting on and in the mother tongue I was able to send a short reply. We hope to meet up with them again in Setubal or Lisbon before we leave this country. He sent a picture of his daughter, Maria with her baby brother together with an invitation to find us somewhere nice to stay! Thank you!

We sat beside the fire and I poured Ted another beer. As I put the empty bottle into the trash, I felt guilty about not recycling. Everything gets put into a black or blue plastic bag and then we have to take it sometimes a couple of miles down the road to the nearest large wheelie-bin, double the size of the ones we have at home.

Anyone and everyone can use any wheelie-bin, which seems a good arrangement to me. Every day each bin is emptied so there is never a pile of rubbish to be collected.

Generally, the Algarve is litter-free but the kind of mess we see is usually around the shacks and consists of anything from old pallets, iron bedsteads, fridges, old cars and dilapidated corrugated iron sheets, which usually represent somebody's home.

Two beers and Ted was anybody's. We must re-stock tomorrow!

Wednesday February 17, 2010

"I must have your phone number in case we toddle off in different directions," stated Ted this morning as he referred to the mobile phone, which Diane left for me to replace my stolen one.

"That won't be necessary, will it Vel?" I replied letting my personal nickname for him slip.

What I meant was that we are never out of each other's sight.

"Vel? What does that mean?" he questioned as he reached over for the Portuguese dictionary. He thumbed through the V's and found the word 'velho.'

"Oh I see," he retorted. "You are saying I am old. Vel-hoooooo means *old.*"

I left it at that. I couldn't tell him that Velcro is a sticky material to which everything sticks, now, could I?

We went to Faro to the new, huge, shopping mall. We had been recommended to go to a place called 'Jumbo' where we were told we would be able to buy a printer.

Trying to get printing done here is very difficult because the library does not allow devices to be plugged into their computers and Internet cafes are a bit dubious. Ted needed to print off insurance documents and stuff.

Once inside the huge city of shops we found one, which sold computer equipment and spent a long time looking at the 'specs' of every printer they had. What we needed was the cheapest, highest 'spec' printer able to scan and photocopy all in black economical printer cartridges! With such a request, it was turning out to be an awkward transaction for the young sales assistant.

"If you buy this one it comes with ink free," he told Ted.

"Oh that sounds good!"

"But you have to buy the cable. It don't come for free."

"Oh! They don't do that in the UK!"

"You are here in Portugal now!"

"Well, yes. But, I mean …. How much is the printer cartridge?"

"42 euros."

"Mmmh. And how much is the USB cable?"

"Come. I will show you," and the young lad began to walk the full length of the store to the USB cables. The display must have had at least 250 different types of cable. I hoped we weren't going to have to look through each one to see the whys and wherefores of each, individual piece of wire.

Delighted, Ted caught sight of one for 1.50 euros.

"Is it any good?" he enquired of the long-suffering lad.

"Of course!" was the bemused reply.

"I mean … is it suitable for Windows Vista? I mean ….. it isn't for a mac is it?"

"It will be good for your laptop if you like it I will put it," came the boy's reply.

"Well, I think we'll go for this one, don't you?" he asked, looking at me for my advice for the first time!

I managed to slip a pair of hair straighteners on to the cash desk while Ted was still talking about the value for money. It was a good deal – for me!

A visit to MacDonalds was surely on the agenda as we had to pass by on our way through Olhao. The last time we went there was with Diane and Clive. A similar situation arose today.

We thought we had ordered beef burger meals and when we got to the window, the Portuguese girl crossed her hands and parted them whilst shaking her head.

"Nao compreenda!"

Another girl who could speak English came to the window to explain that our order had not been taken because they couldn't understand us. And we had spoken in Portuguese!!!! She took our order and asked us to wait. During this time a disorderly queue began to grow. The decorum was exemplary because nobody peeped a horn at us and it was a long, long wait.

After several minutes, which seemed like hours, Ted stretched out of the window to get our lunches. As we are right-hand drive, reaching for tickets in the pay stations has fallen as his responsibility. I won't recall the toll road fee we had to pay because we didn't get a ticket!

Ted spent the rest of the afternoon reading the instructions for connecting the printer to the computer. When I connected the USB cable things began to move. At this rate we shall be taking home twice as much as we brought.

In the early evening we went into Tavira to the farmacia to get some solution for Ted's ears. He informs me that he usually has them syringed. I didn't want to hear any more.

I seized the opportunity to ask for a packet of the cholesterol-reducing pills I have on prescription. Without hesitation the pharmacist produced what she called an equivalent. I was pleased to get these over the counter. I didn't realise just how expensive they were. When she asked for 50.80 euros for a month's supply, I realised how we take our National Health Service for granted. If my NHS card had not been stolen, perhaps I could have had them at little, or no cost. After all, we are in Europe.

Armed with our medicines, we bought a cake to take home to have for our pudding. With no television reception at all now, we realise that the satellite dish has gone into retirement completely. I am pleased in a way because I didn't come to Portugal to watch English television.

Olivia returns tomorrow. I can't wait to use my hair straighteners!

Chapter 29

Thursday February 18, 2010

Whoever forecast rain for eight days looks as though he/she might be right! I am now getting tired and exhausted seeing rain, rain, rain. There is no joy, nor purpose in me going out driving all over the place in lashing rain just for the sake of it. Instead, we sat inside looking at the flames in the fire Ted has made with the remaining pieces of wood, which he collected.

I have read all the books I brought so will have to re-read them.

As the rain continued, the wind howled under the gap in the door upstairs. I suppose it is winter, but we are told that winter in the Algarve has never been like this before. It is usually sunny and warm! I cannot count the number of fine, sunny days we have had. They seem so far away at the moment.

At 4.30pm we decided to pop into Tavira whilst there was a pause in the rain. We managed to run across the road to the vodafone shop without getting splashed. The car drivers, here, have total disregard for pedestrians and sail through puddles and floods making waterfalls and showering anyone in the path. I have seen so many people get absolutely soaked through this carelessness.

I topped up my new second-hand phone for the first time. I have never had a pay-as-you-go before and hadn't a clue how to put credit on it. As I don't have a credit card any longer (and my cards presumably are still not activated) I cannot go online for anything.

Holding my phone like a precious stone, it was a nice feeling to know that I can now make a phone call!

We ran back to the car but this time got soaked. It had to happen sometime!

Who can I ring?

The fire was almost out when we got back to the house. Ted slipped down to Olivia's wood store and brought back a couple of big pieces of dry wood, protected in a large white sack. He looked a bit like Father Christmas with the sack on his back!

We noticed a couple of inflatable Father Christmases still hanging on to chimneys. I don't think they bother to take them down and leave them for the wind to release. Christmas lights are still lit up on a few houses, too.

The kitchen light bulb has blown, the television isn't working, the oven only cooks on one side, the microwave is inoperable, hot water is intermittent, the fridge is so cold that its freeing everything inside. I asked Olivia how the microwave works and she simply said that she wasn't technical and didn't know! She wasn't very helpful, neither was she interested so I don't know how she will respond when I give her a list of jobs to be done!

Lots of rabbits have been playing in the garden today. I wonder if its because of the rain? The rabbits, I have seen are big, fat, cuddly creatures with cute faces. Pippa gets upset with them and constantly wants to chase them. She barks furiously through the glass door, but they don't pay any attention. I suppose they are used to the dogs barking – they bark day and night! Thankfully, we don't hear them as much as we did at the other place.

In the evening we went to O Forno (The Furnace or oven) for supper. Two courses and a small jug of house wine – all for the cost of a pair of tights!! Not bad, eh?

I sat with a view of the kitchen and watched the two ladies working in such harmony to get all the meals ready. Their hair was covered with Daz-white hats, yet they wore jumpers and skirts without aprons! One helper even assisted with her coat on!

The small room was occupied mostly by Dutch people. Lots of Dutch have settled here to live. Ted handed me a poo-bag into which I put Pip's tit-bits while he paid the bill. I was surprised to see that he had left a pile of 1c pieces in the saucer as a tip! We won't be able to go there again!

Friday February 19, 2010

Sun!!

It's strange to see local women in woolly tights, coats, hats and scarves alongside British women in shorts, tee shirts and sandals. How we are all so different and yet made in the same image!

We made Pippa a higher nest by placing the sun-lounger cushions in the back of the car. We then put her bedding on top so that she can be raised up to see what is going on! Perhaps when we make the journey home she can sit on a suitcase because we might need the extra space. We now have a collection of books, maps and a printer extra to what we brought with us. Oh! And my hair straighteners!

We had an appointment this morning at Aldi car park with Rebecca, the letting agent.

She tried to put it off because of bad weather, but I wondered whether it was because the houses she was to show us were damp. These agents have all sorts of tricks up their sleeves, but having worked as a sales negotiator myself, I know them too!

We waited on the car park in the sunshine basking in its warmth. A few stray dogs played on the tarmac. A dear old lady struggled to lift the boot of her car whilst one of the dogs waited patiently at her side, expecting a treat, perhaps. We are told not to feed stray dogs. They don't actually look like strays. One of these was a black Scottish Highland Terrier and the other was a Boxer, both with collars.

Camper vans or mobile-homers as they are often referred to, began to fill up the car park. Taking up to four spaces per vehicle, they park this way to avoid having to reverse the great tanks. It's so selfish.

Rebecca arrived with her little dog seated in the passenger seat of her car. He is crossed with a Portuguese water dog, but doesn't have the webbed feet.

A small woman with long blonde hair, Rebecca was dressed as a local with leather jacket and scarf. She shivered in the wind. We agreed to follow her and drove up the mountains and along the winding road. What did I say about wanting to see mountains again?

She pulled off the road and turned down a red soil track descending the steep path stopping at a double iron gate. The gate was freestanding with no fencing around it. After unlocking it we followed her in an ascent over steep water-eroded soil track to the house standing proud on the top of the hill, or mountain as they call them here.

I could not believe it, because the other day when we had travelled about trying to find the location, Ted had pointed out that particular house wondering whether it was the one for rent!

We agreed to take it from March 1st for one month. It transpired that the owner is Rebecca's partner! One or two things need to be done in readiness for us to occupy – painting and minor repairs, which she promised would be done next week.

The house is situated on the top of a hill in the mountainous region north of Tavira and close to Faz Fato, where Clive's relative lives. It has plenty of surrounding land for Pippa to run around and, apparently, there are no stray dogs.

Satisfied that the right decision had been made, we left Rebecca and dropped down to Manta Rota thinking we could give Pippa a run and roll on the beach but the car park was crammed with mobile-homers. There was a report in the local English newspaper this week about how these people are emptying their chemical toilets down drains in the streets causing concern because of pollution to the ecosystem. It can do significant damage when the chemicals reach the salt flats. To park on the side of the road for more than one night, or to park in the car parks is illegal but the laws here are flouted constantly.

Apparently designated areas have been set for them but, because they have to pay, they just refuse to use them.

We ended up at 'incontinent' where we had a bowl of soup before shopping for paper for the new printer. The centre was very quiet and not many people appeared to be shopping. I wondered whether retailers are finding business hard going.

There seem to be lots of 'kids' stores, as they call them, and I was tempted to go and look. If I were on my own, I would browse. I imagine my grand-daughter wearing that beautiful red dress, or the orange trouser suit. They have beautiful shoes here for children. Lots of leather goods seem reasonably priced to me but I am not here to buy more clothing. My trousers are my friends and we are hardly ever apart!

I boiled a chicken tonight and then added rice to the water – a dish I learned to cook in the Middle East.

Ted enjoyed it – and so did Pippa!

I have learned that the Belgian Buttercups are actually called Burmuda Buttercups!

Chapter 30

Saturday February 20, 2010

Oh what a beautiful morning! When I opened the shutters the sun streamed through the glass, lighting the room and giving instant warmth.

We had a lazy day. Ted was able to sit outside but it was too cold for me to do so. I spent most of the day on the sofa with my various books and papers.

Around 1.30pm he interrupted me and called me to go outside. We had visitors! I had poured out a beer for him earlier and was surprised to see he had covered the glass with his hat!

Olivia and Martin were doing an inspection tour of the estate and had called to 'see if everything was alright!' There is little point in telling her about the few problems we have because she isn't interested.

Olivia sported another 'hair set'. I don't know how many times a week she has it done. I think it's only a recent thing because until a few weeks ago her hair was red and white, looking quite a mess.

They stayed chatting for about twenty minutes during which time I didn't really feel like talking. I had been interrupted from my studying and didn't want to be involved in small talk.

I began to make a move towards the door when Olivia asked when we are leaving.

"We must go out again before you leave," she said. I smiled.

Wondering whether they would be taking Sunday Lunch at the Quinta tomorrow and knowing whether to avoid them or not, I enquired.

"We'll go if you go," was her reply!

"We weren't thinking of going," I told her.

Then, Martin chirped up, "Yes! That's a good idea! We'll see you at the Quinta tomorrow. 1.30pm after church!"

That was settled, then? In my heart I didn't want to go but perhaps we ought. Who knows what might happen?

I asked Ted why he had covered his glass of beer with his hat and he told me that he didn't want them to think he was boozing!!!

The afternoon became cold and Ted lit another of his fires. He is becoming Chief Fire Maker although he does struggle to keep it alight at times.

On a couple of occasions I thought I could smell dinner cooking somewhere. It was quite a nice aroma drifting past my nostrils – perhaps coming from a neighbouring house. I didn't pay much attention to it.

As the smell became stronger I then realised I had cut up some potatoes and covered them with oil as a snack and forgotten that they were in the oven. I reached into the old stove and retrieved a tray of potato bullets. Even Pippa couldn't sharpen her teeth on them. So, lunch had to be leftover chicken and rice.

As we sat quietly in the evening I heard noises outside and discovered that it was raining again and the gale force wind was blowing the patio furniture about. There seems to be no end to this awful weather. The ten-day forecast shows rain almost every day until March.

Our neighbours in Spain have been flooded and lots of people have been forced to leave their homes. Some have lost their lives in Madeira because of landslides. We have witnessed landslides here, to a lesser degree, so have to be thankful that our experiences are not worse.

Sunday February 21, 2010

I woke early and let Pippa out then made myself a cup of tea, which I took back to bed. The mornings are now getting lighter earlier when it isn't raining and today's weather looked unpredictable. Pools of water lay on the paving stones, which could quickly evaporate if given the chance, but it wasn't long before it began to rain again. The force of the strong wind sent cascades of rainwater across the garden in bursts.

We had arranged to meet Olivia and Martin at the Quinta at 1.30pm so, giving ourselves plenty of time, we set off with the view to giving Pippa a bit of a run beforehand as she would be left in the car for some time.

Even after our walk, we arrived at the venue before them. I noticed that the yellow haired lady, Jane and her husband Don, were already having lunch with Jane's daughter who is here for a few days.

We sat and ordered our roast beef and Yorkshire pudding before Olivia and Martin came to the table fresh from their church service, which this week was apparently about 'Lent.' We brushed over that one and spent most of the time listening to Martin talking about his deceased wife.

I was glad to make an excuse to leave the table to take some tit-bits to Pippa for her Sunday lunch.

We declined Jane's invitation to go back to her home and set off, instead, for a Sunday afternoon trip, as older people do, not knowing where we were heading. I hope I don't ever become a Sunday afternoon driver!

Our journey into the hills was very pleasant probably because there were no trees on this landscape, making the expanse appear even greater.

I drove through floods, up narrow lanes, across bridges where the river levels were really high and when we eventually returned to Tavira we intended to go over one of the five bridges, but a fire engine was blocking the access.

Three large JCB's were working to remove huge islands of bamboo sticks, which had collected and drifted down the river causing blockages under the arches of the bridge. As one lorry was filled, so another moved in to dispose of the large sticks. Such activity had drawn a considerable crowd of spectators. We became spectators too as I parked alongside the river with a view where we could watch the performance.

It certainly was a community affair. Men were leaning over the bridge with pieces of rope and hooks, trying to dislodge the long bamboos while firemen provided the ladders for others to get to a lower level to release what they could.

A lone fisherman anchored in the middle of the river, occasionally got up to push away drifting pieces of wood from his bow.

Such was the excitement that we stayed for almost an hour!

Monday February 22, 2010

Although it was still extremely windy and wet, we needed to take Pippa for some exercise. During our time here she hasn't had proper set walks and the only trips she has are in the garden or occasionally on a beach.

We thought that Manta Rota might be a good place as the weather was bad, thinking that the motor-homers might not be walking their dogs on the sandy beach. We were wrong!

The place was absolutely heaving with the vehicles. Two large car parks were full of them so we went a little further up the coast to a small beach where we were able to allow her to run and roll in the sand until it brought that broad smile to her face. It is so satisfying to see her happy and carefree and a blessing that the rain was holding off.

We walked amidst the small fishing boats moored on the sand. Pippa tried biting the rope, unravelling it and tossing it from side to side with her mouth. A couple drinking coffee on the terrace of a wooden café smiled at her antics as she fought with it, then moved on to attack a buoy.

When she was tired, we took her back to the car and settled her into her nest. As I drove carefully over the bumps and holes in the road we caught sight of a small café with chairs outside. We had seen this place on a previous occasion and thought we might try it out.

As it was still dry, we walked up to look at the menu displayed in the window only to be confronted by a small dark haired fellow with very neatly cut small beard. He invited us inside, walked towards a wicker chair covered with a blanket then began to talk to it! The chair!

"Peta baby. It's okay!"

Looking into the chair I spied a tiny little dog with a pretty collar.

"My baby!" he explained.

His baby was cuddled up in a blanket on a chair in the middle of his café where he could keep his eye on him. Peter (the dog) was Spanish. We had a potted version of the dog's life history.

I discovered that the waiter's name was Dino – one I shall remember! He was insistent that we should try Portuguese fish and chips. We took a risk.

He called to his 'partner' an old Englishman whose speciality was making English chicken and mushroom pies. Perhaps we should have gone with that because when the 'fish and chips' arrived, he had battered a couple of sardines in a runny flour and water batter. They were tiny but so overpowering in flavour. Neither of us liked the dish but Ted didn't want to leave his, as I did!

We tried to get away by asking for the bill, but Dino presented us with a very small glass dish each (the type we put candle lights in) both filled with the pith of squeezed oranges and a raisin on top. It was quite the most ridiculous gesture and I'm still not sure why he did that.

He waved furiously as we left, probably hoping to see us again but I think the chances are remote.

It wasn't far to Praia de Fabrica, a village that will be nearest to us when we move to our new villa. Ted had the map open on his lap as I began to drive off.

"Shall we go to *Felacio*?" he asked.

"What?"

So we went to Fabrica and drove up and down a few of the streets. I suppose this will be our new Tavira.

As we were close to the new villa, where we shall stay in March, we drove past and were pleased to see a vehicle was parked outside so the repairs were being undertaken, as promised. That was good.

At the bottom of the mountain and almost in Tavira, we encountered a herd of hundreds of goats, being shepherded by a middle-aged goatherd holding a crook and an umbrella. I stopped the car for Ted to take pictures of the lovely creatures. They really are delightful.

We checked on the progress of the bamboo sticks in the river and they had almost all gone. That was a job well done!

Tuesday February 23, 2010

I had a lazy morning watching the sun allowing the rain to blot it out. Its laundry day so the beds were changed and the linen left in the porch for Olivia to collect while we went into Tavira to get fuel.

I lost the car again in the shopping centre underground car park. We had to go up and down several different lifts until we found the area where Pippa was keeping guard of the car!

We met another estate agent in the afternoon – this time we were going to look at a couple of farms. Although we were not serious, we wanted to have an idea of what the inside of a Portuguese farm looked like. Is that naughty?

The first property was being sold because the wife has cancer. They were a Dutch couple; the husband being a carpenter had made several illegal extensions to the property giving himself a bar, a workshop, shed and other rooms. It was all a bit of a mish-mash but interesting to see that they give very little importance to bedrooms. So long as a bed is placed somewhere, then that does. The upper room, which led to the roof was only big enough for the bed and had no doors but was open to the stairs.

The land was flat and although only about 2 acres, had a few olive trees and carobs. It was mostly stone and also had a right of way through it for the community to come and get water from a cisterna. Up until quite recently, perhaps the last twenty years, local women brought their clothing there to wash.

After drinking coffee with them, we then followed the agent to another Dutch person's farm. This was more organised and businesslike. The woman lived alone and got her olives picked by students, then pressed into oil. The carobs were picked and made into liquor, as were the figs, and almonds were harvested too. It was all very impressive as she had two cottages included for letting.

The heavens opened again and we got drenched in rain so made a quick get-away thanking all concerned for giving us such an interesting time with lots to think about.

Found a lump on my arm. I must have been bitten by something. I spent the evening rubbing it and imagining that I might have to go to the emergency room!

Chapter 31

Wednesday February 24, 2010

As it had been forecast a dry, sunny day we decided to go west to the most southern tip of Europe, to Sangres. It was a long distance as we are quite over to the east. We took the motorway and witnessed the changing scenery as our journey progressed. The landscape became flatter and we saw more sheep and goats – all with their shepherds and goatherds never leaving them.

In the corner of my eye I saw a strange animal in amongst one flock of sheep. I pulled off the road to take a closer look. It was a cross between an Alsatian and another larger breed and really looked unusually fierce as it stalked in amongst the bushes. We watched him for some time but were not able to identify him as any animal we recognised.

We arrived in Sangres before lunchtime. The small town has little to offer except a picturesque harbour. Essentially it is a good base from which to explore the superb beaches and isolated peninsular west of the town where we took Pippa out on to the cliff tops. She rolled in the bright red sand and drank the orange water without batting an eye-lid.

As we stood on the cliffs watching the waves crashing against the rocks, I was transported to the west coast of Ireland. Well, it's the same ocean – just different rocks. It was a beautiful place, but wild, I imagine on a windy, wet day.

There were notices banning dogs from the beautiful sandy beaches, so we had to observe from a distance.

We travelled along the peninsula and then back through Vila do Bispo. The grand name means 'The Bishop's Town' but it is only a peaceful tiny village without anywhere to even take a drink.

We continued along the coast dropping down to Praia da Luz, the place made famous by the disappearance of Madeleine McCann. It was a delightful place with the most magnificent golden sandy beach. It would have been nice to walk around but, once again, having Pippa with us restricted us. So, we pressed on to Lagos. It was difficult to find the centre of Lagos, if there is one. I liked the look of the parts we saw. It is set in one of the largest bays in the Algarve and apparently quite a bustling town.

I understand that the site of the first slave market in Europe is now marked by a plaque under the arcades in the town, which also sustained extensive damage by the famous earthquake of 1755.

We passed the smart new marina on the east side of the town as we drove on towards Alvor, another little coastal town.

At first I was equally impressed with Alvor, a pretty little fishing town of white houses. At the top of the town is the 16th century church. I didn't realise when driving up the very narrow street towards the church that it would be a closed-off road. I ascended the hill towards the church, turned a hard right bend to find a few cars blocking the road and an extended Portuguese family leaning on them, chatting and looking at me.

The street was so narrow. There was no way that I could turn. I gesticulated and in broken Pidgin Portuguese asked them to move their cars. They wouldn't.

Ted, always willing to please, jumped out of the car and said he would guide me. After a 37-point turn, I was almost there. Where was Ted? He appeared at the front of the car, flinging his arms in the air, just as I drove into a block of concrete, which was out of my vision. *Crash!*

His open arms went up to his head.

Fortunately it was only my registration plate that cracked. As I was hardly moving at speed the impact was negligible.

Getting out of the town was uppermost on my mind and I needed to escape at any cost. Winding our way back down the road (we always have to turn back when he is navigating) and along some other narrow streets, eventually I found a way out.

We saw a sign post to a Praia (beach) and Pippa was in need of a walk so we headed down a dirt track, which brought us right on to the beach. Of course there was a network of camper-vans occupying a complete section of track. The Europeans sat in deck chairs, drinking wine in the sunshine, with dogs at their feet, taking full advantage of all the elements available to them.

After our little walk and inspection of the beautiful beach, we spied a wooden shack, serving as a café. I found a suitable place to park the car in the shade, and then we climbed the simple steps to be met by a jolly Portuguese man offering us soup.

We sat under an awning, overlooking the beach, only dunes separating us from the ocean. We were joined by lots of little finches that sat on the tables and chairs, almost pecking the bread off the table. The fresh orange juice was delicious and a little finch also enjoyed the slice of fruit placed on the side of the glass.

The sun began to fall and darkness came upon us. It was a long way home. I was tired, but it had been an adventurous day. Sagres was a beautiful place.

Shame it was so far away.

Thursday February 25, 2010

Maria came to the house, for our Portuguese lesson. I didn't feel that I had done enough homework. In fact, I had done none. I had feelings of guilt.

I asked if she would mind cutting our lesson short and taking Ted back to the bookshop where he bought the expensive cookery book. As she is Portuguese, I thought she would be in a better position to negotiate a refund, as the one recipe I had tried for cooked cod was atrocious and obviously had been badly translated.

She agreed to do that and so we followed her into Tavira. I waited, while they went into the shop. After about fifteen minutes they knocked on the window of the car to tell me that they had only been successful in getting a credit. And, the shop doesn't sell English books!

Friday February 26, 2010

We met Jane and Don in St Estevao at 1pm. We had invited them to lunch and afterwards back to our villa so that they could see our new home. They have built their own beautiful home near St Catarina and, as Don was a builder in Cornwall, was interested to 'have a look.'

They were walking around the tiny village near to the church when we caught sight of them in between a lapse in the rainstorm. Jane was wearing her raincoat, fully equipped for the weather.

They had passed the doorway of O Forno and thought that it couldn't possibly be the place we had suggested as a meeting place. Men were standing outside the door smoking. Inside was a dirty looking bar with a wide screen television in the corner. All faces were set in that direction.

Entrance to the small restaurant was through the bar, out into a courtyard and then at the back of the kitchen. Once inside, it was a treasure.

After a few glasses of wine Jane's tongue loosened and we didn't know whom she was talking about.

The cod I ordered was so salty. It reminded me of my catastrophe and regretfully I had to leave most of it. It looked so plump and fat on the plate and everyone commented on how lovely it looked. It was a bad choice.

They followed us back to the villa and Jane was happy to drink brandy in between popping outside to smoke when it wasn't raining. Ted had a hard time keeping up with Don who drinks beer! Everyone here drinks alcohol by the bucket probably because it is so cheap.

Don grew to like Pippa and offered to take her home with him. I was relieved when they left at 5.30pm and so exhausted that I needed an early night.

Saturday February 27, 2010

Whether it was the effects of yesterday, I'm not sure, but I felt very lazy. I didn't get dressed and was caught by Olivia calling in to 'see if everything is alright' and to find out what time we are leaving on Monday. Her eager eye noticed the post-it notes on the curtains. She then made an examination of the room to see how many others she could find.

"So this is how you are learning Portuguese?" she smiled.

Pippa's wet paw-prints on the floor tiles were an embarrassment to me because I felt she was scrutinising everything.

Anxious to greet and longing for praise, Pippa jumped up her freshly laundered slacks but was quickly pushed away and promptly jumped up on to the sofa to my dismay.

I spent the day resting while the gale force winds ripped the covering from the gazebo-type structure outside the door, causing bits of the wooden frame to splinter off and fly over the roof. It really was raging. I wondered what it would be like at the new villa, which is very exposed and half expected the letting agent to postpone our starting date.

Other than taking Pippa for a saunter around the garden, I didn't go out at all today and began to read Sunset House by Lady Fortescue, an account of her experiences of living in Provence, France.

Had another early night – in Provence this time!

Sunday February 28, 2010

At 1.30am I took Pippa out into the moonlight. We walked around the house and I gazed at the necklaces of glittering lights below in the valley. The lighthouse at Olhao shot beams of light over the glassy ocean. It was a full moon overseeing such stillness after the fury of the wind during the day yesterday. Not a sound could be heard except for my feet treading the stones on the path around the house.

Pip was only just visible, her dark image silhouetted against the steel grey silvery trees and bushes. I wanted to stay and linger in the night but she had already pushed open the door with her nose and jumped on to the bed.

The room was warm. I opened the door leaving the shutters closed for security. I thought of how times are changing and when once we were able to sleep with open doors and windows.

We were invited to a Purim Party this afternoon at Portimao, over sixty miles away.

The sun shone, albeit watery. I was able to wash the towels, which had been provided and most of them dried before we left for Portimao. We had been given the option of wearing fancy dress, but we went as we were.

We bought a superb apple cake, a small decorative pot of honey and some sugared almonds to take as gifts and arrived in the town, one of the largest in the Algarve, in plenty of time for the 3pm occasion. Ted had printed out the directions given, on the new printer. It wasn't clear about how far we would have to walk from the recommended parking area. As we discussed it, the heavens opened and torrential rain and gale force winds came upon us from nowhere. The awning of a shop front was blown across the car park and I didn't like the idea of leaving Pippa in the car in such fierce weather conditions.

Ted said he would walk with the printed directions to see if he could find the place where the party was being held. After five minutes he struggled back to the car, fighting against the wind and was soaked. He couldn't find it! That did it! I said we were going home.

With horrendous weather killing so many in France and Spain, I wasn't prepared to take any risks so drove the sixty-five miles back. It was hard work keeping the car on the road as the wind was blowing into my path with such force. I was labouring to make headway being buffeted about and not being able to see ahead because of spray and poor visibility. It was a strain.

Lightning lit the dark sky and rain became heavier. Whilst fighting with the steering wheel, Ted continued to point out beautiful villas somewhere in the hills. I couldn't take my eyes off the road, despite his attempts to distract me.

I was so relieved to get back to the villa. Pippa couldn't wait to get indoors; poor thing had been rocked about so much.

I heated up the apple pie intended as a gift, and we ate some of it ourselves. It was good.

We began packing up our belongings in readiness for our move tomorrow. We now have a printer, more maps, a library of Portuguese language books, all extra to what we brought.

The towels were wetter than when I hung them on the line!

Chapter 32

Monday March 1, 2010

On the move! Again!

I got up early, put the finishing touches to my packing, then placed suitcases, poly-bags and boxes in the hallway ready to select according to weight and size. The heavier suitcases were placed in the car first with lighter stuff on top. Food was shoved into any available space until the rear seats were filled to the roof. Pippa had her belongings in the back of the car where her bed was made up.

Once everything was placed inside the car, I washed all the floors and scrubbed the doorstep. We then drove the few yards down to Olivia's house to return the key to her.

Her door was open and she called us inside. Thankfully the weather was dry and promised to be fine for most of the day. Soft music was playing in the background as she offered us a seat.

Ted tactfully (but only at my previous briefing) went outside to talk with Martin on the terrace. This allowed Olivia to open up to me about how her daughter didn't speak to her any more. She had bought her daughter a house and gave her money but now, after all her generosity, has lost contact.

I was sorry to hear her story but this happens. She had an appointment with her tax consultant so we were able to get away, promising to keep in touch by email.

We were early for our appointment with Rebecca, the letting agent, at the Pottery Place, the agreed rendezvous, so stopped at Papa's Snack bar, which was just around the corner from the villa we were vacating. We ordered sandwiches, as we hadn't eaten breakfast. Papa's assistant, or wife, doesn't speak any English so we had to speak in our best Portuguese with hand gestures. That was easy for Ted who speaks in picture language anyway!

After disappearing into the back of the building, some ten minutes later she appeared with two pieces of bread slammed together with lashings of margarine and cheese slices. The coffee was nice. She asked Ted if he only wanted coffee, resting her hand on a glass in readiness. Looking confused he replied in her language, quite baffled by her question. The men, here, have coffee with chasers first thing in the morning!

We ordered more coffee at the Pottery Place and waited for Rebecca to arrive. A large white goose spoke to us and wandered across towards the table whilst a three-legged dog cocked his missing leg against the wall.

Rebecca told us to follow her, which we did. The gate to the new villa was wide open, so that was welcoming. She spent a while showing us how things work (or don't work in the case of the TV and one heater). The place was warm and comfortable.

After she left, I took Pippa to explore the land, which surrounds. We walked up the hills and then down to the stream and across a grassy patch alongside the water. I felt such a sense of freedom.

The house sits on a hill amongst other rolling hills, with acres of scrubland and small trees on the hills and valleys, not overshadowed by forests or high trees.

Two swallows flew over the pool and into the distant landscape, whispering sweet-nothings as they passed. I wondered if they were saying 'welcome.'

Pippa adjusted to her new home very quickly. She lay on her bed in the sunshine keeping an eye on us in case we left her.

In the afternoon we decided to go to Tavira and do a 'big shop' so that we don't have to go out every day, enabling us to eat at home more now.

Ted spent a lot of time in the supermarket calculating which bottled water had more volume per cubic litre for the value of euros. I left him and then found him working out the alcoholic content of cheap Portuguese wine.

I cooked our first meal at Casa Monte and we sat at the kitchen table looking out on to the floodlit terrace, the lights reflecting in the pool. The moon was full and the whole atmosphere was that of enchantment.

The television didn't work, but it didn't matter. Pippa found her way upstairs and made herself at home on a sofa in my new bedroom.

As I lay in bed on our first night here, the lights on the upper terrace and the moon flooded through the glass doors, I thought to myself, 'I like it here!'

Tuesday March 2, 2010

I had a fairly comfortable first night at Casa Monte. Pippa has claimed the sofa in the bedroom near the French windows. The sound of the heater clicking on and off did disturb me a little but is more than compensated by the wonderful views from both elevations.

Oh to see 360 degrees of skies, the doormat to heaven!

We had been told that someone would come today to replace several light bulbs around the poolside. Gary arrived at about 11.30am to do this task. Whilst he was here Ted got him to look at the satellite part of the television, which took him ages and even then he didn't have an answer as to how we couldn't receive a signal. He asked if we wanted to be connected up to a game boy instead! I told him we played enough games already - particularly mind games!

I had noticed that the French windows in my bedroom wouldn't lock so he fixed that for me.

I put washing out on a makeshift washing line, which Ted had tied from the air conditioning unit to a carob tree. It began to rain! Gary couldn't complete his work and the washing got wetter than when I put it out.

Gary is another example of how the English change their careers once they touch this soil. He was a BT engineer but now is a Maintenance Manager for the letting agency. He told us that he just got chatting in a bar one day and said that he hadn't got work and was offered a partnership in this house management affair. It was so easy.

He is a nice enough chap. He told me how to drive into Tavira by another route to avoid the spot checks that the police are doing regularly now that the tourist season is about to begin. The last thing I want is to be stopped without a driving licence. It hardly bears thinking of to lose my licence (which I don't have) and be unable to drive back! Or, worse, become a criminal!

I cooked some type of meat for dinner. The gas ring nearly blew my hand off when I lit it. The comments in the Visitors' Book had described the hob as dangerous. The meat was tough as old boots – neither of us could cut it and the potatoes had boiled and disintegrated into liquid. I tried to compensate by opening a tin of what I thought were peaches but were, in fact, apricots. Squirted with instant spray cream, who could tell?

I brought in the washing that hadn't dried and left it in the laundry basket hoping that tomorrow will be a good drying day. I think I am becoming an old fart. I have never thought about drying washing before. Is this, I wonder, a preparation for the tough days coming?

Wednesday March 3, 2010

I got up nice and early, washed up the dinner things from last night, as we don't have a dishwasher here. I put out all the washing, pegging each garment securely to the line under the tree. Satisfied, I made coffee and noticed a black cloud coming towards us from the west. I didn't have time to rescue my washing. Too late! Thunder, lightning and heavy rain soon made small lakes in the gravel. The wind blew furiously taking one of my tops sailing across the mountains. I wonder who will find it?

A red river flowed down the track to the small stream at the bottom and formed a moat around the property's boundaries. A lorry slowly backed its way up a dirt track on the mountain opposite – the only activity apart from the swaying of trees in the wind.

I watched the washing on the line being blown and twisted into knots. We heard the cries of the dogs chained up in an old building across the valley. Intuitively they knew their master was driving down the dirt track to feed them. They are kept day and night inside the old shed bounded by a wire fence and gates, which are locked after each of the master's visits. We don't know how many are imprisoned but by the sound of their cries, we are sure that there are many.

A small man in a white van travelled all the way out here today to switch on a light in the pool. It is an underwater light and as darkness fell it produced patterns on the white walls of the house as the water rippled in the wind.

We sat in front of the television that evening watching a blurred image and listening to Portuguese babblings. Enough! I went to bed!

Thursday March 4, 2010

I let Pippa out at 7am and was shocked to see Ted behind me tying up his dressing gown tightly around his tiny waist. He is painfully thin. I know I can truthfully say that I am painfully fat but we eat similar meals and I always give him a larger portion.

He came out to tell me the news that he had received a text message from Maria, our teacher, cancelling the lesson today. Relieved, I thought I could now relax. With still more washing to do and nowhere to hang it, and, with the previous load hanging on the line dripping, my ideas of relaxing went away with that wind.

I managed to find enough chairs to put outside whilst the sun was shining, on to which I draped garments of all sizes and colours. Just as I had finished my colourful display decorating the patio area, we had visitors. The housekeeper accompanied by the kosher satellite expert found their way through the maze of chairs.

Janet, the housekeeper, unpacked some more bed linen and towels whilst Emanuel fixed the satellite connection. Ted, eager to help, was told to leave it alone! I was glad it was not me who told him!

I needed to be alone. I had two bags of rubbish to take down the road to the nearest wheelie bin. I put them in the car before Ted could take off his Wellingtons.

"I'll come with you!" he called.

"I'm only taking the rubbish!" I declared.

Once down the track and on to the main road, I headed towards Faz Fato where our distant relative lives. Outside the row of cottages was a sweet lady whom I mistook for Portuguese.

"Faluz Inglese?" I asked through the open window and was surprised to discover that she is English.

Casey is a neighbour and invited me inside her tiny house to see her art. I was so surprised to find how big the cottage was. Typically Portuguese, the rooms were small and cosy. Great works of art hung proudly on the uneven whitewashed walls. She delighted in telling me about herself. Born in Liverpool she came here to find peace. She has another property in the North Algarve and still has an investment house in Brighton, which provides an income for her. We talked for a while and had an enlightening passage of time. As she bade me farewell she proclaimed, 'It would be nice to see you again but if it isn't to be, well today was special.'

How nice!

When I returned to the villa, Ted was sulking because I hadn't taken him with me. I should not have been able to spend that time with Casey had he been with me. Consequently, later on in the afternoon, he put on his walking shoes and decided to walk in the direction I had driven this morning. He was away for almost two hours – the longest we have been separated since December!

Supper was simple – I cooked pizza, which we ate on our laps in front of the television. Am I tired, or getting slovenly?

Chapter 33

Friday March 5, 2010

Ted walked into the kitchen wearing his wet filing cabinet trousers, which I washed yesterday. He denied that they were wet. I could plainly see damp imprints of his wallet and chequebook in both of the back pockets!

A mist covered the hilltops obscuring the road. I expected thunderstorms. Everywhere looked grey. It was almost like a different landscape. How different everything looks when it's sunny.

We needed to go to Tavira to deal with the credit note Ted had obtained with Maria's help. It had a validity date we couldn't overlook.

I tried driving by the route that Gary, the Maintenance Manager, had recommended. It was much further but extremely quiet. It took us past a large open market, which we didn't know existed and also past a bullring.

I was able to park outside the bookshop so Ted got a ticket from the pay station and we both went into the shop to see how we could spend the amount on the credit note. Other than Portuguese books and a few amateur paintings, the stock was very limited and I had difficulty in finding anything worth purchasing. Our mission was accomplished when, by adding a further three euros, I chose some pretty purses that I can give as gifts. As we had an hour on the parking ticket Ted didn't want to waste it (all of 40 cents) so we had a coffee in a tiny shop next to the bookshop.

I pulled out a chair from a table inside and Ted leaned across indiscreetly to tell me that the fellow sitting on the table opposite was his estate agent friend who completely ignored us. Some friend! I tried explaining to Ted that when people keep saying, "We must meet up for a meal sometime," they often don't mean it! Anyone who means business will make a date there and then.

We wanted to buy candles and some longer matches to light the dangerous stove. We have to be prepared for the eventuality of a power cut out in the hills. We couldn't find matches anywhere in the supermercado so when I got to the till, I asked the girl, "Onde a caixa os fosforos?" and she told me to go over to the far end of the store, then ask at a counter. Thanking her, we continued to put the few items ready to be scanned. She then asked for the amount in Portuguese thinking that we were locals! My efforts couldn't be that bad, afterall! Black clouds appeared and I had to remember to drive out of town by the new route, which I almost forgot. I decided to drive on a bit further than we needed to for a little drive, as it was dull. We would only, otherwise, be sitting in the villa staring at the washing!

It began to rain just a few miles before we got back. Pippa didn't want to get out of the car. I ran indoors with the shopping and unpacked the bags whilst preparing bread and cheese for lunch at the same time. Ted's trousers got wetter.

We spent the evening watching 'The Coast' on English television. I think Neil Oliver is a darling. Is it his beautiful dark eyes, or perhaps his long hair that I find so attractive? Delicious!

Pippa was disturbed by the thunder and lightning when we went to bed. She wouldn't settle for a while and I had to sit with her on the sofa until she was comfortable.

Heavy rain flooded the terraces and I hoped it wasn't going to leak through the roof into the sitting room where evidence showed it had done so previously.

Flashes of lightning lit up the room so bright that it hurt my eyes.

I dreamed that Diane was walking across the road towards me. She had been for a driving lesson. I don't remember more!

Saturday March 6, 2010

Today was a 'nothing' day. We didn't go out because it continued to rain all day. Is there no end to this rain? The front pages of the local English newspaper showed pictures of Tavira's flooded streets. The river had burst its banks. Everyone says it's the worst weather they have ever experienced.

We are now becoming nosy parker pensioners. We saw some activity today at one of the houses on the hill opposite, so got out binoculars to get a close-up of what they were doing.

Ted stood at the window spying on them, giving me a running commentary of when they were standing by their car, when they moved towards the house, when they walked the dog...

Later in the day he said he wasn't well and had a poorly tummy. I asked if that meant he had diarrhoea and he nodded.

I made pasta for supper – something light.

The dog man visited the dogs but there was silence. I am concerned that he has disposed of them in some unseemly manner. Do they eat dogs, here?

Chapter 34

Sunday March 7, 2010

It didn't seem like Sunday today. I don't know why because the days are no longer identifiable as weekdays or weekends – they all seem the same, but today was different.

I didn't have much sleep. I remember looking at my watch at 3am hoping that I would be able to get *some* rest. I had the pains in my stomach again which keep me awake so consequently I was tired by the time Pippa wanted her constitutional.

I didn't want to spend the day unproductively because it looked as though it was going to be fine weather. I suggested we went out and wanted to take the rural routes to Castro Marim, a small town less than 10 miles away from the villa.

Elevated above the River Guadiana, it consists of one main street and is dominated by the walled castle, which spans over the town.

We sat in the sunshine and had coffee, listening to the locals chattering away as they had their early morning 'smokes' with small cups of Turkish coffee. Someone had told us that because of the bad weather they would jump into the hot weather without the usual gradual acclimatisation to summer. I think I understood the meaning of that statement because I found the sun very hot as I sat outside the café.

We took Pippa out of the car and walked her up the very uneven cobbles to the castle where we had a view of the entire town, its saltpans (which are now home to the wildlife reserve) and the bridge connecting Portugal to Spain.

A large sign on the wall of the castle, beside the huge wooden door, quite clearly said 'No Dogs' so we couldn't take her beyond and into the grounds. Imagine our surprise when a German couple appeared at the door after taking their dog around the grounds simply ignoring the notice. They think there is one law for them and another for everyone else!

We had observed and commented on how the restaurants leave their sometimes very elegant tables and chairs out of doors all the time. They don't take them in at night so there is apparently no fear of them being stolen. That wasn't the case, however, in Castro Marim.

A stone's throw from the borders of Spain, we noticed that all the chairs and tables were chained and most of the windows and doors of the houses were barred for security. This only confirmed to me the bad reputation Spain has for criminality.

As the shops closed at noon on Sundays, I wanted to take advantage of shopping so found a Pingo Doce supermarket a little further up the road. Ted now knows how to put the euro into the trolley so he runs ahead to show off his expertise. He has yet to learn the meaning of *entrada* to avoid pushing the trolley through the exit!

When we returned to the villa it began to rain. Again!

An odd couple drove up to the house in a very old dusty car. It was difficult to see what colour it was through the dust and mud. They had come to clean out the pool. I thought it might be more apt for them to begin on the car!

The driver, and apparently the owner of the car, spoke very well – in fact he was posher than Ted! The other character, tall, thin, weather-beaten with long greasy hair pushed back in a pony-tail was unkempt and merely stood to watch as the well-spoken shorter man did all the work. The lazy one has lived here for over forty years and saw the expansion bridge being built between Portugal and Spain. I doubt if he helped in the making! I suppose he stood and watched that too!

The fruit of the carob tree outside the window is growing quite quickly. It looks very much like runner beans growing in clumps directly from the branches.

All types of fruit, here, taste so different. The oranges are sweet and bursting with juice. Grapes are the size of ping-pong balls, also sweet and juicy – and with pips! It's a pity that we won't be here for the harvesting of peaches, figs and almonds.

I heard the dog choir this evening. That made me happy. Well, I say pleased that they haven't been disposed of but sad that being chained up day and night they don't appear to have any kind of decent life.

The coffee table was wet. The floor had a puddle. The roof was leaking in two places. The repairs that the 'Maintenance Manager' (ex-BT engineer) had done didn't last long. The kitchen ceiling is damp where the terrace overhead is leaking. The electric kettle doesn't work and the water now is dark brown and undrinkable.

Monday March 8, 2010

I have been bitten! My finger itches and I have a blood blister. As I armed myself with all types of ointments expecting to be coming to a hot country, I found a suitable cream to apply. Then I seemed to have itches everywhere!

We went to Vila Real Sao Antonio today and before we went into the town, took Pippa to a beach where we had taken Diane and Clive when they visited us.

It's a wonderfully long beach and apart from the cockle fishermen, not many others go there. This morning we were shocked to see great piles of bamboo, washed ashore in the very bad weather, forming a line for as far as we could see, cutting the sandy beach in half! It looked like a different place and was unrecognisable.

I was looking for a post office but the queue inside was unreal. I don't understand their system. You have to go to a machine on the wall and take a ticket (rather like you do at the deli) but once you have your ticket, it's a mystery how they deduce who is next! Not getting anywhere and waiting for ages, I walked out still holding on to my cards. There must be another post office somewhere.

We sat outside a café on the pavement and presently a cheerful young lady came to take our order for coffee. We began to speak in Portuguese, but she smiled and said she was English. Her parents, Lyn and Keith, came from Tenbury Wells! She told us that her father used to have a caravan in Bromyard! The world is small.

As we sat, a dear old lady appeared from her doorway in the building opposite. Dressed completely in black from head to toe and with a black scarf covering her hair, only exposing her thick, weather-beaten, heavily wrinkled face I needed to capture her remarkable image. I reached for my camera and snapped her. At that, she turned her back and closed the door behind her. I suppose she's fed up with having her face on picture post cards!

As we passed the shops surrounding The Square, it was difficult to decide which of them to get an apron from. They all sell the same merchandise. I felt Father had asked me to purchase an apron.

I looked carefully through the rails set out on the footpath. Full-length aprons, granny-type aprons, which looked like dresses and small dainty aprons were hung from hangers in every colour of the rainbow.

'Which one, oh Father?'

A small apron displaying a map of Algarve with waist ties! This was to be the first purchase for me in a proper shop. I struggled with the six euros, not recognising the cents from the euros, but with some assistance from the nice gentleman behind the wooden counter, I popped the treasure into a bag.

'Why, Father?'

'You shall put on your apron of humility!'

And all of you apron yourselves with humility toward one another, because God resists the proud, but gives grace to the humble. 1 Pet 5:5

Now that was a lesson!

I had seen a notice in the English newspaper, advertising 'Women's Day' at Vila Real Sao Antonio. Men were busy erecting a stadium in The Square, so I suspected that it was for this occasion. My reason for wanting to visit today was because I thought samples of cosmetics and free things were available for women. I had been mistaken. The function didn't begin until after dark, and the stadium was in readiness for a Strip Show for women. I wasn't interested in that! A little disappointed, we decided to continue our journey to Monte Gordo, a coastal town just a bit further along the ocean. It was so commercialised and that was a disappointment too. We got lost in the town and seemed to go round in circles recognising that we had already driven along the same road before. Of course it began to rain again and didn't stop for the rest of the day and night.

Tuesday March 9, 2010

A clear sky!!!!!

We decided to go to our nearest village, Vila Nova de Cacela, for breakfast, so drove the six miles where we found the sleepy little place just waking up at 10am.

We discovered that The Square consisted of a small market. Fish vendors had their units set up on the one side and fruit and vegetables opposite. Located between were a newsagent, florist and the W.C.'s.

As we walked around the small town, which is only one main street we made ourselves comfortable under the awning of a café expecting to eat breakfast in the open, only to be told that they just served coffee.

I purchased a pair of scissors from a shop, which sells all sorts – Ted paid for them, and then we returned 'home' without having had a thing to eat.

It was such a nice feeling having no rain today. The sun shone against a keen cold wind. I sat in the bedroom and attempted to make a birthday card for Mary. I haven't been able to buy nice cards here but despite my efforts, the result wasn't satisfying to my eye. I reluctantly popped it in an envelope and we drove back to Vila Nova de Cacela, to the small post office where I knew I would be able to get service.

There were six people before us in a queue, all babbling away. The post-mistress was spending rather a long time explaining something to an old man who sported a huge contraption strapped on to his ear. He looked quite a simple, country character so I wasn't sure whether it was his lack of hearing, or lack of understanding which took such a long time. Then, a woman pushed in front of another old man to pay a bill. As soon as she picked up her change, another old man pushed in front of the first old man. Surely the post-mistress could see who was first in the queue?

When it became my turn to stand at the counter, she raised her neatly pencilled-in arched eyebrows and the whole procedure was over in a few seconds. Mary's card had been posted!

We then took Pippa to the beach where we were able to allow her to do her running and rolling. In the far distance we could see the waves breaking gently. Miles of sun drenched beach and crystal blue waters were stretched before us like a watercolour – a delight to the eyes.

In the evening we tried our local, which is exactly one mile from the villa. Just a shed-like building situated on the corner of a cross roads with a plastic awning reaching out on the roadside.

Once inside, and through the dark bar, it opened up into a fairly large room where tables were laid with white paper cloths. We were the only people in the room and were welcomed by the Portuguese-speaking lady of the house. Her husband, complete with flat cap and apron, was assisting in the kitchen when not outside puffing a fag. With beer in one hand, I could see him balancing freshly peeled potatoes in a bowl, which he then passed to someone out of my vision.

We chose kid from the hand written Portuguese menu and were informed that you have to give notice for it to be cooked so chose kid chops instead. We booked the kid for Saturday allowing them plenty of time to prepare it and catch it!

Wednesday March 10, 2010

The forecast had promised a fine day so we thought we would go to Spain. Partly because we wanted fuel and we also thought it might be nice to travel a little way up north along the borders to see what it was like.

As we approached the bridge connecting both countries, we saw a gang of police standing, waiting at the roadside. I hoped they weren't going to pull me in to check my credentials. They didn't!

We entered the town of Ayamonte, a place we had visited when Diane and Clive were here. It's the closest point for getting fuel, which is considerably cheaper than in Portugal (according to Ted, who holds the purse-strings.) We passed through and continued northwards to Villablanca. We were struck at how all the houses and shops were painted white, hence the name no doubt. The sun reflected on the paint and almost blinded us.

We didn't find anywhere to have coffee. We hadn't eaten breakfast and I was getting quite hungry so we found a supermarket tucked away in a back street and attempted to get something to substitute as breakfast.

The assistant on the till didn't speak to us, nor acknowledge us in any way. She didn't even look at us but simply threw our few items through the scanner and demanded payment. She was most rude. This was to be the attitude of all the Spanish people we encountered during the day.

The roads were of extremities. They were either new, freshly tarmacadamed roads, or dreadful unmade gravel paths filled with huge craters and potholes. We continued north to San Silvestre de Guzman and then on northwest towards the borders.

I liked the flat countryside and thought the landscape was beautiful in places, but the people put me off the country completely. I also still had the remembrance of being robbed in Spain.

We drove into Sanlucar de Guadiana, a small town beside the river, which forms the boundary between the countries. I was surprised to see that it was exactly opposite Alcoutim in Portugal where we had, with Diane and Clive, looked across the river wondering what this place was like!

When we entered a canopied building to ask for coffee, Ted was brusquely corrected for ordering coffee in Portuguese! As the Spanish hate them and vice versa, we were off to a bad start. The landlord poured out the coffee and shoved the glasses towards us then turned his back on us to speak to an old fogy drinking wine at that time in the morning!

In front of me, but behind the bar, was a side of bacon set on a wooden frame, completely exposed with his old jacket slung over the leg of the beast, which served as a coat hanger. A deep hollow had been made in the meat where the dirty knife had carved pieces off in the same place. Flies hovered above it, feasting on the rind. We took our coffee outside and sat at a table next to a Dutch couple. They began to speak to us and told us that they, too, come here for the winter and went on to tell us how in twenty years of visiting they had never experienced such bad weather. Some consolation to us!

We travelled for miles along wonderful new roads built with funds from the EU. Some led nowhere and one such road led only to large gates across it. As we approached, we were in time to see a fellow locking them. He got into his car, drove past us and laughed. Spanish! Uggh! We had to turn and go back. I began to get tired of avoiding potholes on a disgusting road, which went on for miles. I wanted to get back on to Portuguese soil but the journey seemed unending. At last we arrived back at Ayamonte and took a quick look at Lepe before heading back to the bridge.

As we passed over the bridge, we noticed that the gang of police were still there but were holding several people and cars hostage. One fearful looking person dressed in black with a balaclava hiding his face and head was on the alert with a gun ready. I was glad to be getting back to Portugal and extremely relieved to get back to the villa.

If one lived to be 200 years of age, it would be impossible to visit every place in Spain. It is so vast and I realised that we had spent one whole day travelling and only covered a miniscule part of this country.

Thursday March 11, 2010

We were up nice and early expecting it to rain so thought it would be a good idea to go to Faro to see if we could meet up with the couple who had invited us to the Purim party, which we had to give up on!

Ted, armed with his map collection and sat-navs also had explicit directions taken from the website so surely today we wouldn't have to do the usual trick of having to turn back and start again.

Getting into Faro was the easy bit and we recognised where the heritage centre was. We had already, previously, tried to park in that area and got stuck up a dead-end road. It was another of those difficult times when I had to practice my 50-point turns.

We arrived at lunchtime when the heritage centre was closed so went out of town to give Pippa a bit of a run and then returned to the new shopping complex to have lunch. I parked in the underground car park, opened the rear door to take out my handbag (the new one which now contains nothing except my journal, some pens, my new second-hand phone and the glasses case Mary had given me) then realised with horror that I hadn't disposed of the rubbish. The black bag was still sitting on the back seat and had been cooking gently all day! Ted said he would get rid of it and I didn't realise how, until I saw him trying to stuff a full-sized black bag into a tiny rubbish bin erected on one of the concrete pillars.

Trying to disown him, I walked quickly to the elevator, which took us up to the shopping mall. I was certain that he had been captured on the CCTV cameras.

We didn't really know what we were ordering and when the plates were given to us through the serving hatch of the 'eatery' we were surprised to see the contents. Ted had lots of very thin slices of meat, rice and salad. I had three chicken legs, rice and beans with a large helping of shredded green stuff soaked in vinegar and oil. The chicken was so salty I wondered whether they had left it marinating in the salted cod. Unable to eat it all, I popped a lot of it into the poo-bag for Pippa. I would later regret this.

The Jewish Heritage Centre was simply a memorial to the Jews in the form of a cemetery and small building housing pictures of how it had been restored by a Jew and is now a living memorial to him. We met the couple, now in their seventies, who invited us to a Passover meal to be held at their home on March 29. After the previous attempt at finding them, I think it is unlikely that we shall repeat that scenario.

Before going back to the villa, Ted picked up a couple of copies of the East Argarve Magazine, a nice glossy mag which this month published my poem. Vanity! Vanity!

Friday March 12, 2010

Pippa got me up three times in the night! I shouldn't have given her that salty chicken.

Hooray! A fine day has been forecast. I didn't hesitate to do a load of washing and hang it out on the new line Ted has erected for me at the front of the house. He has tied this one to a lamp on the wall from the down pipe on the house. It starts off by being quite high, but hangs low by the wall light.

We picked up the kitchen table to take outside and as we lifted it, an unseen drawer fell out and smashed on the floor. Immediately Ted turned to his emergency kit and got out the glue and two red rubber bands (the ones that the postman ties up the mail with) and set about sticking it together again.

I made coffee and took it out to the table, now placed beside the pool. Ted put up the umbrella and we sat to drink our elevenses at 10.30am. The washing machine bleeped and I took out the load to peg on the line. By the time I had put a couple of towels on, it began to sag and the washing ended up resting on the floor.

The clear blue sky clouded over and black clouds approached. We have such a vast expansion of sky here. The clouds appeared to be overlapping each other at different heights forming unusual patterns and emitting wonderful colours where the sun was exposed.

Our curiosity was aroused when we spied a white van on the horizon over the top of one of the nearby hills. A man dressed in white emerged from the van and began to engage in some activity, which required us to get out the binoculars.

On closer inspection we realised he was a beekeeper. What we didn't realise was the other neighbour was watching us through his binoculars!

In the evening we tried a restaurant a mile away from us in another direction. Once again we were the only people there and the owner only spoke Portuguese. We managed well to order a simple, local meal, which was cheap and cheerful.

A young waitress appeared after we had finished. She had spent most of her time standing behind me watching the television whilst we were eating. She could benefit from going on a training course. It was apparent that we, as customers, were secondary to the Soap she was concentrating on.

We were back home at 8.30pm. My bedtime! I am an old age pensioner now!

Chapter 35

Saturday March 13, 2010

A day of glorious sunshine! It was hot on the balcony and wonderful weather for those sun-worshippers, which I am not any longer.

We are very exposed here in the hills, so can expect wind most days. Today's wind was quite chilling but out of it, it was hot!

We had a quiet day. I caught up with my journals, which had been neglected over the past week. I feel extremely agitated when I haven't written. It's such a relief when I have brought my notes up to date, such as they are. I suppose I should be more disciplined, but I do get tired very easily these days.

Pippa moved from the balcony to the sofa when she got hot, and from the sofa to the balcony.

I heard a great commotion and looked up to see the dog man's pick-up at the gate of the dog den. He, and another person, stayed there for a long time and when it became silent, I was anxious that they might be preparing the dogs for Sunday lunch (grilled barbeque).

All the Portuguese houses have purpose-built barbeques outside the living quarters. It is here that all the cooking is done out of doors, winter and summer alike. Usually they are covered with corrugated roofing, but all have large chimneys. It is very apparent to know which are the British or Northern European owners' homes because their barbeques are usually built away from the houses, perhaps alongside the pool. This, of course, would be impractical to use for several months of the year.

It's hard to believe that we are almost halfway through our tenancy here. I have been thinking of 'home' a lot lately. We need to find accommodation for the week over Easter and then will make our way towards the north of Portugal. Our only experience of the country so far has been the Algarve, 'home to tourism.' We are looking forward to seeing how different it is in the north.

Ted has a new habit of patting down his hair from the crown towards his face. I think its because it's getting long but it does look as though he is stroking himself! He now has silver curls around his neckline – a wee bit afro-like while the rest of his hair has gone wavy. He has been smiling a bit more since I took a photograph to show him how miserable he looks!

He spent the day sitting in the sunshine. At one point I noticed he had hung his hat on the washing line. It had, no doubt, blown into the pool again.

It's a strange feeling knowing that I am not exactly on holiday and neither am I resident here. It's a sort of limbo experience.

We have booked to go to our local tonight. They should be cooking our kid for us! We haven't been there on a Saturday night so I am hoping that won't be a limbo experience, trying to get a table!

We arrived at the appointed time to find that two tables in the restaurant were already occupied and the family was using one long table for playing dominoes. Adults and children alike were all concentrating on the game oblivious to the fact that it was a restaurant.

Framed photographs of children were sitting on the counter on top of the cakes and fruit, in amongst ornaments and a few cups, obviously coveted by football fans.

We waited for the kid, which had been pre-ordered. Tables began to fill up with locals coming in. I must say that it is easy to recognise the locals who all have a sort of 'inbred' look about them. We waited. And waited.

An hour later the middle-aged waitress brought one oval dish of bones together with a smaller dish of beans and a carrot. I couldn't imagine why we had to pre-order such an offering. Cut through the spine in chunks, the kid had hardly any meat and was presented in two-inch wedges of bone. I was once again disappointed.

Children were screaming and running in between the tables when I would consider they should have been in bed. After all, it was past my bedtime anyhow!

A group of ten British folks seated themselves at a long table next to us. They looked and sounded like the cast of Eastenders. The one woman looked like a witch with long unkempt hair falling down her hunchback. She could hardly raise her arms because of the weight of gold around her wrists. They shouted above everyone else and with the screaming children, I could hardly wait to get out. We skipped pudding and I left the room to give Pippa her big helping of tit-bits.

Saturday evenings are obviously a very social occasion here. Families get together and friends join up to eat, drink and be merry. Ted and I hardly exchanged two words. It was just as well because I shouldn't have been able to hear him.

When he came out to the car he complained about the cost. It was only a mile to the villa. It was a late night for me – 9.30pm to bed! I wonder what tomorrow will bring?

Chapter 36

Sunday March 14, 2010

The sun rose just before 7am and we were walking Pippa on the beach at Fabrica before 9am. It was already warm and so still. The ocean looked like glass crystal and the sand like white gold dust.

We could see a few Lowry people cockle-picking in the far distance. One lone woman (from the motor-homes) had already taken her deckchair on to the beach and was sitting reading. She must have been German!

The tide was out leaving small fishing boats tilted on their sides in the muddy sand near the estuary. Of course Pippa chose to roll just there and when she spied a stork in the water, ran after it only to find she was sinking in quicksand. She didn't quite understand what was happening to her and dragged her little body back to the fine, warm nice sand, bewildered and defeated.

My phone made a sound. I found a text message from Mary wishing me a happy 'mothers day.' That was so sweet of her. I hadn't realised what day it is not that I recognise these commercial 'days.'

We needed to get another supply of water. Since the water in the system has turned brown, we are buying large bottles. We couldn't find a supermarket nearby and drove into the coastal town of Altura. The only supermarket open for business was a small one in a side street. We were able to get what we needed and then came back to the villa for late breakfast.

The sun shone fully all day. Ted decided to fill all the potholes in the long dirt track leading up to the house. The track is about half a mile long with big rocks protruding due to the vast amounts of rainwater washing away the red dirt surface. It's really rocky driving up or down the very steep track because we are situated on the top of the hill.

He prepared himself by using two empty paint cans to carry stones, and an old spade, which he found in the cupboard where the propane gas cylinders are housed. He soon realised that it wasn't easy trying to dig up earth, which had dried out like concrete, but he was determined to persevere, stiff upper lip and all that. After all, it was a challenge! I now need to wash those filing-cabinet trousers again.

The dog man was present at the dog den again today. We thought we saw him making concrete. I hope he isn't going to bury any bodies anywhere. The dogs don't seem to be making any noise. Perhaps the 'kid' we had last night was, indeed, dog!

The warm sunshine is bringing out the wild flowers. I noticed a field of white narcissi and the bushes near to the house are sprouting large white flowers. The hills here are terraced and have been planted with young pines. They are only the size of small bushes at the moment, but the pungent smell of pine first thing in the morning is quite heady mixed with the fragrance of lavenders and milk vetches.

There is an abundance of those lovely marigold-like flowers, which come out in the sunshine and close up at night. I don't remember what they are called, but they are just growing wild here. Pale purple and deep mauve in colour they mingle with orange marigolds all over the countryside.

Ted wanted to light a fire in the afternoon. He was holding a cardboard box, packaging from the bottled beer, and a box of matches. I made it clear to him that I didn't want him starting a forest fire with so many bushes and bracken about. We have had too much rain and not enough sunshine to dry anything, but, nevertheless, I needed to warn him.

The evening was spent wastefully. I didn't cook because I had prepared a hot meal in the afternoon. Listless and bored after thumbing through local magazines, I took Pippa out for her last 'convenience' then retired to play with my words. There wasn't much to report so the journal was shorter than normal. Tomorrow is another day!

Chapter 37

Monday March 15, 2010

Tomorrow is another day, indeed!

I watched the sun rise at 6.50 as I lay in bed. Morning has broken! The condensation on the window looked like snow resting on the panes as the sun's rays spangled the droplets. We missed all the snow they have had in the UK. An airplane trail had left a line of lace across the sky, which melted into the high cloud.

Two fat little birds sang a song to me through the window as they perched on the sill. I tried not to frighten them away as I pulled back the curtain to see where the chirping was coming from. We have lots of interesting birds around here. The other day we saw a couple of hoopoes. Their brown bodies suddenly change as their wings fan out and display beautiful patterns of black and white. A few eagles live nearby too.

We drove into Vila Real Sao Antonio again today. It isn't far from here and sits almost on the Spanish border. We took Pippa to the beach where the bamboo, which had washed ashore, still separated the soft silky sand from the harder, wetter sand. A lot of the bamboo had been removed. We saw one old man collecting it and putting it in the boot of his car. Good firewood, no doubt!

We walked along the sand for quite a distance allowing Pippa to have her freedom. No other dogs seemed to be in sight so we had the beach to ourselves, apart from the few old fishermen. They set themselves up on the sand letting the ocean take the rods off into nowhere. Seldom do we see anything caught.

When we had dusted her down, we put Pippa into her bed in the rear of the car and I 'investigated' a dirt track, which ran parallel to the coastline. We were surprised to find a couple of wooden walkways, which had been erected from the side of the track, over the dunes and down to the beach. The track was dreadfully pot-holed and the car rocked from side to side as we drove to the end. Pippa gets disturbed when we drive on bumpy roads. It came to a dead-end occupied by a couple of motor-homers! They were quite well established with a washing line and flowers planted in pots. I suppose because the location was so remote, they had set up home there.

A visit to Lidl completed our little journey. We stocked up with water, which is extremely cheap to buy at this supermarket. 5 litre containers are .29c each! Even cheaper in English money!

I remember talking with a Scottish woman who now lives here permanently. She told me that she can live here much more cheaply than in UK. The vegetables and fruit are less expensive and by looking for local brands everything is cheaper. I was surprised to find that Spain was more expensive than I thought, despite hearing that property there is now dirt-cheap.

In the afternoon Ted went for a walk. I seized the opportunity to drive down to the post office ON MY OWN! I sang to my praise CD as I drove into the sunshine, looking down to the ocean before me, which glistened in the sunlight.

A small queue had formed in the post office. It was 'dole day.' They produce a cheque, which is handed to the post-mistress and she then clicks away on the computer after which she requires a signature from them on the back of the cheque before she counts out 355 euros to each of them. I'm not sure if this is a weekly payment, or monthly but they all seem to get the same amount.

She greeted me with a smile when it was my turn to be served. I had a package and two envelopes to be weighed. Her eyebrows were not in the same place today. The pencilled half-moons, which she had the other day, were now lower and straighter. After asking me if I wanted standard or express, I wasn't sure so told her that I wanted them to go by plane! She understood and pressed a sticky label on each before serving the next person who was already edging in to the counter in front of me.

I sent a copy of the magazine containing my poem to Diane. Vanity, vanity!

In the evening we watched a 'Despatches' programme on television about Gaza's children. It was quite upsetting and biased against Israel. I felt they should have had the viewpoint of both sides. Small children are being taught in the schools that they should not hate the Jewish children because it is their fathers and uncles who are killing them. Consequently, the homeless kids play shooting games, pretending to capture the Jews and torture them. Such aggression is being encouraged to this generation. It makes me wonder what will be happening in five or ten years' time when this hatred takes revenge.

Upset at seeing small children suffering – and that was the purpose of the film – I decided to have another early night.

There was no moonshine. Just a few lights glittered on the hills and stars twinkled in the navy blue expanse. If it wasn't so cold I would sleep with the door open but I still need the heater on at night.

Tomorrow I need to contact the agent to remind her to find us some accommodation over the Easter holiday. We are now into the second half of our stay here.

As I prepared to go to bed Pippa decided she wanted to go out. The sounds of the dogs crying in the dog den split the silence. It's a cruel world.

Chapter 38

Tuesday March 16, 2010

It looked as though we were going to be blessed with wall-to-wall sunshine again today. I lay in bed thinking. Thinking of what would or would not be. I had dreamed of being in Malta with my friends. I also dreamed that I had left a baby in a hot car. Dreams are strange and I wonder whether they have a hidden meaning sometimes. Mine are mostly strung together with unconnected events.

I cut up an orange and an apple then took the dish out to eat whilst I sat on the concrete bench outside the pool. The wind was cool, but the sun was warm. I was in reflective mood. Ted sat in his usual place on the sofa in the sitting room pretending to be reading.

The house sits on the top of a hill, which drops down on all sides so it really is like a castle perched on a peak. It has a low, white, wall all the way round the house, patio and pool with lamps studded at equal intervals. At night when lit up it is quite a spectacle from the high main road and looks like a small village.

The dirt track slopes steeply down from the main road into a dip where a stream runs the whole way round the hill on which the property stands. A concrete bridge connects the two tracks over the stream. Then, a very steep ascent brings you to the house, about half a mile from the very quiet road, which runs along the top of the next hill.

This morning I took Pippa down the slope away from the dirt track, down the terraced 'mountain' now covered with wild lavender just coming into flower.

I walked carefully over the stony uneven surface, past wild fig trees, just producing fresh green leaves. The old wild olive trees look dusty and grey. They don't shed their leaves at all.

At the bottom of the hill was a small area of luscious grass, which Pippa began to eat. I sat on a large stone beside the stream, effectively, a moat. Old trees had fallen into it, yet the water still seemed to find a way around to continue its course. The trickling of the water was the only music to be heard above the gentle wind. I watched the sparkling liquid pour over the stones, all so gentle and clear so unlike the red gushing roar of floods last week.

The Eternal shepherds me, I lack for nothing; He makes me lie in meadows green, He leads me to refreshing streams, and revives life in me... Ps 23

Bees vanished inside the trumpets of little yellow flowers set amongst the stones. It was a beautiful place to be. Quiet and beautiful! We stayed for some time until Pippa became hot and on the way back to the house we actually found a golf ball!

Several people have been strimming the grass around their homes. Usually this is never done because the hot sun burns the grass before it can grow too long. This year, because of the enormous amount of rain they have had, the country is greener than normal.

My watchstrap has broken so I have put my watch in my new handbag for safekeeping! I am now learning to tell the time by the position of the sun. Obviously when it rises, it is before 7am and by 8.30am it has reached the edge of my bedroom window. At mid-day it is directly in front of the house, which faces south. This is all very well but the sun doesn't shine every day! Those days will be called Timeless!

We had planned to go to Silves today to the Cork Museum. There are so many cork trees in this region and I am not certain of how they are harvested. Some say once every seven years – others say once every ten years to allow new growth. We have seen large piles of cork stacked up in the fields as we have travelled around the area. Strange that the local wine has screw tops!

Ted rang the Tourist Information office to find out when it was open, only to be told that it was closed until further notice. It would have been interesting to find out the history of the cork.

I did some washing this morning and when I went to peg it on the line, discovered that Ted had moved it. It now extends from the down pipe of the house to another lamp on the wall around the pool, but he has hung it over the children's paddling pool so in order to put anything on it, I have to balance on the side of the pool to reach the line. I'm not sure which of us is 'losing it'.

After a light lunch of lettuce, tomato, two slices of cheese and five grapes I felt very disciplined. I need to eat more healthily. We cannot buy cheese how we do in the UK. All cheese here is sliced. I have seen the assistants in the supermarkets cutting up blocks of it and wrapping it for sale.

I made myself a cup of vanilla tea and brought it up to my room, which has patio doors onto a terrace. Pippa came with me and lay out on the terrace while I checked my emails and did some 'work' on my laptop.

I noticed Ted wandering about downstairs, looking at the washing line, so seized the opportunity to take a bar of chocolate out of the kitchen cupboard. I brought it upstairs and attacked it with vigour.

Pippa's little head looked up at me as I gobbled the delicious drug, trying hard to capture the true flavour as it melted before I swallowed. I gave her a tiny piece without much guilt. Why did I do it? I immediately felt the conflict within my stomach. My ulcers were trying to reject it. Why, I ask myself have I let myself down on Day 1. It was cheap chocolate – 38c a bar and yet, so delicious!

The sun moved across the sky to two-thirtyish. Ted was sitting in a plastic chair against the white wall with the pool in front of him. I watched him pretending to read as his head toppled backwards and forwards as he slept. Of course he denies being asleep!

I wonder if we shall ever be able to use these pools. The temperature is going to have to rise considerably before my toes touch the water. It seems a shame that they have to be maintained and cared for throughout the winter months when it's too cold to use them.

Clouds appeared from nowhere and disorientated me. A few moments ago it should have been about 4.30pm but, now, I haven't a clue what the time is. I am counting the days to our homecoming. 36 days till we hit the ferry. Tomorrow will be our 100th day away! If we prolonged our stay by another 50 days we could qualify for residency, no inheritance tax, cheaper food – not sure about the sunshine!

Chapter 39

Wednesday March 17, 2010

St Patrick's day! And, another warm day! How lovely!

We walked Pippa in the Forestry Commission along a narrow red soil track, which seemed to have no end. It was so liberating for us all. Pippa was able to run and investigate without the fear of having stray dogs appearing from nowhere. At the bottom of a steep bit of road was a ford. We hadn't brought our Wellingtons otherwise would have walked up the other side but Pippa was happy to lick up the water and plod about in it for a while.

We had met a couple who casually invited us to 'drop in' any time we were passing their villa. To pass it, one would have to make a detour off the main road so unless we were particularly seeking them, it wouldn't be a case of 'dropping in.'

It is not a village, just an area. On the way home, we turned off the main road into a dirt track where we thought they lived, and followed the potholes down to a dead-end. There were about six shacks in between a piece of ploughed soil. We saw a local old lady in the field, complete with scarf and straw hat perched on top. She blanked us as we passed but that was okay. Surely this couldn't be where they meant?

We had to turn around (again) and retrace our tracks, as there was no other way out. It was just a simple community of old, Portuguese people living in a frugal environment.

Almost at the top of the track, and on a sharp bend, was another track feeding up the hill. Ted felt that it must be the way to their home. It was another dead-end and I couldn't get any further forward anyway because a car was parked at the hammerhead.

There was only one house perched on the top of the hill so Ted got out to see if it was the right house only to be welcomed with shouts of joy from Bob, the builder. Yes, really! Bob was a former builder, now retired, and his wife, Belinda, had both been coming to this area for holidays for over twenty years. They built the villa about ten years ago, but today, were suffering damp and mould problems. We had called on them (at their casual invitation) whilst they were trying to clean the mould off the walls.

We stayed and chatted for about an hour and arranged to meet for dinner on Saturday night. They live in Northampton but don't have plans to come here to live permanently. We had a happy time discussing the Portuguese language and sharing our experiences of mistakes we have made!

In the evening we went to a place just off the road junction to Spain, recommended by our new friends. Some nice cars were in the car park. There were too many waiters lingering at our beck and call but the food was very good indeed only spoiled by three men in a table in close proximity – close enough for their cigarette smoke to reach me. I thought smoking in restaurants had been banned but it appears that rules and regulations don't always apply.

The portions were 'double-portions' and we were so full that we could hardly move. Pippa had a big bag of tit-bits afterwards.

It was a late night for retiring at 10pm and a bad night for stomach ache!

Thursday March 18, 2010

We had a Portuguese lesson booked for this morning – the first for over two weeks but we had to cancel it due to my aching stomach. I hadn't had a good night's sleep because the dogs had been barking for most of the night and my stomach was really painful.

Two stray dogs approached the house. I dashed out to chase them away and grabbed my white nightdress off the washing line to use to shake at them. Fortunately Pippa hadn't noticed them. One was an Alsatian and the other, a large black unidentifiable breed. They ran away to the top of the track and made their way back towards the dog den. I don't think they are part of the dog den family because I have seen them roaming around for a few days.

Ted asked me if my lavatory was ok. I said it was slow to drain the water once flushed, but why? He said that his was blocked. It certainly was!

We had nothing available to unblock it so had to go into Tavira to his favourite ironmonger to get plunger, acid and a flexible pipe to do the job. Armed with a Portuguese/English dictionary he went into the shop only to find that they speak English. He had been practising the Portuguese for 'blocked' 'cistern' 'lavatory' all the way into Tavira!

When we got back to the villa I went up the stairs to flush mine to check it out and somehow the water ran down from mine and filled his lavatory pan even more until it began to overflow on to the floor. In a wild panic Ted began to hop from one leg to another. He then ran into the kitchen, grabbed the flexible hose and tried to untie it. In his fury he ripped open the plastic tie and started pushing the hose down the lavatory. It did nothing. The pan overflowed brown effluent all over the floor. He was standing in it and his hands and arms were also covered.

We spent all day trying to unblock these lavatories. Ted lifted the manhole covers and tried wriggling the hose up, all to no avail.

At 4pm and still getting nowhere, he decided we needed to go back into the town to get a stronger solution and some bleach. Off we went and I dropped him off at the ironmongers, as there were no available parking spaces in the street. I drove up and down a couple of times and then waited at the top of the road. I saw him come out of the shop but although I was parked where he should have seen me, he didn't. I waited and waited while he walked in the opposite direction; laden with his wares and then, he turned around and noticed me. He began to run up the road banging the bags on his legs as he ran.

Back at the ranch we continued this ordeal of trying to unblock the lavatories. Ted poured some very strong liquid down and as soon as it hit the water it turned black in colour and smoke began to rise. He said it was very hot. We waited the recommended twenty minutes after which I poured boiling water down but still we couldn't make progress.

I suggested that we use a small glass cárafe to empty the dreadful stinking contents into a bucket. Ted bravely volunteered to do this job with a handkerchief tied around his face. The stench of sewage and chemicals was dreadful and enough to cut your throat.

At about 7.30pm we finally heard a 'glug' and the offending blockage was released. Both lavs began to operate as they should and all that was left for me to do was to mop up sewage from the bathroom floor and disinfect everything.

We didn't eat supper that night!

Friday March 19, 2010

The atmosphere was very warm. The patio stones were soaking with humidity. Pippa got up in the night and found a huge, big, fat toad crawling alongside the wall of the house. She walked past it, gave it a sniff and moved on. Toads I have seen always jump, but this one crawled slowly almost as though he had been injured.

The birdsong was sweet. We have swallows, stonechats, finches and pied flycatchers here, all singing together as dawn breaks. The humidity had soaked the pines giving off that heavy scent across the valley.

Ted found a bright green spider in the doorway and had gathered it up with a piece of tissue before I could really have a good look at it. I asked him why he had thrown it away and he said he had done the same with a toad last night! Threw it over the wall and out into the scrubland beyond!

We had agreed to meet Jane and Don today at their home in Moncarapacho. She had suggested around 11am so in order to go the scenic country road, thereby avoiding the N125 and the police checks on the roundabouts (or rotundas as they are called), we needed to give ourselves enough time.

Jane doesn't like dogs so Pippa had to remain in the car whilst we had coffee with them. She also had to stay in the car when we went for lunch. It was easier for me to drive everyone. That way Pippa was able to stay in her own bed.

We drove to Rocha da Gralheira, a restaurant in the hills just above S Bras de Alportel (www.rochadagralheira.com). There were 40 steps up to the restaurant, which overlooked the town and Faro beyond that.

The meal was a buffet lunch but the waiters brought it to the table. A large skewer was placed on the table and a chef cut pieces of beef vertically on to our plates. The same thing happened with chicken, sausages and pork.

A large tray of rice was placed in the middle of the table, with dishes of beans and shredded cabbage. We were able to go up to the salad bar and help ourselves to salad too. There was fruit available at the same station.

Shortly after the dinner plates had been taken, a waiter brought another skewer to the table, this time paring off slices of hot pineapple for each of us. And, if that wasn't enough, after that, a young waiter brought out a tray so wide that his arms were outstretched to the full. The tray was laden with twelve dishes of puddings for us to choose.

Included in this gourmet buffet was white and red wine. When the bill came it was only 28 euros!!! We shall be going there again, I feel.

Pippa is now used to getting treats after being left in the car. She wasn't disappointed.

We took Jane and Don back to their home, had coffee whilst she surreptitiously drank vodka in a glass cup. I know all those old tricks.

When I felt I had had enough, I began to make a move. A loose arrangement was made for them to visit this villa where we are staying, before we leave. Don is particularly interested in looking at houses. They had already visited us at Olivia's place so that he could have a sniff round. Next week he has lots of doctor's appointments so it's an arrangement to be confirmed.

Chapter 40

It was a quiet day. I didn't get dressed until almost mid-day. When I let Pippa out we walked down the track and across the hilltop amongst the newly born yellow buttercups. It amazes me how they just appear overnight. It had rained during the night and the moisture in the pines produced that heavy, heady scent. It reminded me of men's aftershave. The lavender had more heads today and the white flowers on the bushes were a few more than yesterday.

Ted and I spent about an hour learning how our mobile phones work and what options they offered. I learned how to use the capital letters button on mine. All very thrilling!

I cooked late breakfast so we didn't bother with lunch. We were going out for supper with Bob, the builder and Belinda, his wife.

As I backed the car away from the wall of the house, I spied the toad in my headlamps. He was crawling half in the undergrowth and half on the gravel. I put on my main beam and he jumped into the darkness. He was still able to jump!

We arrived at Bela Vista, (place with a view) before our new friends and sat at a table waiting for them to show up. Fifteen minutes later they walked in just as the young lady waitress handed us the menu.

I had heard how delicious the black pork is. As I don't particularly like pork much and don't eat it anyway, I was fascinated to hear about how the pigs are fed only on truffles and figs so that the meat is 'out of this world.'

Well, one for an out-of-this-world experience, I wanted to go along with this.

There was a whole section of different pork on the menu so I chose the one described by the waitress as being "soft." I was to wonder whether it was I who was soft! I almost ordered the one described as 'secreto' (secret) but she revealed that it was just fat! Good thing I didn't!

I don't seem to be having much success with meals out. When it eventually came, the meat was far from soft. I could hardly cut it and it was so salty, I just couldn't eat it so there were no treats for Pip.

Belinda and Bob's conversation was a bit heavy. They are keen church-goers and are unwavering in their churchified pagan thinking. Being 'members' of their church prevents them from coming to live in the home they have built, here in Portugal. It is a substitute family and they just couldn't leave it! It was a time for me to keep quiet!

At almost midnight we left the restaurant, much to the relief of the staff, as we were the only ones left. Poor Pippa didn't get any treats. I rolled into bed. I am not used to going to bed so late. My bedtime is more like 8pm these days! Just think how beautiful I shall be when I get back home!!!! Early to bed, early to rise, makes you... beautiful!

Sunday March 21, 2010

We thought we would go and visit the nice Dutch people who are selling their farm near Moncarapacho. She has cancer and red hair. I should have looked more carefully to see if it was actually a wig.

We had only driven a few miles down the road to a junction where I was about to turn right when Ted told me that we needed to turn *left*. In obedience (!) but stupidly, I listened to him and recognised that it was the wrong direction so I had to turn around and go back *again*! I was annoyed. This happens every time we go out. What is it about having to go *back* all the time? Is this significant? Does this hamper progress?

The narrow road suddenly became crowded with vehicles parked on either side leaving little space to drive between them. I then noticed dirt-track driving taking place in the valley and up the hills in the distance. A small policeman was on duty to direct the traffic, mostly 4x4's and some souped-up racing machines.

Suddenly out of nowhere came a small boy riding a motorcycle. He could only have been about six years of age. He drove into my path and continued wobbling along the road for about a mile when he disappeared in the same fashion as he had appeared.

We later passed an open tractor – with no safety hood – being driven by a young man with his little son on his lap! No rules here!

When we reached the farmhouse we met the tenant of the adjoining rental property, outside collecting wood from a stockpile. She wore her dressing gown as most people here do. They wear them all day, particularly on Sundays.

She was Dutch but spoke good English and was able to tell us that the couple was out in Fuseta but would be back by about mid-day. Their dog tried to get into our car because he could smell that I had Pippa inside. Once she caught his scent, she began roaring like a lion so I had to make a quick exit with a promise that we would be back later.

We drove on to Fuseta only about five miles away hoping that we might see them but we didn't. This was a place we liked to bring Pippa in the early days of our stay here. We now are staying too far east to make this a daily trip.

We didn't go on to the beach today because we had only begun to walk a short distance from the car when it started to rain. We ran back and sat watching the fishermen bringing in the fish. The smell of fish reminded me of proper seaside places!!

I moved the car more towards the town and we made a dash to one of the small restaurants alongside the wide pavements. Their boundaries are clearly defined by the colour of the chairs they have outside. A man and woman, from neighbouring establishments, were in charge of large oil barrels set up under umbrellas serving as barbeques. On homemade grills perched over the hot coals they had scores of chicken pieces smouldering. The woman was busy turning them over with her hands clothed in marigold gloves whilst the man turned his head to one side to blow away the smoke from the cigarette he was holding.

We had coffee and a 'tostie' (toasted bread with a chicken filling) then made our way back to the villa.

On the return journey it was necessary to cross the river at some point and we found a narrow concrete bridge inland to avoid going back into Tavira.

I waited for a vehicle to get over the bridge and began to drive forward. There were two people walking over it. This is a bridge without railings, just simply slabs of concrete open to the elements.

I stopped as I reached them only for the fellow to shout abuse at me through the passenger window, which was open on Ted's side of the car. He ranted at me for being inconsiderate. I asked when it had been pedestrianised and he sarcastically replied, "This morning!" He looked as though he was going to thump the car so I put my foot down and left him standing there.

I asked Ted why he hadn't said anything. Why had he allowed the fellow to shout abuse at me? He had no explanation as usual and this made me really angry.

We got home and I didn't speak to him for the rest of the day. I watched an interesting programme on the television about the Sahara and went to bed.

It is important to keep our spiritual slate clean at all times. Harbouring any unforgiveness or unconfessed sins will definitely hinder prayers. Father, please forgive me!

The agent can't find us another property for next week so I suppose it is my faith that will carry us through! Bed at 9pm! Not so much beauty sleep tonight!

Chapter 41

Monday March 22, 2010

I took Pippa out as the sun was rising, so it was probably before 8am. I then returned to bed and, using the bed as a table, began to look through my notes and diary. I opened the doors on to the terrace and allowed the sun to flood the room. I wasn't sure how long I was going to keep up this 'no speaking' policy so decided to write a note to Ted explaining how I felt. How I felt about him never supporting me and never taking my side. I doubted whether it would have any affect but left it on the bed.

I checked my emails and nobody loves me today.

It was really hot. I put Pippa's bedding out on the terrace to air. She lay on it for a short time but found the heat too much. Someone told me that Staffies feel the heat more than other dogs and advised putting a bit of lemon on their tongues in hot weather. Perhaps this helps produce more saliva.

I painted my toenails. Women here always have painted toenails – that is if they are not wearing Nora Batty stockings! I straightened my hair and spent a whole day in my room and on the terrace with Pip. The sun was so strong that neither of us could sit out for long periods. I was glad when the gentle breeze passed over in the afternoon as the cloud built up making the sun warm and hazy.

I read and then checked my emails. Still, nobody loves me! I imagine that the silence game will be over by tomorrow as Jane and Don have confirmed that they can come in the morning.

I left my note on the sofa in the place where Ted always sits. There was no reaction as he continued to sit and sleep on the patio. You would think that a man, blessed with such a wonderful person as myself as a wife, would be masculine enough to apologise, give some explanation or *something*! Nothing!

That was it! At 6pm and before dusk, I changed and put Pippa in the car. I took the house keys, which also had the gate key, and drove off. I needed to get milk, anyway, so went to 'incontinent.' Before going into the food store, I looked around C&A's new shop but didn't see anything I liked, then went to the upper floor and ordered myself the Dish of the Day. It was a strange feeling being able to handle cash. Diane had left me her change so I was able to use that.

I sat in the mall and ate the vegetable soup and borrita, then moved further down nearer the cinema and ordered almond ice cream and coffee from another place. Well satisfied, I then wandered back to the supermarket to get milk and dog food. Pippa was thirsty when I got back to the car so I gave her a drink, then drove into Tavira. I like the little town at night. It has a sparkle and the river is spangled with pretty lights. Few people were about as I parked and watched the lights dancing over the water through the open window of the car.

A little shuffle in the back told me that Pippa probably wanted to have a wee, so I took her out and walked her in the garden beside the water. There was a bit of grass so she was able to do what she had to do comfortably. We had a short walk around the square and then back to the car.

I rang Al on my new mobile phone. It was so uplifting to hear his voice. He is so sensible and had some words of encouragement. And, of course, some sound advice,

"Don't be out late. You don't know who's about!"

I had a little spin around town, peeping into the cafes and restaurants most of which were empty of customers. Perhaps it's because Monday is a quiet day?

As I drove off the main road and on to the narrow road towards the villa, I was overtaken by a pickup, which had its reversing lights on permanently. I slowed up to let him go because his lights were blinding. The total disregard for law abiding is prevalent everywhere.

After putting the milk in the fridge, I began to walk upstairs and noticed a message left on the bottom step. I'll read it tomorrow!

Chapter 42

Tuesday March 23, 2010

The sun appeared later this morning because of the cloud, but once it burned through it began to get very warm. Most people say that the winters are warm. If only we had experienced sunshine earlier in our stay, it would have changed things enormously.

I could hear the 'tut-tut' of a tractor over on yonder hill. It sounded rather like a scrambler bike as it crawled along the man-made terraces on the hill. A little old man wearing jacket and hat, hung on to the wheel as though he might be moving at 60mph! It was obviously not going to be hot enough for him to remove his coat. As he moved to the other side of the hill the sound went with him and was replaced by the disturbed dogs at the dog den.

I brushed all the floors and 'swept the house clean.' Ted had written a note and left it on one of the steps of the open plan stairs. As I brushed the stairs down, I swept the paper on to the sitting room floor. When he went outside I strained to read his reply without moving the paper.

I have been blessed with eyesight that can see a bird perch on a tree a mile away, but cannot see anything in front of my fist. I climbed on to the first stair to make myself taller, therefore extending my distance in order to read his tiny writing without disturbing the position of the paper, which I knew he had observed.

He had written that he was sorry but felt useless because he couldn't drive or use the computer on his own. That did it! What about trying to explain the nights of silence or the lack of support? The silence will continue.

Oh do I need to eat the words of Galations 5. I am haughty and proud. I should humble myself and have compassion on him although he treats me like rubbish. But I am finding that hard to do. I need to put on my apron of humility. I'll wait just a bit longer!

Some gentle tapping echoed across the valley. People were now coming out on to the land to work it. The dreadful rain has set them back by at least a couple of months, but the pace of work here is painfully slow.

I was surprised to hear a fast bike approaching the house down the dirt track. A motorcyclist (complete with helmet) had come to read the electricity meter. I watched him opening the meter boxes set on a purpose-built concrete wall about 6ft high but only 3ft wide. It looks a bit silly, but that's how they build them. He then scrambled up the track leaving a trail of red dust behind him, only to repeat his business at a couple of houses on the roadside. I expect the bill will be high. We have been running heaters day and night, until the sunny weather, to dry out the damp.

At 11.15am I put Pippa in the back of the car and prepared to go to the new golf club complex (which Jack Nicholas has put his name to) where I had agreed to meet Jane and Don who hadn't been to this villa before. The idea was to lead them because giving directions here is difficult.

I had intended going on my own but as I was backing the car, Ted ran out with his waterproof mac (21 degrees today and sunny!).

We met them as arranged and they followed us back to Casa Monte with gasps of "How lovely!" "How beautiful!" "What a beautiful spot!" "Oh the house is lovely!" but once inside they showed their disappointment.

The house was built purely as a holiday-rental and structurally is not sound enough to withstand the winters, such as the one we have just had. In many ways it's similar to the first villa we rented. Built mostly of concrete, it has no damp course because that's the way they build the houses here.

Don, an ex-builder (aren't all the men here ex-builders?) examined the white ceiling in the sitting room and smiled at the Picasso that the Maintenance Manager (ex-BT engineer) had created with the black bitumen.

Jane was keen to have a glass of wine at 11.30am. I struggled to open the bottle with the flimsy bottle opener so she took the bottle out for Ted to open. The two men talked together outside behind the house while Jane and I sat in the sunshine beside the pool.

I had forgotten that she smokes so provided her with a small glass yoghurt pot as a substitute ashtray. I listened to her grumbling about Don. I wondered whether all marriages suffered similar problems when couples reach my age!

Because of Pippa's disposition, I drove everyone to Manta Rota to the little Portuguese restaurant where we had lunch. This was to be our last get-together with the couple before we leave.

Apart from the odd question Ted asked me, eg. "What are you having?" No further communication took place between us. His whole personality had changed to silly schoolboy while he was with Don.

The couple stayed until 5pm and we said our goodbyes with promises to meet again. Jane asked me to go and stay with them – she said she would miss me! I shall put her on my list of people I have to visit in the future.

Instead of going to bed I put on the television and flicked through the channels to find a programme that I thought Ted would least like and opted for Camera Cops Action! Cameras followed the police at riots in the city centres with yobs shouting and showing their bottoms to the police. In the corner of my eye I could see him crossing and uncrossing his legs. That is a sign that he is uncomfortable! It was having the right effect!

He tried to interject with insouciance by saying he had left me a note and had I read it. I didn't respond immediately and then told him if he wanted to play 'silence games' I would be better at it. It was then time for bed!

Chapter 43

Wednesday March 24, 2010

I had been looking on the internet for somewhere to stay over the Easter holiday as this villa has been booked. Places are getting harder to find, as it's the start of the tourist season proper. I found what I thought was a suitable place at Santa Catarina – a villa in the countryside with space for Pippa to walk. The owner had responded positively to my email but before making the commitment, I needed to talk to Ted. As we hadn't been speaking this was difficult so I put on my 'apron' and went downstairs.

"I think there are some decisions you have to make," I said speaking into the mirror and not at him. I hadn't tied up the apron strings tightly enough!

"I think you ought to look at your emails," I told him, only slightly moving my head in his direction but still avoiding eye contact.

"When are you going online?" he asked.

"Whenever you are ready."

That broke the ice; tightened the apron strings or whatever you would like to describe it.

He seemed to be okay about the property. Well, at short notice, there is not really any choice. We had been offered a semi-detached on the main road with no parking space and no garden. That was the best the agent could do at such a busy time.

He later rang the owner who happens to be German, living in Switzerland but is in Portugal at the moment. We agreed to meet her, at the property, on Friday morning so it looks as though we are now fixed up for the first ten days of April.

We had a cup of tea and both apologised to each other asking each other for forgiveness, acknowledging our shortcomings and pledging to be more understanding in future. This bloomin' apron of humility was so tight it was cutting into my stomach!

SO! Back to where we were, it was a good opportunity to go out. We drove to our nearest little town and had coffee outside on a pavement café near a roundabout (or rotunda as they call them). Suddenly, out of the blue, Belinda – Bob the builder's wife, came walking across the road towards us closely followed by Bob. They had seen us sitting at the roadside and stopped to join us for a drink. We chatted for about fifteen minutes; they drank their coffee and got up to go on their daily walk along some beach somewhere. They didn't even say thank you – just left us! Without being judgemental, I felt it wasn't a very godly thing to do, as they were deeply religious!

We had already decided that we would take Pippa to the Forestry Commission again because there were no stray dogs and she had plenty of freedom. We stopped at the local supermercado and bought some bread rolls, cheese, crisps and beer and picnicked by the small river at the bottom of the valley in a clearing. We watched Pippa walk in the water, which cooled her from the hot sunshine and spent almost two hours watching the water trickling over the rocks while she tried putting her head under to pick up selected stones.

As the water ran over the road like a ford, I walked to the edge of the concrete road and noticed some fresh flowers had been thrown into the water and two gold candles had been lit against a large stone. I thought that was very strange but thought little of it and dismissed it from my thoughts.

We were going to investigate where the track led but I realised I was on a reserve tank of diesel so our plans had to be changed so that I could get into Tavira to a fuel station.

We got back to the villa just as a few spots of rain hit the windscreen. It didn't really turn into anything significant. We watched the early evening news on television then Ted suggested we go out for an omelette 'to save me cooking!'

I wonder how long this will last? 10.30pm to bed. Is life becoming more interesting?

Thursday March 25, 2010

I have discovered what is making the meowing sound and it isn't cats, thankfully! It's the call of the jays. They have many different calls and can imitate other birds – and cats!

Our Portuguese lesson was at 11.30am in Tavira at Maria's apartment. She is about to have her baby any time so to avoid her having to drive; we said we would go to her home. I wanted to look in C&A's at 'incontinent' to find her a little gift for the baby, as this was to be our last lesson with her. There wasn't anything suitable in that store so I walked across the mall (sorry, *we* walked across the mall as Ted is still stuck to my side) into a Kid's store where I found some blue trousers for a newly born little boy who is to be called Lucas.

We took Pippa for a walk along the saltpans because she would be left in the car for two hours during our lesson. It began to rain so I knew she would be okay that the temperature wouldn't be too hot for her.

The two hours with Maria were spent just chatting with her. She admitted that our lessons were the weirdest she had ever taken. I don't remember how we got on to the subject, but she told me that there are lots of witches in Portugal and that most of them come from Brazil bringing their bad ways with them. She described how the women make potions and do strange things for different purposes and gave us an example of how her brother found some perfume pots on the beach once. They had been arranged in a tray with flowers and candles. He trod on them and smashed them and then took the perfume pots back home. He proclaims that since that event he has never been able to have a relationship with a female. Maria went on to say that some women use the perfume pots and candles to cast spells over their husbands to make them love them more – or to attract a man that they like!

As she spoke, I remembered the flowers and the gold candles I had seen yesterday at the stream. I described it to her and she, with a wave of her hand, said it was probably a woman making a wish for a man or something! It happens all over Portugal!

I won't be buying candles, no fear.

She then went on to tell us of an encounter she had the other day when driving to a junction. It was her right of way, but an old man drove out in front of her. She blasted the horn and he got out of his car and came to her window and began shouting at her. I looked at Ted. He cast his eyes down to his notebook and flicked through the pages.

I urged her to continue.

"He was a bad old man. He came to my car and he was shouting at me. He looked down to me and he saw that I am with baby but he still shouting 'bitch' to me... If my Miguel was with me, I don't know, I don't know what he would do….."

Eager not to let this one go, I leaned towards her,

"Maria! That is terrible! What do you think Miguel would have done if he had been with you?" I looked over to Ted. He still had his eyes in the book.

"He would bloody get out of the car and oh I don't know. He would kill him for speaking to me like that."

Satisfied with her answer, but wanting to make it absolutely clear I continued ..

"Do you *really* think he would have **hit** the man? I mean it's dreadful to talk to a woman in that way and a man *should* stand up for his wife."

"Of course!" she replied. I wondered whether I should milk it a bit more, then remembered that I had put on my apron of humility this morning so let it go. Ted didn't react in any way but I hoped he had digested. Isn't it wonderful how we have these opportunities?

As we were so close to 'incontinent' we went back to have the cheap soup on offer at lunch time but the queue was about 35 deep so Ted bravely suggested going to the Chinese buffet lunch. I'm not sure whether the waiter recognised him from the time he thought he had helped himself to soup but mistaken the soy sauce instead.

We both had soup, but this time he followed me, copying me, so that he wouldn't make that mistake again. When the waiter had taken the bowls, we both got from the table at the same time to help ourselves to the buffet. When I returned to the table a woman was clearing it. She had almost removed the paper tablecloth and the drinks were about to be put on her tray. Obviously she was very apologetic and tidied the table up, but she had mixed up the drinks. Which glass was mine? OK, it shouldn't have mattered, but I am very particular about drinking out of someone else's glass. I asked for another.

I didn't particularly want to come back to the villa straight away. It was rainy and dull and there wouldn't be anything to do so suggested we tried to find the way to the villa we are about to take possession of. We have the appointment on Friday so it would be useful to know exactly where to go ahead of time.

We drove past the Quinta, which we haven't been to for a long time. I haven't missed the Quiz Nights, nor the Sunday lunches. I wondered how they were getting on.

So far as we could see from the roadside, the property is a long way down a track and probably situated on a hillside.

The sun began to break through just as we got back to 'our' villa. I made a cup of tea while Ted hosed the car down. It was so dusty and sandy.

He took his place at the edge of the sofa, as usual. We watched Ruth Watson giving business advice to some dimwits who owned a country mansion somewhere in Staffordshire and I wondered how long this sweet harmony is going to last.

When I looked at my emails, I was surprised to see that I had a message from the editor of the magazine asking me to proofread for them. They are willing to pay me 30 euros for the privilege!

Chapter 44

Friday March 25, 2010

I am re-reading 'To Kill a Mocking-Bird' by Harper Lee. It was a Pulitzer Prize Winner based on the story of a lawyer in Alabama, in the Deep South, who was called to defend a black man charged with the rape of a white girl. It is so compelling that I struggled to finish it last night when I went to bed. Too tired to read another word, I just had to put it down leaving only 9 pages to read. Perhaps my tiredness had something to do with the fact that I slept so soundly and can't remember a night of such sweet sleep.

I remembered our appointment with the German landlady so had to get my backside into gear. I had already put on a load of washing last night and it was waiting to be pegged on the washing line. I have now discovered that the children's paddling pool is nothing of the sort, but is a Jacuzzi.

We turned off the tarmac road on to a red soil dirt track. We are now accustomed to these tracks, referred to as roads. It was only about ten years ago (with EU funding) that tarmac roads came into existence in this part of Portugal. So, it is quite acceptable to the locals to use these rock infested, soil tracks liable to subsidence and landslides.

We ascended a very steep hill for almost a mile and eventually came to a little community of three or four cottages. An elderly fellow was at the gate of one of them and seemed pleased to see other humans. We asked him where the Vila is and he was glad to point out that he was neighbour.

It was the last house up the track. We turned into the gravelled entrance and were greeted immediately by two dogs. I prayed that Pippa wouldn't turn into a lion.

We met the German owner and her husband. She was a small woman with very tight curls and spectacles, which slid down her nose often. It was obvious that she is a dog lover. She explained that the large brown dog belonged to her English neighbour (the fellow we had just spoken to) and she allowed him to just come and be friends with her own little spoiled Peke, which she brought to Portugal on the plane in her handbag!

The house is small but very homely. Well elevated but sheltered it has been built into the hillside all on one level. She pointed out to us that the kitchen was new. I shouldn't have liked to imagine what the old one looked like! It was all very basic but for ten days, I am not concerned about that.

The master bedroom has doors that open on to the terrace with an outlook over the hills. Beneath the terrace, on a lower level is the pool where a barbeque and sun-loungers are positioned. As I leaned over the balustrade to see the pool area, I knocked her husband's cup of coffee off the corner and it smashed down the steps. I was so embarrassed and thought of how I had locked Jane and Don out of their home. I guessed it was a special cup, too. I carefully picked up the pieces and she provided me with a poly-bag assuring me that it was all all right.

She pointed over to the steep hill in the distance and explained that they get their drinking water from a well set in between the trees there. That should be interesting! At least it won't be brown water like we have had here at Casa Monte.

We had a tour of the small house, which she had built about fifteen years ago to an English architect's, design. She also has two apartments in other parts of the Algarve. Alistair, her appointed maintenance guy, manages them all. I immediately *knew* in my heart that this was the same chap who maintained the first dreadful villa that we had stayed in. The one Ted had booked for 9 weeks, but we had to vacate early because of mould and damp.

"Did you say *Alistair?*" asked Ted.

I tried to cut him a look, but he wasn't going to look at me.

"Yes, Alistair," she replied pushing her spectacles back up to the bridge of her nose.

"What's his other name?" went on Ted.

"Alistair MacPherson. Why? Do you know him?"

"Noooo. I don't think so!" I quickly interrupted.

Ted looked puzzled and scratched his head. "Yes, I think we do. It rings a bell."

"*No! I dooon't think so!*" I tried to emphasise it to Ted without being obvious to her.

"Mmmh. Rings a bell," he wouldn't let it go. I am nearly sitting on the ceiling.

She sat at the table and opened a book of writing paper and asked me to put down our names and address. I hoped this was enough of a distraction for her to forget the conversation.

We paid over the rental in cash, as we don't have a bank account here, shook hands and arranged to pick up the key from under a stone on the roof terrace on Tuesday morning. She apologised that her husband had gone off to do some gardening, but explained that he didn't speak English very well. They are both social workers in Switzerland. She works with normal children, but he works with drug addicts. I didn't tell her that I work with a child, too!

One thing I know for sure is that the neighbour's dog won't be visiting Pippa for friendship!

I had left my apron behind. As soon as we got down the track, I tried to explain to Ted the consequences that might arise, after he gave too much information to our new landlady. He didn't get it. To simplify it, I gave him an example of how, when we were working, decisions were made at boardroom level and eventually shop floor personnel would see the results of them. They, in turn, would interpret these changes in their own way. I told him that the same thing would happen with 'Alistair, the Maintenance Manager' (ex-Welsh plumber). He would not have seen that we had paid up front for 9 weeks at the first villa. All he would have seen was that we had 'done a bunk.' He didn't deal with the financial side of the lettings. He was only called on to fix problems and there were many.

The probability now was that this German woman would ring him and ask if he knew Ted. Well, with a name like that, who would forget? Of course he knew us. They were the couple who just 'up and left'. That would obviously make her feel nervous, even though we had paid her for our rental. I explained that it wasn't necessary to tell her that we knew him. He still didn't get it and I was getting tired.

We took Pippa along the beach at Tavira where there were only a handful of fishermen sitting with their rods secured in the rocks. She had a wonderful play in the sea, trying to pick up rocks. The sand was soft and pale and the water level dropped quite sharply so at times she sank up to her belly quite suddenly. She was happy to play her own game while Ted and I stood guard watching for strays or other dogs.

We stayed for over an hour until a woman sauntered her elderly white Labrador over towards us. I clipped Pippa on to the lead and we took her back towards the car, walking across the top of the promontory. Although she couldn't see the Labrador, she could smell him and her little nose began to twitch as she pulled on the lead. Her mouth opened and she began to show her teeth. That's my girl! It was *her* bit of beach first!

We had agreed to meet Ted's old school friend for a meal that evening. It was suggested that we met at Bishop's Square in Tavira. It's a small garden over the old bridge and in the 'restaurant section' of the town. Previously when we had been in that area on a Saturday we had found it very quiet so much so, that we had remarked about so few people being around. Not so this evening! Crowds of young people were thronging the roads standing on corners and blocking the road access to vehicles. We looked at each other!

We sat on a bench overlooking the garden and in front of the large church feeling a bit vulnerable. There was no need to have those feelings, as the high spirits were only those of kids on vacation.

James and his wife approached us. Ted had been concerned that his friend wouldn't recognise him with his long hair! I told him that he didn't recognise him anyway! When they first met, James spent several seconds puzzling who Ted was.

They took us to a very busy tiny restaurant off the street. Obviously well known and easily recognised, we were shown to the table his wife had thoughtfully booked. There were two long tables set out for parties, one a party of men and another a party of women, quite unconnected. People entered the restaurant for meals well after 10pm. The Portuguese apparently are late eaters.

At one point the lights went out and I thought there had been a power failure, but a waiter then brought out a cake lit with candles and presented it to one of the old ladies in the women's party. The whole restaurant broke out into clapping and shouting. It was quite touching and the old lady got up from her chair, looked around smiling, also clapping!

The meal was nice and I enjoyed James's wife's company. I think her name was Janice, but the noise was such that I couldn't hear it clearly and didn't like to ask again.

We talked about how they had come to Portugal and that moving here was the best thing they had ever done. Ted and James were talking about school days well over sixty years ago. Strange how he can remember that far back and can't remember something two seconds ago!

We left the restaurant at almost 11pm and said our goodbyes on the cobbled street with promises to catch up for coffee next week. We were invited to visit their home high on the hills overlooking Tavira. I am expecting some delight as, being an estate agent; surely he could pick and choose from the bunch!

Pippa didn't have any treats tonight as we were on our best behaviour and with people that we didn't know well. She was curled up in her bed in the back of the car when we lifted the boot. Despite all the noise she seemed unperturbed.

We put forward the clock one hour in line with UK and went to bed at 1am (midnight) having had quite a fulfilling evening.

Chapter 45

Sunday March 28, 2010

The hillside this morning had a pale purple haze. The lavender flowers are blooming and give the landscape that of a delicate pastel or watercolour. The heavy perfume overpowers and the buzzing of busy bees feeding sounds like an aircraft flying overhead.

The loss of the hour did have an affect on me. My solar clock has had to be discarded. The sun rose at 7.30am, which would have been 6.30am yesterday so I have resorted to using my watch again. It is a comfortable heat, and, being exposed here, there is always a bit of breeze even on the stillest of days, today being one of them.

I have been trying to empty the fridge because I don't want to take a lot of food with us to the next place, so our stocks are low. This morning we had half a bread roll each for breakfast. Ted wanted to go out (I think he was hungry) but our local village is closed up on Sundays.

Taking Pippa out in the car in the heat is a problem because I can't leave the car windows open having been warned that the car could be car-jacked. She has to come with us everywhere we go and gets very hot quickly.

As I began to prepare for our departure I became aware of the reality of what we are doing. We are soon leaving a place (Algarve) where I have felt at home. I have grown to know the area very well and have met some acquaintances who will be friends.

Ted was keen to use the swimming pool before we leave – just to say that he had swum! We had been advised that people don't usually swim in unheated pools until about June and even then it could be cold. According to some of the comments in the visitors' book the water has been cold in August in temperatures of 40 degrees – too cold for children to swim.

Nevertheless, he had to use it, so came out in a large pair of swimming pants, shivering before he touched the water. His face and hands are really brown but the rest of his body is milky white. Slowly he stepped in and with a great splash almost knocked himself out with shock but with the old stiff upper lip did a few lengths. When he came out commented:

"It isn't *that* bad. Not as bad as I thought! Not as cold as the sea at home."

"When did you last swim in the sea, at home?"

"Mmmh. Oh I suppose with the children."

They are in their forties! I give up!

We did the usual Sunday afternoon thing which most Portuguese families do. We drove to Santa Luzia, parked, ate ice creams in the car and people-watched. I am not sure that sitting in the car suited Ted who is now so athletic after his cold swimming, but it was interesting to see families taking out their old grand-parents for lunch at one of the many waterfront bars. The youngest member of the family would open the car door for the oldest who tried to get out unaided, but usually had to have help.

A group of young men drank bottled beer beside the jetty as the fishermen brought in their catch. As they emptied the beer bottles so one of them collected them up and put them in a nearby bin before going to buy more. It was all very sociable and made me think of how the yobs back home would probably have either thrown the bottles into the ocean or smashed them against a wall!

It was early – 5.30pm. We hadn't eaten properly and most places were either closed or packed with families. We drove afar to Altura by which time some of the restaurants had opened for the evening. We had an early supper as dusk fell. It seemed strange to see the sun set at 7.30pm.

Chapter 46

Monday March 29, 2010

Our last day at Casa Monte! With nothing in the fridge, we went into the village to have breakfast of coffee and pizza at the café on the roundabout.

I washed the towels and had left them on the line but it began to rain so I wasn't sure that they would dry in time for tomorrow, our day of departure.

The young Portuguese man at the café offered for us to sit outside and said he would dry the chairs but we chose to sit inside not trusting the rain clouds.

We made a little diversion on the way back towards Faz Fato and found ourselves going up a dirt track towards a cute little ochre coloured property perched on top of a hill. The 360 degrees views from there were stunning stretching over to Spain in the east and somewhere and nowhere to the west.

The small, typical Portuguese, property was unoccupied and had a sale notice pinned to the gate. We walked up the drive and looked around because we are always interested in houses. Ted rang the telephone number on the sale board and spoke to an Englishman who said the property is owned by an English company who were disposing of it, desperate to sell! We are going to look around it on Thursday!

I know its naughty of us but I do like looking inside other people's houses! On the way 'home' I joked to Ted:

"If that house belonged to me, I would paint it white with pink around the windows."

Immediately I felt a voice in my spirit saying, "It must remain yellow!"

Being light at 7.30pm seemed strange even though it was cloudy and raining. The most magnificent huge rainbow appeared over the house enveloping us in its colours. I wondered whether we were sitting on the pot of gold!

Ted had printed out a Passover format and as part of it wanted us to go out to eat lamb. We went to a rather smart restaurant as it was a special occasion but I have to admit that I don't always like lamb. It was greasy and smelled of blood so I suppose that was my sacrifice!

Together we read out a passage from the printout as we sat in the crowded restaurant and then finished the reading when we got home and raised our glasses with some red wine. So we had a little, quiet Seder just by ourselves.

Sleepy we retired at 10.30pm, ready for the move tomorrow.

Tuesday March 30, 2010

I got up early to finish packing everything ready to leave Casa Monte, which has been our home for the past month. There was such a lot to do – fridge to clean, floors to mop and suitcases to be packed into the car in such a fashion that we didn't look overloaded.

Once everything had been done and Pippa's bed had been placed on top of suitcases, we sat outside waiting for Rebecca, the agent, to come and collect the keys. She was very prompt and arrived at 10am as arranged. I wanted her to inspect the house and when she was satisfied we drove off without any feelings whatsoever.

In order to avoid the police checks, we took the back road into Tavira and then continued to Santa Luzia where we had a 'tostie' and coffee for breakfast. This set us up for the rest of the day. As we ate on the roadside, I thought about how we had eaten ice-cream just around the corner with Diane and Clive when they visited. It seems an age since they came.

We reached Santa Catarina after midday. The car bumped its way up the rocky soil track. Once inside the garden of the new villa, Ted tied the gate up so that Pippa could be free to investigate what was to be her home for ten days.

It wasn't long before an old Englishman sauntered up to introduce himself and tell us that the owner of the villa, encouraged his dogs to play with hers and that they were harmless. We are now neighbours.

"The brown one might just jump over the gate to get in and say hello," he said slowly with much gesticulating. Is this what older people do?

If he jumps over the gate, I thought to myself, Pippa would make mincemeat of him. Harmless or not!

We took all our possessions out of the car and then walked around the garden and into the adjoining field, which belongs to the property. It is all set on a very steep hillside and as Ted stumbled I thought he was just being clumsy again until I saw him shaking a huge, thick snake off his foot. It was at least a metre long and as thick and round as a saucer. It slid under a rock but I could see that Ted was taken aback.

There I was, concerned about other dogs and now I had something worse to consider.

We then went to the nearest supermarket in Sao Bras to get some food and before bringing it back to the new villa, took a fork to the left off the dirt track, down into the valley where the landlady had told us we can get fresh drinking water from a well.

We drove through mud over a really narrow track and found the steps leading down to a cave under the mountain. It was filled with water like a small reservoir reaching far back into the darkness. Ted filled two 5L plastic containers and I then had to reverse until I could find a place to turn. We ploughed through deep mud and then up and over rocks jutting out of the track.

As we ascended the track towards the villa, I asked him if he thought it was worth all the hassle when we can buy water at 29 cents for 5L. It must have knocked £50 off the value of the car! He agreed we would get the water from the supermarket in future.

We sat on the veranda and drank coffee until the heat left the sun and it became cold. I set about making a cooked meal in a properly equipped kitchen. What a treat!

The tiny sitting room was cosy and Pippa found her way to the bedroom while we were eating. She soon discovered where her duvet had been placed and settled down happily.

I hadn't had much sleep last night – I remember seeing 3am on my watch before I finally fell asleep so was tired. It took a little time to adjust to another bedroom, but it wasn't too long before I nodded off.

Wednesday March 31, 2010

I slept quite well in the new bed although the bedding leaves a lot to be desired. An old winceyette duvet cover and pillowcases with colours washed out. There is no washing machine here only a stone rectangular tank on legs with a washboard incorporated on the one side. I am quite sure this is an ornament or does she really do her washing in it? I certainly am not!

We ate our cornflakes under the veranda. I watched one or two big, fat, juicy ants scuttling along the brick tiles. They are big!

I didn't get dressed until almost mid-day. It was so still and quiet – unlike Casa Monte, there are no dogs barking and as we are between extremely steep hills, the silence is more apparent.

Opposite is a field on the mountain, which is almost vertical. We thought we would take Pippa along the dirt track to see where it went but soon realised it was a dead-end with a couple of Portuguese houses at the end guarded by dogs. So that is where the little old lady lives. She passes the house on a moped and must be in her seventies.

We came back to the house through the field, which belongs, treading very carefully hoping not to see any snakes. I tried to look up on the computer what it might have been, but couldn't find anything that looked like it.

I had been expecting to hear from the editor of the East Algarve Magazine with my first assignment of proofreading but no contact had been made until I found an email asking me to meet him in the afternoon.

We haven't been to the Quinta ever since we stayed at Olivia's villa and it seemed strange going back there after such a long time. They were just photocopying the copy for me to take away and proof read. The editor greeted us both enthusiastically as he handed over the parcel and I agreed to meet up with him tomorrow at his house when we could go over it on his computer.

We have an appointment to look at the 360 degrees cottage tomorrow morning.

We had a visitor from next door whilst I was indoors. Ted said that the brown dog jumped over the wall and came up to the terrace where he was sitting and rolled over hoping to get his tummy tickled. Apparently Pippa smelled him and her nose began to twitch but she didn't see him. She was quickly ushered inside while Ted chased it back over the wall.

We then discovered that the English neighbours have four dogs!

Ted barbequed some chicken for supper and I made rice and vegetables so it was a joint effort. The television only has German channels so we sat and watched a programme about storks not knowing what the commentary was but the photography was very good.

I completed my proofreading assignment by which time I was ready to retire.

Thursday April 1, 2010

Another month and only 20 days until we ride on the ferry back to the UK.

We ate breakfast on the veranda again this morning while the sun got warmer. This is becoming normal practice now. We had an appointment at 10am with an agent to show us over the property high on the mountaintop. He was running late and we had to wait for him.

We looked over the small house and as we were about to thank the agent for his time, it transpired that he, too, is a Believer. When we told him that we believed in Jesus as our Messiah, he burst into praise on the doorstep.

We told him that we didn't know our purposes in all of this, but we all agreed to pray there and then so joined hands on the top of the mountain asking Father for His Will.

We discovered that he, also, used to be a builder so his expertise was a valued attribute. We had such an interesting time with him that it turned into lunch on a pavement café in Tavira. He invited us to go to his church tomorrow for an Easter Service. We told him we don't go to church but I felt it was right to accept his invitation. It should be fun!!!

I took Ted back to our new home and asked him to look after Pippa while I delivered the copy to the editor of the magazine. We were to meet at the Quinta, his family-run business. He was already waiting for me when I got there and took me back to the villa they are renting just a stone's throw from the Quinta.

We went through the corrections together on his computer and the whole job was finished in thirty minutes. He then returned me to the Quinta to pick up my car and we sat and talked for about twenty minutes. He is such a lovely young man. I felt good being able to have the freedom to be on my own for a while. He shared some sadness he had had in his life and the time was very special.

I returned to the villa and sat in the shade of the hot sun until evening.

We decided to take a short drive to Sao Bras which is now our nearest big town and saw a small roadside eatery so had supper out. The sun went down and it was the end of a very exciting and busy day!

Friday April 2, 2010

We had agreed to meet 'Geoff', the estate agent, in Tavira by the railway station at 10.45am. He would then take us to his 'church' for an Easter service. I wasn't looking forward to going but felt we needed to support him.

We had been informed by the owner of this new villa that 'Alistair' would be coming on Friday mornings at 9am to clean out the pool. We left the house just after 10am so I was rather relieved that he hadn't turned up.

Geoff came walking across the road waving both arms in the air beaming from ear to ear. With the greeting of a hug, he took us a short distance down the street and into a building where about fifteen chairs had been set in a semi-circle in a small room. A woman, who seemed very pleasant, greeted us and presently two other couples came in.

The service was in the format of typical Church of England. The vicar's wife handed us sheets of paper with instructions of what to read. She controlled the whole meeting not allowing any freedom whatsoever. I remembered why I don't go to church! I couldn't wait to get out of there.

Geoff introduced us to his teen-aged son - a lovely young boy who had been given the job of operating the computer-based overhead, for the hymn.

After the service we all went to Santa Luzia for lunch together when Geoff shared his testament.

He went on to testify that when he met 'G-d' face to face, he changed and became like a lamb. He would go into the fields and pick flowers and just give them to people and his mates thought he had had a breakdown.

He has worked tirelessly for this church finding them a building and doing building work for them. It was apparent to me this morning that they did not appreciate him. I didn't hide my dismay.

We had promised Ted's old school-friend that we would meet him in the road near his home at 3pm so we had to cut short the lunch with Geoff to get to our next appointment on time.

James arrived just after us and we followed him for nearly two miles up a rocky dirt track high in the mountains to his home, which was cut into the rock-face on the summit. We enjoyed their company around the pool and met his daughter who was staying with them for a short holiday. She lay sunbathing but joined us with some hearty conversation.

We all ate cake and drank soft drinks until after 5pm. The sun was hot and the views were such that I felt it was surreal. The river was so far below us that it became an optical illusion appearing to be rising upwards. Houses miles away in the distance looked like pinheads. It made me feel quite odd because I couldn't focus on the reality of such a landscape – as one might see it from an aircraft. We were two miles up in the air! Incredible!

They were going out that evening so we said our goodbyes promising to keep in touch when we leave and got back to our villa before sunset only to discover that the pool had been cleaned after all. I am so glad we missed seeing Alistair!

The Portuguese don't celebrate Easter much with eggs. The shops have been filled with sugared almonds, which appeal to me more. They may be celebrating a pagan festival, but at least they don't follow the fertility god's rituals with eggs.

Ted fell asleep in front of the Moscow TV channel – the only English speaking one I could find on the television so I turned it off and we both had an early night.

Saturday April 3, 2010

Breakfast was taken in the usual fashion, to which we are now accustomed. The birds were singing in the carob trees. Pippa lay at my feet waiting for scraps of toast and the sun rose higher getting warmer and warmer.

We had a leisurely day moving from the sunloungers by the pool, to the shade of the veranda, then to the little wooden bench on the hillside in the grassy piece of land adjoining the garden.

Ted stood like a century on guard, getting up almost every fifteen minutes to monitor the temperature on a thermometer strung to the security bars on the window. It was in the shade so didn't give a true temperature.

"It's gone up to 21 degrees! And that's in the shade!"

I decided to turn on the ignition of the car and see what the temperature gauge showed me. 34 degrees! I think that was because the car was closed up and perhaps it just gives the internal temperature.

When the clouds came over, the temperature dropped very quickly. I was wearing a short-sleeved blouse some of the time but wrapped in my fleece when the sun was clouded. This meant that Ted had to leap up the steps to check how quickly the temperature had dropped by how many degrees in how many seconds!!

I am sure that I have become acclimatised to the weather and still feel cold, when, perhaps, I would have been warm in the past.

A little old man peered above us in the grassy patch, which belongs to this property, then vanished.

Shortly afterwards we heard bells ringing and discovered that he had brought his sheep and rams into our field. Ted put Pippa indoors and said he was going to see the old man to tell him that she didn't like the sheep. I wondered how he was going to manage to communicate to an old, Portuguese man who didn't understand any other language.

Pippa followed me out and didn't pay any attention to them whatsoever! We then witnessed the arrival of the old man throwing stones at the sheep. When Ted returned he said he couldn't make himself understood. The man simply, without expression, came into the field, threw stones at the sheep and took them elsewhere.

I asked Ted what he had said to him and he told me that he had bent down like a dog and barked, then waved his arm towards the house. He then gnashed his teeth to imitate a lion! The old dear must have thought Ted was round the bend.

After the successful removal of the sheep, we watched a little red tractor tilling the soil on the mountain opposite. His tractor was almost vertical and we wondered how anybody could plant a thing on such a steep slope. Occasionally the sound of striking rock echoed across the valley as he continued mostly in reverse gear.

We heard the sound of church bells ringing in the distance. Everyone is having Fiestas in villages and towns all over Portugal. They will bring out their statues of idols to parade in the streets and throw flowers everywhere. Families will be out in their droves so we shall be spending quality time chilling at the villa.

Chapter 47

Sunday April 4, 2010

I opened the west facing kitchen door to let Pippa out and met floods of sunshine. A cuckoo sang in a nearby olive tree, his message was so loud. I have never heard a cuckoo at such close range. It wasn't long before another cuckoo in the distance answered his call. I thought that was so sweet.

It was a cool breeze, which necessitated full covering. It was too cold to sit in short sleeves.

I needed to do some washing. As there is no mechanical means of doing it I resorted to hand washing in a bowl. Of course I can't wring it out so dry so it was hung to drip.

We sat on the sunloungers beside the pool in the sunshine away from the cold wind and listened to the planes coming and going to and from Faro Airport. The weather is ideal for golfers who come in droves to play the beautiful courses here.

The new Monte Rei Course (which was closer to our last villa) boasts a 45-hole course. They have a gateman at the entrance 24 hours a day. We were allowed access (I am sure it was only the car that got us in – certainly not our Armani suits!). and walked around the clubhouse, which is sleek, but no better than some hotels I have been in. If we had been able to find a shady place for Pippa we would have had a coffee in the small café overlooking some of the greens but it wasn't to be.

It was a cloudless sky with acres of blue. I could have been looking at a photograph as the hills before us were still and bright - the sun casting shadows which dropped down the slope. Stones glistened like precious gems and the red roofs of the two cottages on the horizon were like blobs of crimson on an azure board.

Ted had heard from the man who came to do the pool at the previous villa, that he no longer needed to wear glasses because one day he just took them off and his eye muscles strengthened enough for his vision to return.

He came down to breakfast under the veranda without his glasses this morning. I knew why! I didn't ask!

He spent some considerable time closing his eyes and then opening them. I knew that he was trying to exercise his eye muscles!

A plane flew overhead at low range. It was white with a blue tail. Normally the planes are either BMI Baby or Easyjet but this was neither of those.

"Oh! What's that one?" I asked.

Ted ran indoors to get his glasses but was too late – the plane had probably landed! He continued to wear them for the rest of the day!

A gate leads off the pool terrace into a grassy area of mountainous land (where the sheep were evicted yesterday). It's blooming with wild flowers and is ablaze with yellow buttercups and wild orchids. I suppose the place does live up to its name.

We spent all day under the umbrella beside the pool setting up a regime. We watched the planes making patterns in the clear sky. I didn't realise how many planes use this airspace. We didn't hear most of them because they were flying so high.

Ted found himself some entertainment for almost an hour as he watched an army of ants carrying a piece of bread across the paving and up the side of a concrete flowerpot. Each time they got it to the curved top, it fell. After three attempts he helped them by flicking it over the top with a stick then rushed in to get the video camera. I think he has made a film of it!

As the sun went down we took Pippa on up the dirt track past the house, to the top of the mountain where we saw the magnificent setting sun throwing indigo, violet and crimson brush marks across an otherwise clear sky.

Darkness crept upon us as we walked over the top of the mountain – not as high as James's mountain, but just as beautiful.

As we came back down, we saw the twinkling lights of Tavira in a tiny crack through the mountains in front of us. We then sat on the sunloungers for some time just looking at the stars and watching the occasional plane coming in to land at Faro Airport flashing red, white and blue lights towards the heavens.

Monday April 5, 2010

After spending two days at the villa and not going anywhere, we decided to go further up this mountainous road towards the north of the Algarve.

We set off about 11am before the sun got too hot. It was very pleasant with a lovely breeze – just the weather I like.

We drove for about six miles up the mountain passing temporary road works where the road had caved in and slipped down the mountain face. The beautiful new tarmac road had sunk and dropped into craters so I had to really concentrate on where I was driving.

Ted had a map on his lap. Pippa seemed a bit unsettled so I stopped to let her out for a walk. Ted showed me the map and said we would have to go "Up there and turn across the land on an unmade road to meet the other main road over there!"

Leaving it to him, we put Pippa back in her nest and I began to drive in the direction he had given me. About half a mile up the mountain he declared:

"I think we are going to have to turn around and go back!"

That did it!

Every time we go out he navigates us up the garden wall. I turned the car round in one shot and began to drive back.

"I did tell you..."

Without another word I leaned across and took the map and threw it out of the car window.

As we approached a sign post he said :

"We have to turn right here."

I continued straight. I was having none of it. We were going 'home.'

Back at the ranch, as they say, I had to go all the way through the forgiving/repenting process again. It was all soon forgotten and we took our places on the veranda once more. I presented him with lunch and we then moved down to the sun-loungers and sat under the umbrella in the shade. This routine is now getting boring. His telephone rang. It was Geoff. The people who owned the house on the hill would be happy to reduce the price and would accept an offer.

The topic for the afternoon was the ochre coloured house, which I had said I would paint white with pink windows if it was mine!

We went out for supper to a nearby Horta or garden pub. It was nothing special but had a garden for children to play in. We had a simple meal and half a jug of wine all of which cost £1.80

When we came 'home' I made coffee, Pippa went to bed and Ted looked through the Visitors Book where he found a map of Beja.

"Oh! There's a street map of Beja here. I might take a photocopy of it."

"Carry on and you'll soon be able to open a map shop. You will have all the maps there are of this region with the exception of one!" I said, referring to the little incident earlier.

"Yes," he agreed, "that was the most expensive one that I had!

Chapter 48

What an extraordinary day! We spent most of the morning in Tavira, the morning being the best part of the day. In the afternoon it became humid and dull.

Ted decided that he would attempt to use the car wash. There is a pressure spray wash close to the villa but the instructions for use are all in Portuguese. He spent a long time working out how much it cost and by some miraculous means, actually got it to work! He sprayed heavy foam all over the car and then the 50c he had put in was used up. The car was covered with soap.

He had to put more money into the machine to get the clear water for rinsing, which he managed to do but that also ran out so we drove off in a streaky car.

When it hasn't been raining the dirt tracks are very dusty and the car gets coated in red dust. So his attempt at washing it was an improvement.

In the evening we followed the owner's recommendation and found a small eating-place on top of the nearby mountain. It was actually a kitchen and the man and woman had turned a room into an eating area. Neither of them spoke a word of English and they didn't seem to understand our version of Portuguese. The menu was hand written and difficult to read and try, as we might, we could not make sense of a lot of it.

The short, stout, elderly wife had a surly manner and stood at the table with her hands on her hips sighing because we didn't understand what she was saying.

Playing safe, I ordered frango (chicken), which I understood. Ted also ordered chicken but she gabbled something at him and he nodded, not knowing what she had said. He got out the pocket dictionary and discovered that he had ordered chicken stew. He frowned.

Eventually, after they had cooked the meals between them, they were duly delivered in a couple of bowls. I thought we had been given each other's meals so we swapped. Instead of getting on with it Ted tried to ask her which was which. She became impatient and we couldn't understand what she said so she stormed off.

Mine turned out to be turkey which must have been an anorexic because there wasn't a bit of meat on the bone and Ted's chicken was just bones. Both dishes were so oily that the paper tablecloth was stained through with oil marks where it had splashed off the bowls.

The old man came out and took away the bowls. He was just as surly as his wife.

Ted said to me:

"Did you notice his hands?"

I hadn't. It was most unusual for Ted to notice anything so I asked what he meant.

"Wait until he comes back to the table," he smiled.

Well, I almost exploded! I have seen cleaner hands on a chimney sweep! His whole hands were black with grime and you could have grown a row of radishes under his fingernails.

He popped his fingers into the glasses to collect them, straightening a paper napkin on another table on his way to the kitchen.

I couldn't stop laughing. We both laughed so much that I could hardly get Pippa's tit-bits in the poo bag without dropping them on the oily tablecloth.

Aching from laughter, we drove back proclaiming that we would never go there again!

We later found out that the establishment had been closed down the previous year, but the locals don't pay too much attention to the law.

Wednesday April 7, 2010

We spent the whole day in Tavira then took Pippa for a short walk along the saltpans, which have now dried up and left a dark crusty residue of salt crystals in the soil. It's hard to believe that this material can be transformed into salt, as we know it. These saltpans, marshes, barrier islands and lagoons are most visitors' first view of the Algarve from an aircraft. It's one of the most important wetland areas in Europe and covers nearly 45 acres stretching all along the coast.

On our way back to the villa I took the back road once again taking us through Santa Luzia where we saw the fishermen loading up octopus traps. Santa Luzia is, apparently, the octopus capital of the Algarve.

We saw some adventurous tourists eating tentacle slices on the pavement near the waterfront. These are charcoal grilled after being air dried on wooden racks – not everyone's taste!

The road from St Estevao had recently been given a tarmac surface. It looked like a long piece of pastry stretched out before us with wrinkled edges at the sides. Being so narrow, most cars drive in the centre, and then veer off to the side if there is an oncoming vehicle.

A large Mercedes people-carrier approached us and the driver put out his arm to flag me down. Suddenly a million thoughts ran through my mind at once. Should I stop?

Is he just flagging me down to tell me something?

It was the editor of the magazine. He just recognised our vehicle and wanted to say 'hi'. How silly of me! That is how most people are around here. We have met so many friendly ex-pats and locals whose company we really enjoy. I mustn't let that first experience dominate and influence my feelings about this place.

Thursday April 8, 2010

The sun quickly burned up any small clouds and displayed its heat very suddenly. We took the computer outside on to the table under the veranda to see if we could get better reception. Ted wanted to get online to his bank.

The gentle breeze was welcome as it blew softly across the valley. Apart from the bird song, it was perfectly quiet. The House of Tranquility!

Today is our last day here. The ten days have passed in the twinkling of an eye.

Yesterday we had a change of plans. Ted rang Nuno, our new friend in Setubal, without realising that he was in Germany. We are not, now, going to stay with him over the weekend as previously planned and are now staying the last week back at Olivia's. I didn't feel happy about staying in the very busy Setubal area now that the tourist season has begun. We need to keep a low profile because we shall be packed to the hilt for our return journey home.

We called in to the vodafone shop to ask whether the dongle we have will be ok to use in France but were told that it is only useable in Portugal. I seem to remember that we were able to use online facilities at a couple of places when we drove down here.

Once again, I was emptying out the fridge in readiness for our departure so we ventured out to find the restaurant we went to with Jane and Don. They do wonderful buffet lunches at a great discount. (www.rochadagralheira.com)

We were not disappointed. The waiters brought the food to the table unlike other buffets I have had. We ate five courses for the princely sum of 7 Euros and that included a large jug of red wine! Eating out is so cheap, that I wonder whether it's worth taking shopping home.

Pippa was relaxing on the sun bed and suddenly leapt up and poked her head through the balustrade. She had seen something and was panting with excitement. Neither Ted, nor I could see a thing. We waited patiently and then he said he had seen a 'rabbit' running across the grass. I thought rabbits hopped! We both stood with baited breath waiting for the 'rabbit' to reappear when I saw a huge rat run up the hillside towards the wall of the house. I'm not sure that I shall be happy to let Pippa out in the middle of the night again. After all, I walk around with her thinking that there is nothing out here (apart from the snake).

There are mosquito nets at the windows, but not on the doors so inevitably the little so-and-so's get into the house.

Ted and I spent the evening with fly swats in hands trying to catch one of these little blighters. In the end we had a sword fight using them as weapons. It must have looked funny seeing us waving little plastic 'hands' at each other!

We saw the old shepherd man outside the gate, waiting for the sheep to have a meal on the luscious grass on the side of the track.

I wanted to try to speak to him and noticed that he had a huge gash from the back of his neck to the front. The blood had almost dried. I asked him what he had done and he just waved his hand towards the barbed wire so I took it that he had fallen against it. It really was a nasty cut and one, which I think he should have had medical care for. Instead, he put his hand into the inside of his jacket and pulled out a broken bit of mirror which he looked into then popped it back without much concern.

I didn't bother to unpack any clothing since the last move and have only taken things out of my suitcase, as I needed them. Ted, on the other hand, has unpacked everything so has the job of getting it all together for our move tomorrow.

The mosquito saved his own life and we had another early night. Tomorrow is another day — we'll be in another place and a few steps further on our return journey.

Twelve days to go...

Chapter 49

Friday April 9, 2010

We planned to leave our final 'home' at about mid-day but had already packed, and I cleaned the house by 10am by which time the sun was getting hot. The temperature showed 20 degrees in the shade.

Ted slotted everything neatly into the car and Pippa became restless. She didn't eat her food and then I noticed a community of big, fat ants (about half an inch long) were devouring her untouched meal. I quickly gathered it up and threw it into the bushes, then washed the dish. I turned round to find her eating it out of the bushes, no doubt complete with ants!

As we rested under the veranda, we heard the sound of tyres on the gravel. I knew it would be Alistair! He seemed a bit cagey at first as he walked towards us, but soon got over it. He told us that the people who owned the first villa we had occupied (which we moved out of) were still having problems with the damp. He said that he had been to paint it and the paint had peeled off because the walls are so wet. They have had dehumidifiers going and the heating on, but still it hasn't resolved the dampness and mould. The owners apparently came out about a month ago. I needed to tell him that we had forfeited three weeks' rental when we left. Being a busybody and knowing so many people, I didn't want him going round giving us a bad c.v.

The purpose of his visit here was to clean the pool. Ted had already paced it and measured it with his feet. It was much smaller than any of the pools at the other villas and, Alistair 'the Pool Man,' (ex-plumber) (ex-Maintenance Manager) informed us that it was, in fact, a plunge pool. In other words, a short swimming pool!

When Alistair had gone, Ted began to do his Hitler impression by pacing out the pool to check if what Alistair had said was correct!

We left the villa and made our way towards Luz de Tavira. We had plenty of time to spare because Olivia had suggested 2pm as a time for returning to the second villa we stayed in during February.

The ice cream at Santa Luzia doesn't vary in quality. We both ate cornets in the car while Pippa peeped out of the window. She was jacked up so high having her bed resting on top of the suitcases.

After killing time, we turned into the familiar road, past the orchard of peaches which are now fully in leaf. The smell of the orange trees was heavy in the pure air – trees bearing fruit and blossom at the same time!

Olivia gave us the key and said she would see us later. I hope that she isn't going to be coming up asking if we are all right as she did before. She didn't look well – her eyes were puffed. Martin appeared at the door behind her wearing shorts and showing off a bronze tan. He had to put in his two pennyworth!

When we got inside the villa we found a bowl of fresh fruit and two up-turned glasses on either side of a bottle of white wine. That was very generous of her!

Pippa made herself at home at once. I wondered whether she recognised the place. It all seemed the same except that the garden was alive with white irises, the fig tree had leaves and the most extraordinary feat of nature I have never seen before is that of orange and lemon trees bearing fruit and blossom at the same time!

In the evening the blossom was heavy and heady. The air was filled with the musty perfume of oranges and lemons.

It didn't take long before Ted was pacing out the measurements of this pool with his feet. He then took out his psion and made note of the statistics in comparison with the plunge pool we had just left. I am quite sure that all this information is extremely relevant and worth storing!

The last time we sat on the green plastic chairs it was cold and windy. Today was just perfect.

We connected the computer and got online with a fairly good signal so were able to book our ferry crossing back to the UK on the 22nd. As there wasn't a crossing from Cherbourg, our preferred port, we booked to go from Caen to Portsmouth.

It's strange being here again at the end of our journey.

Saturday April 10, 2010

The swallows nose-dived into the pool in pairs catching the bugs and then flew off only to repeat the game several times while we sat outside first thing this morning. Two very pale green birds flew over towards the carob trees. We weren't able to identify them and wondered whether the hoopoes are still here. This is a fantastic place for bird watching.

The noise from the motorway was constant. Had we heard it before and not noticed, or was it because we have spent so much time in the hills listening to the stillness and nothingness that suddenly our ears are exploding.

Olivia and lover Martin drove past the house and stopped. They walked over the garden to the fence, which encloses the patio area, to ask if everything was alright! I wondered whether this was to be the format for the rest of the week and remembered how she had appeared from nowhere when we were here before, to ask the same question.

It was so much warmer now than when we were here in February and we welcome the breeze rather condemn it as we did then. Pippa lay under the pagoda on her quilted mat and was quite happy to sleep. Ted and I read and he frequently fell asleep doing his usual 'sleep reading.'

We opened the complimentary wine, which had been left for us and ate soup and cream crackers for lunch. I hadn't been shopping and this was all the food that we had. It was all very pleasant.

Not content with spying out the first damp villa from his binoculars Ted had to take some more photographs of it so that he could blow them up to get a better view. He had already stepped out the measurements of the pool, again, and taken out his notebook to record the temperature at hourly intervals. Gathering this information seems to be important to him.

I took some pictures of the irises, (iris in Portuguese means 'rainbow') which are in abundance in this garden. I also took a sneaky picture of him sleeping with his mouth open.

Christening the pool was an occasion, which had to take place today. I am not sure whether he thinks he needs the exercise, or if it is just a challenge to withstand the cold water. Whichever, he wasn't getting me in the cold water even if the temperature outside was 24 degrees. Locals don't venture into unheated pools until June and I consider myself a local now!

Ted wanted to make another list of things to do tomorrow. He delved into his filing cabinet trouser leg and brought out a handful of bits of paper - old lists he had been keeping. He has a file bulging with receipts dating back from December when we began this adventure. It will surely take him twelve months to check them all out, or perhaps he just wants to keep them along with all the other stuff he hoards.

Shopping
Milk
Bread
Newspaper
East Algarve Magazine (a must!)
Small screwdriver

Torch battery
Check bank
Pippa walk
Cash machine

"I must get my hair cut sometime! It's getting long!" he combs his fingers through his curly locks which now are shoulder length and long enough for that pony tail!

I tell him that he ought to keep it that length now because if he cuts it all off the sun will burn his head.

Satisfied with those words of wisdom, he strokes it forward, then strokes Pippa before putting his list back into his leg pocket ready for tomorrow.

Chapter 50

I had a disturbed night and couldn't sleep well. The fire alarm system was triggered by a power cut and I had to go and reset it. Pippa then wanted to go out and I think I went back to bed at 3.30am.

We had planned to go out early this morning before the sun gets too hot to take Pippa for a walk. We wanted to go shopping afterwards knowing that she had been exercised and would want to sleep in the car.

We left the house before 9am and took her to the beach beyond the saltpans in Tavira. Unfortunately a lot of fishermen had already taken over the sandy beach so we walked around an ancient monument and along the sand dunes in the opposite direction. She ran and rolled enjoying her freedom and appeared from behind the stone wall of the fort almost red in colour with sand stuck all over her body.

A campervan was parked on the other side of the track and the young male driver got out to urinate on the roadside. They do it all over the place without shame. I am told that they are afraid of getting gallstones and that is why they have to do it when they need to irrespective of where they might be, or who might be watching.

I wondered whether a blind eye might be turned if I decided to drop my apple-catchers and expose the moon on the roadside somewhere!

With Pippa safely settled in the underground car park at 'incontinent' we took the elevator to the first floor to get some of the things off Ted's list.

We were walking up the aisles where the pastas are displayed and he stroked his hair forward again.

"I must get a comb some time," he remarked.

"What happened to yours?"

"I didn't bring one!"

"What!"

"Well, I didn't need one when my hair was short," he patted his head again.

By this time I had reached the checkout and was putting the food on the belt. He stood looking disorientated with his hand on the top of his head.

"Ask the assistant where the combs are," I told him pointing to a young girl busy ripping up boxes.

He came leaping over to the trolley smiling like a child and put the comb into the trolley for me to take out again and put on the belt. The next time I looked at him his curly, fluffy hair was combed tight to his head and looked longer than ever.

We passed a circus unloading for a show. I was upset to see cages with camels and tiny ponies all shut up together. A queue of men had formed at the entrance of the enclosure and it was still only 10.30 in the morning. They don't appear to recognise the cruelty to these animals.

We seem to be gravitating towards Santa Luzia. Today was no different. We had coffee in The Square where we could keep an eye on Pippa. The church doors were open but nobody seemed to be going to mass. One old dear dressed in black with hat covering a headscarf clutched her handbag as she climbed the step to enter. She made the sign of the cross with her right hand and then walked into a side room. Perhaps she was going to dress the priest in one of the many robes hung in the foyer.

When we drove back to the villa we passed a donkey tethered in the hot sunshine. I noticed it the other day and it hadn't been moved since. It had no water and no shelter from the sun. I stopped the car and wanted to do something to help the animal but there wasn't anything I could do.

Like the animals in the circus, it was obviously suffering. The Portuguese don't care about their animals. They leave their dogs chained up day and night and most suffer cruelty in some form or another.

The British ex-pats do get together and have founded animal sanctuaries in various parts of The Algarve. They also have sterilisation campaigns on the go and contribute a lot towards animal welfare. I suppose because they are mostly retired they want something to do to remain active.

We watched an ant carrying a piece of crisp across the tiles. (We have such an exciting life!)

"Isn't it amazing!" said Ted, "I mean, imagine being low down like that – it must seem like an incredibly large car park. How does he know where to go?"

In the evening and just before sundown we went out for a coffee to a nearby pavement café. As we sat towards the melting sun, I had a running commentary from Ted on what a fellow was doing on a table behind me.

"That fellow behind has brought out a tin and has opened it."

"He's now rolling up a cigarette."

"He's got the paper out and is putting tobacco in a line and now he's rolling it up!"

"What's wrong with that?" I ask.

"Nothing, but it's quite unusual these days to see someone rolling cigarettes, isn't it?"

I sometimes wonder which stone he has crawled from under!

Monday April 12, 2010

I used the washing machine and was reminded that it jumped across the kitchen. The oven still only cooks on the one side and this morning I discovered water leaking from the down-pipe under the sink. Not long after that we had no water at all. We went to bed last night with the kitchen light left on because the switch has gone peculiar. When we turn off the lights under the kitchen cabinets, the main light goes on. When we turn that off, the lights under the cabinets come on!

When the water returned I got soaked as it spluttered brown liquid all over me. There is so much which needs attention in this place that I fear Olivia has just given up and that's why she has put it on the market (persuaded, of course, by Martin – I am convinced.)

We went into Tavira again because Ted needed to go to the bank and then we drove out into the hills. It was such a humid warm day that we felt we needed the fresh air of the hills to cool us.

We were surprised to see the acres of flowering bushes that have blossomed in the last few weeks. Miles upon miles of large white flowers could be seen all over the hills.

We saw the most beautiful coloured bird sitting on a fence. I instantly took a picture but it wasn't very clear. Ted took some time to get the other camera, change the flat batteries and fix the focus by which time the bird had flown.

I am covered with bites and found a black blood bruise on my chest this morning. I don't know what bugs are getting at me during the night. I have a bite on my cheek and another on my eyelid. It's so hard to resist rubbing them and it looks like I have a black eye.

The orange blossom perfume is stronger than ever today and really is quite sickly but absolutely wonderful.

We spent a frustrating time on the computer trying to find pet-friendly accommodation in the North of Portugal for Friday. In the end I had to give up because I was so tired.

I had a natural facial scrub tonight – the brown water had sand in it. Good can be found in all things!

Tuesday April 13, 2010

Had another unsettled night. I got bitten about five times all over my arms. I creamed myself over with hydrocortisone and managed to get a few hours sleep.

We needed to go into Tavira early. It was cloudy and the weather forecast – such as it is – had predicted showers but it was hot.

We met Geoff, our new friend, and as we walked up a narrow street with him to a place he recommended for coffee, he told us that last year the builders were knocking down a wall there and he happened to be walking past when he saw a man squatting down doing a poo on the pavement. As he did so, he was saying 'hello' to people as they walked by. As I have already said, the men here have no shame.

Ted spent most of the afternoon on the phone trying to get accommodation for our journey back on Friday. He was successful in doing so but I noticed that he had forgotten some French words and was getting mixed up with the Portuguese he has learned while we have been here.

The oven only half cooked the supper leaving the other half burned. She really should do something about all the things needing attention here. I noticed that she had been in the house whilst we were out. She had placed a couple of white plastic chairs by the pool. She simply cannot stop interfering!

Ted had observed that diesel prices have risen from about 87p a litre to around £1. I had an email telling me that petrol was now over £1.20 a litre in UK. I wonder what he will think when we get back and have to pay more!

He is busy making up files for the places we are going to stay on the return journey. This afternoon I put some of my clothes into a black bag to go to a charity shop in order to make the baggage lighter.

I am very much aware, now, that the end is nigh and I have mixed feelings about leaving.

Wednesday April 14, 2010

Rain! Rain! Rain! The wonderful sunny days were soon forgotten as we ran from the door to the car. It washed all the dust off the car so that was good. Some good can be found in everything!

Very much aware that we only have one day left here, we tried to tie up a few ends in Tavira. I left the black bag of clothing on the steps of the church charity shop and came back to the villa for a lunch made of everything left in the fridge. The rain was exceptionally heavy and reminded me of all those dark days we have had. The days which locals claim they have not had for decades.

Ted had some phone calls to make and we waited for confirmation of our accommodation bookings. It looked like all was set for our homeward trip.

I began sorting out some of the vast array of possessions we have acquired since December. I tried to get some of the new books into the spaces where the clothing would have gone. We don't want to look overloaded when travelling through Spain.

We shall leave here early on Friday morning and head towards the North of Portugal, staying one night and then will undertake the long journey through Spain (non-stop hopefully) to the South of France on Saturday.

Sunday we are staying in Poitiers and then will head up towards Caen – the ferry port. We need to find a vet there to give Pippa her treatment before we can leave for home on the 22nd.

So, as the rain and wind howled and rattled the windows this evening, I reflected on my time here. My feelings, yes, they are mixed. We have made friends here and begun to learn their language. It has been home to us for nearly five months, but I miss my family and want so much to see them all.

Pippa made her way to bed. I turned off the dishwasher. The suitcases are almost packed and I stepped over them wondering if I had left anything important. Extremely tired, I hoped for a decent sleep with sweet dreams. Tomorrow is another day – and the last!

Chapter 51

Thursday April 15, 2010

I had another restless night being bitten by silent, invisible bugs. They cannot be mosquitoes because I don't hear a sound.

Thunder rolled and lightning lit up the room. The rain hit the shutters like hail stones. I heard the patio furniture being blown away, scraping along the tiles. Pippa slept.

I lay in bed thinking of the events of the previous day. Thinking of Mary and how she must be feeling about her father having a heart attack and her granddad being in the same hospital. I thought of how they are coping and wished I could be near to them.

I looked at my watch. It was 3am. Is this significant in some way? Several times I have still been awake at that time.

I scratched my nose. One of these creatures had bitten me again. Pippa continued to sleep. Do bugs bite dogs? If so, do they feel it?

At 7.30am the sky was austere. The wind was fierce and determined. I took my shower and heard someone knocking at the front door. It was Olivia. I heard Ted saying, 'No thank you. We are busy!" I cringed.

With my hair still wet I came out of the bathroom to ask what the conversation was about.

"Oh she asked if we wanted to go and have coffee with her but I said we were too busy."

I walked down the shingle drive to her house to apologise and to explain that sometimes Ted comes across as being rude but I am sure that he doesn't mean to. We had coffee together and she told me of her disappointment that her daughter no longer wants contact with her. We sat and talked for about twenty minutes in between rain showers.

She told me about her days as a psychiatric nurse and how the establishments were then known as lunatic asylums. She explained that there were rooms underground, called dungeons where the patients would be locked in solitary confinement, probably for the rest of their short lives.

Such an establishment was built at Powick and some years ago the land was acquired for building dwellings. I am not sure whether the underground rooms, or dungeons, were filled in or not. Those must have been really cruel times in the 1950's.

As it was our last day here Ted wanted to go and have lunch at the cheap buffet place where you can eat all you can for 7 euros. We had to drive 20 miles to get there!

I had finished my meal and the waiter was about to take my plate when Ted proclaimed, "What about the pineapple?"

A toasted pineapple was brought to the table on a vertical skewer, the sides coated with sugar and cinnamon. With a sharp knife, the waiter pared slices with a downward swipe for me to deliver with a special pair of tongs.

Stuffed like a taxidermists pension I left the table, descended the 40 steps and gave Pippa two sausages, which had been carefully dropped into a poo bag as her treat.

We drove on to the Quinta to say goodbye to those we have grown to know since New Year's Day. With promises to come back one day, we left them with a coach load of Dutch customers sitting by the pool drinking beer and coffee. I noticed that their fig trees are already loaded with fruit, far more advanced than the fig tree after which this villa was called. It doesn't have a single fruit.

I wanted to take the opportunity of getting the vodafone shop to top up my 'pay-as-you-go' phone so we parked the car in the shade of the Lidl car park and walked across the road to the shop. The young man wasn't able to do it for me so that was a waste of time.

We passed an under-inflated Santa Clause clinging desperately on to a chimney pot as the wind blew him in all directions. The Portuguese never seem to take down their decorations. Underneath him was a statue of Our Lady of the Waves! I only knew that because there was a plaque 3ft wide stating so.

We returned to the villa. I dipped the car for oil in readiness for our long journey tomorrow. Ted saw me doing it and then wanted to inflate the tyres with the battery operated tyre pump he bought from a supermarket here because mine had burned out.

He spent over half an hour walking around the car going back to the filler cap to check what the pressures should be. He then blew up a tyre only to lose the air when he took off the connection so had to repeat the process. I have never seen such a palaver.

Another downpour of rain brought him inside. I gave him the job of vacuuming the floors upstairs and that occupied him for over an hour. There are two bedrooms and he only cleaned the one.

I packed up most things and cleaned as much of the house as possible then took a glimpse of the pretty lights glittering over the small town of Tavira before whispering goodbye. It looks as though we shall be leaving here during rain, just as we arrived during rain. We might encounter ash tomorrow if we run into the volcanic matter, which grounded all flights in the UK today!

Chapter 52

Friday April 16, 2010

With all the preparations done last night, we were able to make an early start this morning leaving Tavira and heading towards the north of Portugal. Olivia and Martin were having breakfast when we called to return the key of the villa. I felt emotional and hugged her tightly. She is a small woman who has been strong in her lifetime, but now in her twilight years has become frail. She responded in a way in which words are not needed, and then asked me to come back.

We had only travelled 18 miles along the road when Ted realised we were on the wrong road! I had given him an ultimatum about having maps and satellite navigation systems telling him to simply make a list of the different towns en route. It was all too simple for him. He needed to make it complicated. We had to turn and *go back*.

The journey took us through wonderful Portuguese countryside where fields were spread out like purple carpets unrolling before our eyes. Storks were feeding their young in nests high in the trees, rather than on the top of telegraph poles which we had become accustomed to seeing in the Algarve.

There were times when torrential rain hit us then blue skies and sunshine followed.

Occasionally we got stuck behind a slow moving truck and it was difficult to see oncoming traffic being right-hand-drive but, on the whole, the roads were fairly quiet by our standards, although it wasn't motorway.

I suppose we made good progress although it was a long day. I was driving from 9am until 5.30pm with a stop for fuel and then a bite to eat. Ted remarked about how expensive the diesel is!

When we arrived at the 'dog-friendly' accommodation it certainly was dog friendly. There were five dogs (two Alsatians) lying in the road basking in the sunshine outside the reception area. They quickly picked up Pippa's scent and ran towards her as I lifted her out of the car.

Naturally, she needed no help in defending herself and put on her lion act much to the amazement of the children coming out of the school opposite.

The Alsatian set about Pippa and she tackled him around the head. A fight ensued. The Manager of the hotel came out and grabbed his dog by the scruff of the neck while the other four dogs watched from the bank opposite.

Pippa needed to walk, so I managed to take her across to the public gardens and on to the grass when it began to rain. We found a shelter under the veranda of the health clinic and waited until it stopped. I needed a stick - a rod of correction, to carry with me back to the hotel. There, before me lay three poles! I selected the shorter one which was very long to carry, and began to walk back towards the hotel.

The pack of dogs was lying in wait at a 'keep left' sign and arose with one accord. The Alsatian began to run towards Pippa who was biting at the bit and as I raised the stick, the Manager came rushing out to rescue us again.

Once inside the room I looked out to the front of the hotel and the five dogs had now become a pack of eight.

The garage, which the hotel had boasted, was difficult to drive into and rammed full with rubbish. Fortunately it had access to a lift taking us directly into the hotel so that enabled us to go up and down to the car without having to venture outside.

We had dinner in the restaurant there with a coach load of French speaking Portuguese. I was able to take Pippa a few pieces of calf's fillet, which she ravaged in one swallow. She was desperate to go to out again but I couldn't get beyond the front door because the dogs had taken residence there for the night.

I asked the receptionist if there was a back way to the hotel and obligingly she took me out into the dark beyond the sheds and into the shadows of the unknown. Pippa wouldn't do her business because they had set up a dog kennel out there for the stray dogs. There was no way she was going to do it in the vicinity of other dogs.

Disgruntled we both tried to adjust to sharing a room with Ted. Was I being unreasonable? I was tired, had driven over 400 miles and needed sleep. Some hopes!

Saturday April 17, 2010

I had a dreadful night. The dogs, which had set up camp outside the front of the hotel barked unceasingly. At 11pm last night I went down to the reception in my dressing gown and told the receptionist that she must do something about the noise. I had hoped that Ted might have taken some authority but he didn't. The duty receptionist gave me the keys to a room at the back of the building which was quieter but at 4am the neighbours decided to come back after partying and continued the festivities in their room.

With very little sleep under my belt, I had a long journey ahead. Pippa was desperate, again, to go to the loo. I hadn't been able to take her out because of the dogs so we made a hurried departure and got on our way.

We were less than two miles into the journey and Ted said we were going the wrong way! I nearly exploded! I stopped the car in the middle of the road and took Pippa out for her long awaited walk. The road was quiet and she was able to run freely getting some exercise while I defused.

This was to be the format for the 600 miles journey that day. We left the hotel at 8.15am and by 9.15am had only done 8 miles because we had driven round in circles.

I realised that Ted is no longer capable of map reading. He had written a list as I had asked him to do but had put all the wrong place names down so we were going to Timbuktu instead of trying to get out of Portugal.

We encountered some heavy rainstorms, which flooded the roads in places. Until I could find my way back on to the motorway I had to manoeuvre roads so narrow that the sides of the car almost touched the houses.

I drove for nine hours, only stopping for Pippa to stretch her legs. I ate a sandwich as I drove along because we needed to get back on track, recover lost time and get out of Spain into France.

The countryside was breathtakingly beautiful in Northern Portugal and once in Spain we felt the change in atmosphere. The land was very flat and, at times, full of huge boulders.

Ted was keen to fill up the car with cheap diesel in Spain so I drove off the motorway to a service station situated some way down another road. As I waited inside the car, I noticed a fellow get out of his car and walk over to a wall where he urinated in my full view.

I needed to 'spend a penny' so asked Ted to watch the car while I went into the service area toilet block. There were three cubicles. One was locked and the other two had unlocked doors. I pushed open the door only to be astonished to find that very man performing a lewd act in the ladies lavatory. I screamed with fright knowing that he had already pee-ed outside. This didn't improve my attitude towards the Spanish.

A dubious couple of men were kicking stones around by the car and I was pleased that Ted had closed the windows while I was away. I really couldn't wait to get out of that country.

When we eventually arrived at the place in Biarritz where we were staying for the night I discovered that it was on an extremely dangerous piece of road.

The large iron gates had to be opened whilst I waited on the busy road.

The arrogant French woman showed us up a long, dark, wooden staircase to a shabby apartment. The ceilings of the chateau were very high and the tall windows had wooden shutters some of which didn't open. On the table was a basket of plastic fruit. She seemed unconcerned about us actually and said flippantly that her daughter was having a party in the garden that evening. So much for a nice quiet evening!

A dog and cat were in residence so that made it awkward for me to keep Pippa under control.

Madame recommended a few places nearby where we could get some food. Ted asked if there was anywhere in walking distance. If he thought that I was up for a walk after driving for nine hours non-stop, he was going to be enlightened!

We put Pippa in the back of the car and found a pub nearby where we chose the dish of the day, which was dreadful. It consisted of watery soup with blobs of oil swimming on the top, a bottle of sour wine, a small dish of pasta between us both and some cooked meat, which I put in the poo-bag for Pippa. It was a complete waste of money. The waitress was grumpy and impolite.

When we returned to the chateau the party was in full swing. Loud music was playing and drunken people were screaming and shouting. Then, wheels began to spin on the gravel car park and two young high-as-a-kiters spun a little white car round before taking it at full speed on to the road with no lights.

Madame said we could leave our car in that car park but I am glad that I left it at the front of her 'manor house' instead as I settled for another sleepless night.

Sunday April 18, 2010

The seating arrangements had been made in another building so we had breakfast on a shared table with a French couple who, merely nodded to us cordially in greeting.

Ted went to pay the bill but there was nobody around and when, eventually, someone did appear, she overcharged him although he didn't say anything. He told me he would send an email!

Our journey to Poitiers was fraught with stress. I think every French family was driving home along the main holiday route from Spain. I was caught up, no end of times, by drivers who deliberately taunted.

Driving around Bordeaux in heavy traffic with Ted clutching his map and sat-nav was a nightmare. I was subjected to dreadful driving behaviour, being cut up and almost run off the road by the French who, recognising my British registration number deliberately targeted me. I gave as good as I got but it meant concentrating which was hard when Ted was telling me to go left when I was in the right lane.

The sun beat down as we faced north and Pippa got the full brunt of it. She was uncomfortably hot although I had the a/c blowing. We had to stop to re-arrange her bedding and put her on the back seat in the shade. After that she settled down.

Our journey was short in comparison with the previous two days. I was only driving for just over five hours!

When we arrived at the hotel in Chasseneuil (www.ribaudiere.com) there was no wind and the sun was blazing. We asked for coffee and cakes and sat in the shade of the large gardens watching others drinking champagne whilst sunning themselves.

When the waiter brought the cakes they were so small I needed a magnifying glass to find them on the saucer. We hadn't eaten since breakfast and my head was thumping like a drum beat.

Ted couldn't rest and wanted to make no end of visits to reception to ask the girl to get online for him. He didn't have details of the place where we were going tomorrow!

After two nights of little, or no sleep, it was all beginning to take its toll. My patience was almost shot. The French people are so arrogant and unfriendly.

We had been to this hotel before just after we were married. I don't know why Ted wanted to return. I think it has something to do with wanting to go back all the time (including his navigation skills!)

We had dinner in the restaurant at the chateau. It was all very grand and I ate more than I should have.

After dinner, and on the way across the courtyard, we met a Portuguese couple sitting under the night sky having a quiet drink together. We began talking to them and discovered that they have a house in Portugal. They and their two children couldn't get back to Holland because of the cancellation of all flights in Europe so they were driving back instead. We had a nice chat about Portugal and they enquired about our dog. They have dogs and horses at home in Holland, apparently and had taken a shine to our Staffie. They thought she was beautiful and wanted to see her so as we left them to their romantic time together, we promised to show off Pippa tomorrow.

Monday April 19, 2010

I had forgotten about the hour being forward in France although it hadn't made much difference to me. I took Pippa out early and we walked around the large gardens of the chateau. The grass was cold and wet with dew and it seemed like an autumn morning, rather than spring.

Unfortunately, the Portuguese family had not turned up for breakfast by the time we were ready to leave so they missed a formal introduction to Pippa.

We had an awful journey to the northern part of the country with traffic racing, overtaking and undertaking. I had to keep my wits about me at all times.

Ted continued to navigate. He had reinstated his map system together with sat nav assistance.

"Wait a minute!" he told me as I was in the middle lane of a three-lane motorway approaching a slip road. There was traffic on either side of me and he wanted me to stop the car whilst he decided whether we should turn right or not.

The stress level was at overload. Apart from a refuelling stop I drove continuously for six hours.

Why do such dreadful people have the nicest countries? The French don't like us. And, we don't like them.

We arrived at the hostelry at almost 3pm. The grounds were vast and the accommodation was spread over three buildings. The car parking was half a mile from the accommodation so I didn't bother to take much out of the car. I was tired, hungry and frustrated.

Ted booked dinner in the main house where the owners lived. I wasn't going to change and turned up in the clothes I had worn for two days.

My observations of the French were confirmed tonight when the owner completely ignored us and spoke only to another guest in French for the whole night. We were completely ignored. The wine was put on the table and not served. After the other paying guest picked it up and poured it out for himself, I decided to do the same for myself.

I thought that a small glass of calvados had been poured to drink alongside coffee but no coffee arrived because the wife had decided to just leave the table and do the washing up. I poured mine on the carpet under the table while the two French men gabbled away in their mother tongue.

A couple of times Ted had offered conversation in French, but they were just not interested. They were so rude – it was almost unbelievable.

When we left the house to walk across the garden to the accommodation in the block adjoining the chateau, I felt relieved to be out of their company if you could call it so. I hoped to get some sleep. I was so tired. Would I have sweet dreams?

Tuesday April 20, 2010

I took Pippa into the large manicured gardens of the chateau at 7.30am French time. The chill in the air reminded me of autumn as the watery sun began to rise across the grey sky only to be obliterated by heavy mist – or was it the ash from that volcano?

A young boy had three black rabbits running loose which Pippa wanted to catch. I had to keep her on the lead, as she pulled frantically to move towards them. They stood on their hind legs rubbing their little hands together as she looked in amazement.

Again we were ripped off when Ted went to pay the bill. The lady of the house overcharged for the meal we had last night and charged 8 euros for home made cider drinks, which, according to the information pack, should have been inclusive. I gave the information sheet to Ted and told him to go back and tell her of her mistake. In her arrogant way (which only the French have) she simply said it had changed.

Disgusted, I took the information pack to the car and will complain to the agency she uses.

We drove away from there towards Caen where we had booked a family run hotel for the two remaining nights. Pippa had a vet's appointment at 8pm so it was convenient to stay nearby.

We arrived early because the distance was only 60 miles. Ted had already telephoned to inform them that we might be early and was told that it would alright. He went inside to check that all was well and came back to the car saying that the Manager had told him it would not be ready yet. I suggested that we have some coffee so we both went back to reception only to be confronted by a dishevelled, dirty looking man looking over to us with evil eyes. When Ted asked for coffee the man ran both hands through his unkempt hair and shouted "*No!*"

I walked out and told him to forget it. He pretended not to understand.

We have found this a lot with the French, as with the Welsh. They understand you perfectly well but because you don't speak their language want to punish you. That is why we were excluded from the conversation at the table last night.

We left the hotel and drove along the coast visiting the little seaside places until 4pm when we returned. A lady (wife) told me to park alongside the hedge. She then asked me to move the car back a bit to allow people to walk past. Then, the monster, whom we had encountered in the morning, came out and told me to move it to a completely different place. I obliged but was getting very impatient.

The lady said that Pippa could have a run in the garden at the rear so I led her towards an unhinged gate left leaning against a post. As I began to move the gate we were almost attacked by a large dog, which 'the monster' quickly took under control.

The wife came out to the front of the hotel to apologise. I asked who is the boss. She said *"He is my 'usband and I am sorry."*

I could see that she was genuinely sorry and embarrassed. She asked if she could do anything for us and so I asked for a drink. She obligingly suggested tea or coffee – either would be acceptable and no problem. We settled for coffee, then waited rather a long time outside at the front of the hotel beside a small table on to which I put my sunglasses and car keys.

'He' came out with a tray which he banged on the table – picked up my sunglasses and banged them down in a different place and then asked me if I spoke French.

"NO!" I emphatically replied. Even if I did, I would not have done so. He rambled on in French about it being a hotel and not a restaurant that they do not do snacks and coffees and then stormed off.

That did it! I didn't want to drink from his cup. I left it there and told Ted that we were going. Ted wanted to drink his coffee and had picked up a piece of cake, which I told him to put back and we left. I felt relieved once I had made that decision because the atmosphere there was dreadful. I knew that when we got to the vets he would tell us where we could get accommodation with Pippa and he did!

Ted had already paid up front for two nights but I told him that it wasn't to be an issue. I knew in my heart that we were not to go back (go back) there and that we would find somewhere more suitable.

The vet suggested King George V Hotel but didn't give us the address. Remarkably we found it and when Ted made enquiries they were fully booked but the kindly Manager rang a friend of his and booked us into a small hotel in Lion-sur-Mer just a few miles up the road. The owners were very nice and we got a ground floor family room fully equipped for disabled persons!

I was anxious about having to park the car in the public car park because we were still heavily loaded but the owner's wife moved her car from outside the hotel for me to use her parking space. Everything fell into place. She even booked a table for us at a nearby restaurant so we even got a meal before they closed.

Ted was anxious about having the key to the other hotel room but I told him not to worry that we would drop it back on the way to the ferry.

We settled down to what was to be the most peaceful night yet!

Wednesday April 21, 2010

Today was really about wasting time. Breakfast was simply bread and preserve with coffee. We left our baggage in the hotel and took Pippa along the seafront. The sun was pleasant but it was bitingly cold. We spent three hours walking up every narrow street in Lion sur Mer.

I noticed that all of the dogs here are kept on leads. That was fortunate because Pippa was definitely in fighting mood.

We were surprised to be invited to take her into a small restaurant on the corner of the street near the hotel at lunchtime.

"It is ok. No problem. My dog it is in the kitchen!" said the young woman with a very heavy French accent and a safety pin through her lip. I wondered how she could eat anything without it catching, but didn't feel like asking. There was no need for a poo-bag because Pippa was able to eat her treats right from the table!

A dear old woman sat at the window with her half carafe of wine, demolishing apple tart. She was then served with her main course afterwards. It is a long time since I have seen that custom. I remember some Danish friends inviting me to their home for a meal and we had all the courses back to front.

The day seemed to drag but we passed the time by walking Pippa around so she was quite tired by the end of the day – and so was I.

Ensuring that everything was packed up ready for an early start, I fell into bed and into dreamland without any effort at all.

Thursday April 22, 2010

We got up before dawn. Ted took Pippa around the corner near the church where there was a grassy patch for her to do her business. We then loaded up the car for our final leg of the journey. We dropped off the key to the dreadful hotel and managed to get lost again before getting to the ferry terminal.

We lined up for embarkment and were told that we had to take Pippa into the terminal for screening. That was an experience!

We were supposed to form a queue but there were two other dogs before us and the boxer took a dislike to Pippa. There was no way that I could join the queue so Ted had to stand in for us while I kept Pippa at a distance.

The terminal was crowded because of the air disruption. Pippa was causing a spectacle as people were looking over towards her as she flashed her teeth and roared like the lion she is at times.

When we eventually got to the desk we were told that she needed a muzzle and were provided with one. She wasn't going to wear that!

The screening procedure went smoothly and we were able to get back into the car without too much delay. I settled her into the bed, which now was on the back seat, and we joined all the foot passengers on to the vessel.

There were several restaurants on the boat. We went up on to the top deck and sat down to a buffet breakfast. Ted was able to eat as much as he could, and got up for preserves, bread, cake and more.

We finished breakfast and found a couple of seats. Ted bought a bottle of water and spent about an hour reading the label. He seemed quiet and something was bothering him but he wouldn't share with me.

The crossing was smooth and uneventful until we got down to the lower deck where the cars were parked.

I got Pippa out of the car to give her a drink. The car door was open. I tripped over a raised pothole, smashed my head on the car door and fell on to the concrete deck cracking my forehead on the hard surface. I was out!

I remember some people helping me but don't remember too much apart from lots of people, a wheel chair and a nurse trying to get me away to take my blood pressure. They wanted Ted to drive the car, which I was not going to allow under any circumstances.

Not knowing what was more painful, my head or my knees, I managed to get into the driving seat. I thought I might have smashed my kneecaps. The nurse didn't want me to drive. More people arrived on the scene. The English Manager came over and spoke to Ted and after an assurance from me, allowed me to drive off the boat.

The journey to Al's was very difficult for me. I was in such pain but so wanted to see the family again that the joy of meeting up with them somewhat over-rode the pain.

After we left them and continued the journey 'home' I felt pressure on my neck, shoulder, arm and legs. What a way to end the journey – walking with a borrowed walking stick!

THIS IS NOT THE END!

Author's Note

This is a true account of an adventure made by my husband and I in the winter of 2009.

Father had laid it upon our hearts to make this journey of faith. With little forward planning we moved around The Algarve at His direction not knowing His Purposes, which always seem to unfold step by step.

Ted is an Aspergers sufferer and the journal is a diary of events and circumstances in which I found myself during the wettest winter in remembrance.

Those who have Aspergers Syndrome (a form of autism) often have obsessive behaviour; live in their own world and Ted's world is that of a mathematical mind. His profession was engineering – a typical career for someone with that type of Aspergers.

In a humorous and sensitive way, I hope I have described the times when, without my faith, I would have crumbled. I have shown how, by standing on the Word, I was able to gain strength in times of great weakness to enable me to carry Ted on my faith.

I hope you enjoy reading this account of our journey from east to west of the Algarve allowing yourself to share the confrontations and situations that only a seasoned Believer can overcome remembering that we always have the Victory in our Messiah, Jesus Christ, Yahshua Mashiach!

S Amos